The BRISKET Chronicles

HOW *to* BARBECUE, BRAISE, SMOKE, *and* CURE *the* WORLD'S MOST EPIC CUT *of* MEAT

STEVEN RAICHLEN

Food Photography by Matthew Benson

WORKMAN PUBLISHING
NEW YORK

WITHDRAWN

Library of Congress Cataloging-in-Publication Data is available.

Paperback ISBN 978-1-5235-0548-7
Hardcover ISBN 978-1-5235-0779-5

Cover and interior design by Becky Terhune
Original photography by Matthew Benson
Food styling: Nora Singley
Prop styling: Sara Abalan

Additional images: **Adobe Stock:** pp. 17 (electric cooker), 27, 28. **Alamy:** Karl Allgaeuer p. 241; Cannon Photography LLC p. 162. **Courtesy of the Author:** pp. iii, 2, 4 (top), 7, 20 (top), 21 (top), 55, 60, 99, 104, 105, 129 (left), 179, 253; Strauss Brands p. 12; Weber pp. 21 (middle), 22 (left); Weber-Stephen p. 17 (water smoker); Yeti p. 24. **Creative Commons:** The following image from Wikimedia Commons is used under a Creative Commons Attribution-Share Alike 4.0 International (https://creativecommons.org/licenses/by-sa/4.0/deed.en) license, Author: Chiswich Chap p. 3. **Public Domain:** p. 4 (bottom). **Shutterstock.com** pp. 6, 10, 17 (stockpot), 23 (bottom), 64, 115, 163. **Special thanks to the following for courtesy use:** Big Green Egg p. 19 (top); Companion Group pp. 23 (top & middle), 25; © 2018 Crowd Cow by Steve Hansen Images p. 11; Franklin Barbecue p. 262; Ha Noi House p. 157; Hometown BBQ p. 225; Horizon p. 20 (bottom); Lodge p. 22 (right); Masterbuilt p. 21 (bottom); Mile End p. 128 (left); Pit Barrel Cooker Co. p. 19 (bottom); Poggio Trattoria, Executive Chef/Partner Benjamin Balesteri p. 167; Snowdon Deli pp. 128 (right), 129 (top right); Staub USA p. 17 (dutch oven).

Text on page 4: Excerpt from COLD MOUNTAIN, copyright © 1997 by Charles Frazier. Used by permission of Grove/ Atlantic, Inc. Any third party use of this material, outside of this publication, is prohibited.

Steven Raichlen is available for select speaking engagements.
Please contact speakersbureau@workman.com.

Workman books are available at special discounts when purchased in bulk for
premiums and sales promotions as well as for fund-raising or educational use.
Special editions or book excerpts can also be created to specification.
For details, contact the Special Sales Director at the address below,
or send an e-mail to specialmarkets@workman.com.

Workman Publishing Company, Inc.
225 Varick Street
New York, NY 10014-4381
workman.com

Printed in the United States of America
First printing March 2019

10 9 8 7 6 5 4 3 2 1

To Barbara

The smoke that scents my brisket.
The spice that lights up my sauce.

ACKNOWLEDGMENTS

This may be a single-subject book (what a subject!), but I drew on the wisdom of many experts in a wide range of disciplines and literally from around the world.

My immersion into brisket science began at Camp Brisket, a two-day seminar organized by Foodways Texas and Texas A&M University in College Station, Texas, and directed by four professors—Dr. Jeff Savell, Dr. Davey Griffin, Ray Riley, and Marvin Bendele—whose erudition is matched only by their ability to make learning fun. Another Camp Brisket instructor, Aaron Franklin of Franklin Barbecue in Austin, has been a constant source of inspiration and education for me, as he has for millions of brisket fanatics across the planet.

A huge thanks to my former editor at Workman Publishing, Suzanne Rafer, who commissioned *The Brisket Chronicles*, and to my new editor, Kylie Foxx McDonald, who, with great discernment and creativity, has ushered it into print. Thanks also to the many dedicated folks who contributed their many talents: Sarah Curley, Kate Karol, Barbara Peragine, Jessica Rozler, David Schiller, Carol White, and Doug Wolff. As always, Workman CEO Dan Reynolds, publisher and editorial director Susan Bolotin, and associate publisher Page Edmunds lent their guidance and expertise. Gratitude as well to Carolan Workman.

Workman photo director Anne Kerman led a tremendous team that included photographer Matthew Benson, food stylists Nora Singley and Kristina Kurek (who also served as recipe testers), prop stylist Sara Abalan, and fire wrangler Ezra "Stokey" Dunn. Designer Becky Terhune graced *The Brisket Chronicles* with its handsome cover and layout. Material support for the photo shoot came from the Adams Fairacre Farms in Newburgh, New York; Breville; Creekstone Farms Premium Beef; Environmental Dreamscapes; The Companion Group; Lodge Manufacturing; Kai USA, Ltd. (manufacturer of Shun Cutlery); marbledmeatshop.com; Staub USA; Strauss Brands Inc.; and Roger Davidson of Horizon Smokers.

Molly Kay Upton, Erin Kibby, and Moira Kerrigan keep our website (barbecuebible .com) and social media humming. (Be sure to subscribe to our *Up in Smoke* newsletter—if you haven't already.) Publicists Chloe Puton, Rebecca Carlisle, and Jocelynn Pedro will make sure that everyone on the planet knows about *The Brisket Chronicles*.

A big thanks to my TV production team, which includes Matt Cohen, Ryan Kollmorgen, John Pappalardo, and Gwenn Williams of Resolution Pictures, and Steven Schupak, Stuart Kazanow, Frank Batavick, Donna Hunt, and many others at Maryland Public Television. On the home front, my assistant, the inestimable Nancy Loseke, helped in more ways than I can count, from researching to recipe testing to proofreading to just being there as a friend 24/7.

Finally, thanks to the next generation of brisket lovers, Ella, Mia, and Julian, who eat my experiments with gusto and remind me of what's really important. I couldn't do any of this without my wife, Barbara, who truly is the fire in my smoker and the wind beneath my wings.

CONTENTS

INTRODUCTION

ABOUT THIS BOOK

Brisket has been part of my life almost from the moment I started eating solid food. For decades, braised brisket was the centerpiece of the Sabbath dinners that took place at the home of my grandparents Ethel and Sam every Friday night. No holiday dinner was complete without my aunt Annette's magisterial brisket made sweet with dried fruits and kosher wine and enlivened with chunks of fresh lemon and freshly grated horseradish.

As a teenager, I ate my fair share of corned beef and pastrami at Baltimore's landmark delis. And at college I had the good fortune to work for a delicatessen that did all its curing and smoking on the premises. After college, I moved to Paris to study the history of cooking and modern French cuisine, and there I experienced a different sort of brisket—slow simmered with red wine and root vegetables and served by the stylish name of *boeuf à la mode*.

Back in the US, I became the restaurant critic for *Boston Magazine*. My beat often took me to Chinatown, where I discovered red cooked brisket (braised with soy sauce, rock sugar, and star anise). As a roving freelance food writer, I ate *ropa vieja* ("old clothes" literally), brisket stewed in cumin-scented tomato sauce in Miami's Little Havana, and *bollito misto* (a two-brisket boiled dinner) in Italy's Piedmont region. From there it was on to what we then called Saigon (today's Ho Chi Minh City) as a travel writer for *National Geographic Traveler* to report the pleasures of Vietnam's brisket-rich beef noodle soup, pho.

My immersion in the most famous brisket culture of all—Texas barbecue—came relatively late. The year was 1994—I just started work on the book that would change my life (and I hope many of yours): *The Barbecue! Bible*. I crisscrossed Texas, feasting on briskets the color of coal, cooked in metal and masonry pits that look like relics of the Industrial Revolution. Said briskets not only smelled of smoke—they were the essence of wood smoke, just as the meat was the quintessence of beef. Tender? Let's just say that no knives were provided and none were required. If this was brisket,

what had I been eating all these years? I wanted in, and I wanted more.

This book tells the story of my brisket obsession and education. And it's written in the reverse order of how brisket came to play such a significant role in my life.

We start with the reason many Raichlen readers and viewers will pick up this book—barbecued brisket—in all its glorious manifestations, from Texas Hill Country packer brisket to Kansas City burnt ends, and from obscenely rich Wagyu brisket to a fiery Jamaican jerk. And—gasp!— there are two briskets you actually cook in minutes directly on the grill. Chapter 2, "Brisket Barbecued and Grilled," is by far the longest chapter in this book, just as barbecue casts an oversize shadow on America's culinary landscape.

The next chapter deals with another distinguished branch of the brisket family tree—cured brisket. In it, you'll find that triumvirate of great brisket deli meats: corned beef, pastrami, and Montreal smoked meat— all of which owe their rich umami flavor and inviting rosy hue to a curing salt called Prague Powder #1. (Later on, you'll learn how to use these meats to make the ultimate deli sandwich: the Double-Down Reuben, lavished with both pastrami and corned beef.) And you'll learn about corned beef's lesser known, but eminently worth discovering cousin: Irish spiced beef.

In subsequent chapters, we'll explore brisket braised (including those steaming slabs of beef I grew up on), brisket boiled, brisket sandwiches, brisket appetizers, brisket side dishes, brisket for breakfast, the best sauces and rubs for brisket, and, yes, even a brisket dessert. Together we'll circumnavigate the globe, just as I have done many times in my pursuit of the world's best barbecue.

But first (in chapter 1), we'll master the brisket basics, from how to buy, trim, cook, carve, and serve this majestic cut of beef to the necessary cookers and gear.

So fire up your smoker and haul out your stockpot and Dutch oven: *The Brisket Chronicles* is about to begin.

A CRASH COURSE ON BRISKET

B risket. Few words have the power to make you palpitate, salivate, and levitate. Whether smoked in a pit, braised by a Jewish grandmother, or simmered for half a day by a Vietnamese pho master, brisket ranks among the world's most revered meats. Corned beef, pastrami, Montreal smoked meat, or *bollito misto* all start as brisket.

Brisket is easy—Texas barbecue, for example, requires only three flavorings: salt, pepper, and wood smoke. But easy doesn't always mean simple. Brisket comes in a bewildering range of grades and cuts. Its chemistry and physics would daunt an honors student. Myriad are the ways you can cook it, but each involves insider knowledge and techniques. Fear not—you'll find all the basics, plus some fascinating history and culture, explained here.

WHAT IS BRISKET?

Picture a steer. We'll call him Sam. Born of Angus stock and weighing 1,400 pounds, Sam just celebrated his 16-month birthday. True, he's less the man he was at 6 months, when a cowhand relieved him of what we politely call Rocky Mountain oysters, but he's still a barnyard bad boy. Sam leads a good life, spending his first year grazing on grass under a big Texas sky, rollicking with his buddies. More recently, his diet switched to grain, and Sam feels bigger and stronger than ever. Hey, you know the saying: When a boy fattens up, he gains muscle. When a man bulks up, he gains fat.

Unlike a human being, Sam walks on all fours and, unlike us, he lacks shoulder blades. But he definitely has chest muscles. In a human, they're known as pecs (short for *pectoralis major*). In Sam, we call them brisket.

BRISKET ANATOMY

Actually, two muscles comprise Sam's brisket. The first is a flat rectangular muscle nestled against Sam's breastbone under the first five ribs and known as the *pectoralis profundus*. Butchers and brisket lovers call this the **flat**.

On top of the flat (but lower and more forward on the steer's undercarriage) is a second muscle, this one thicker at the shoulder end, thinner at the other, and generously marbled with rich veins of fat. This second muscle, the *pectoralis superficialis*, goes by the name of the **point**. (In delicatessen circles, it's called the **deckle**; we'll use the term *point* throughout this book.) Connecting the two is a thick seam of pearl-white intermuscular fat called the **seam fat**.

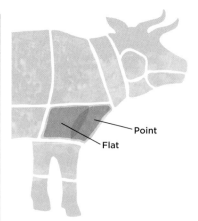
Point
Flat

Each of Sam's untrimmed briskets (he has two—a right and a left) weighs 12 to 18 pounds. This represents just 3 percent of his edible meat, but that 3 percent serves an outsize role in Sam's well-being. They help Sam move—striding toward food, running away from danger. They enable him to stand up—and get up after he lies down to rest. Most important, they support his not inconsiderable weight— roughly 350 pounds per brisket.

As a result, Sam's well-exercised briskets have a

A BRIEF HISTORY OF BRISKET

1400s
The first written appearance of brisket (*bru-kette*) in the English language.

1500s AND 1600s
Brusket, briscat, and *brysket* enter the lexicon.

1700s
Mrs. Raffald publishes the first printed brisket recipe in *The Experienced English Housekeeper*.

1800s
American food writing of the period is strangely silent on the subject of brisket, although Texans, Kansas Citians, and other Americans surely ate this versatile, flavorful cut of meat.

very different composition, texture, and taste than one of his lazy muscles, such as the *psoas major* (beef tenderloin) or *longissimus dorsi* (prime rib). No, the brisket is as bad-boy as its owner. It's a lot denser and tougher than steak, but when properly cooked, it has a rich, beefy flavor that just won't quit.

BRISKET PHYSICS

Being such a load-bearing, hardworking muscle, Sam's brisket is laced with a connective tissue called collagen. Collagen consists of amino acids wound together in triple helixes to form elongated fibers called fibrils. Collagen (named for the Greek word for "glue," of which it was an early ingredient) gives the brisket muscles their strength but also their toughness when cooked.

On account of this collagen, if you tried to cook Sam's brisket like a steak—quickly over a hot fire—you'd wind up with a mouthful of shoe leather. That makes brisket a poor candidate for grilling (with one exception—the paper-thin-sliced Korean grilled brisket on page 83). But the same collagen makes it an excellent candidate for slow, low, moist-heat cooking methods, like barbecuing, boiling, and braising. (More on that on page 15.)

As you cook a brisket, this tough collagen gradually turns into tender gelatin— a process that begins at around 160°F. At the same time (at around 140°F), the fat starts to render (melt). For both transformations to take place, you have to raise the temperature slooooooooowly; otherwise the meat fibers will contract and toughen. That's why barbecue pit masters insist that you have to cook brisket "low and slow."

BRISKET HISTORY

Brisket's big flavor and historically affordable price have made it a popular meat throughout history. The word *bru-kette* first appears in an English-Latin dictionary published in 1450. Over the centuries, you could read about *brusket, briscat,* and *brysket.* In the seventeenth century, *brysket* referred to the chest of a horse as well as a steer. (Sam would not be amused.)

The first brisket recipe appeared in this book in 1769.

1900s
The first wave of brisket mania in North America, as European immigrants introduce pastrami, corned beef, and Montreal smoked meat.

1910
The first written mention of smoked brisket in Texas—it is served at the deli counter of two Jewish-owned groceries.

1950–1960s
Texas barbecued brisket makes its debut at Black's BBQ in Lockhart and begins its ascension to cult status.

2000s AND BEYOND
Destination barbecue joints such as Snow's, Fette Sau, and Franklin Barbecue elevate barbecued brisket to the culinary stratosphere.

Beef in the nineteenth century. Talk about smoky!

In 1709, we learn from a period tabloid called *The Tattler* that the Black Prince (one Edward of Woodstock) was "a professed Lover of the Brisket." The first printed brisket recipe appears in *The Experienced English Housekeeper* by a Mrs. Raffald in 1769. (That's seven years before the founding of the United States! You'll find the original recipe on the facing page.) In colloquial British English, if you're angry at someone, you might punch him in the brisket.

Pork appears extensively in the culinary literature of Colonial America. Brisket does not. Nor does it surface in the nineteenth century, but here's how writer Charles Frazier imagines it in his Civil War novel *Cold Mountain*:

When Ruby finally returned, she carried only a small bloody brisket wrapped in paper and one jug of cider. . . .

Not hardly four pounds, she said. She set it and the jug on the ground and went to the house and came back carrying four small glasses and a cup of salt, sugar, black pepper, and red pepper all mixed together. She opened the paper and rubbed the mixture on the meat to case it, and then she buried it in the ashes of the fire and sat on the ground beside Ada. . . .

After Mars had risen red from behind Jonas Ridge and the fire had burned down to a bed of coals, Ruby pronounced the meat done and dug it from the ashes with the pitchfork. *The spices had formed a crust around the brisket, and Ruby put it on a stump butt and sliced it thin across the grain with her knife. The inside was pink and running with juice. They ate it with their fingers without benefit of plates and there was nothing else to the dinner. When they finished they pulled dry sedge grass from the field edge and scrubbed their hands clean.*

Brisket's golden age in America wouldn't arrive until the twentieth century. First with Jewish immigrants from Romania who pioneered the brine-cured, spice-rubbed, smoked, then steamed

Brisket debuts on a Texas menu. No, it wasn't barbecue.

THE OLDEST BRISKET RECIPE

Based on linguistic evidence, the English have enjoyed brisket for more than six hundred years. The earliest brisket recipe appeared in a cookbook called *The Experienced English Housekeeper: For Use and Ease of Ladies* by one Elizabeth Raffald, published by an R. Baldwin in 1769.

It's a splendid, surprisingly modern preparation that uses bacon to moisten a brisket flat's inherent leanness. Oysters may seem like an odd touch—until you consider the popularity of Worcestershire sauce (which contains anchovies) and fish sauce, which remain popular brisket flavorings and condiments to this day. Red wine becomes the base for the "gravy" (read: barbecue sauce). They even serve it with pickles, as do twenty-first-century pit masters, to counterpoint the fat.

The only note that would be jarring to modern taste buds is nutmeg—an enormously popular seasoning in eighteenth-century Europe (perhaps because earlier papal authority had proclaimed it a cure for the plague). But nutmeg does turn up in some modern barbecue rubs—used in moderation, it adds a pleasing musky sweetness.

You'll recognize the method as braising (in red wine), so cook it in a Dutch oven. The instructions are easy to follow; the result is out of this world.

TO MAKE BRISKET OF BEEF A-LA-ROYAL

Bone a brisket of beef, and make holes in it with a knife, about an inch one from another, fill one hole with fat bacon, a second with chopped parsley, and a third with chopped oysters, seasoned with nutmeg, pepper, and salt, till you have done the brisket over, then pour a pint of red wine boiling hot upon the beef, dredge it well with flour, send it to the oven, and bake it 3 hours or better; when it comes out of the oven take off the fat, and strain the gravy over your beef; garnish with pickles and serve it up.

---

brisket we enjoy today as pastrami (see page 93). (They introduced it at an equally revolutionary new type of restaurant where you could eat it—the delicatessen.) Their Canada-bound cousins branded the preparation "smoked meat" and made it a Montreal sandwich icon (see page 123). Around the same time, Irish immigrants brought brine-cured, boiled brisket to Boston and New York, where corned beef became an indispensable symbol of St. Patrick's Day.

You may be surprised to learn that Texas-style barbecued brisket is a relatively new phenomenon. Undoubtedly, Texans have been eating brisket ever since Lone Star State pit masters first put meat to fire—but it was part of a barbecued whole animal or forequarter. According to *Texas Monthly* barbecue critic Daniel Vaughn, the first written mention of smoked brisket occurred in 1910—it was served not at a barbecue joint but at the deli counter of two Jewish-owned grocery stores: Naud Burnett in Greenville, Texas, and the Watson Grocery in El Paso. Watson's clients, for example, could choose among "cooked brisket," "smoked brisket," and "corned beef."

HOW BRISKET MAKES PEOPLE HAPPY AROUND THE WORLD

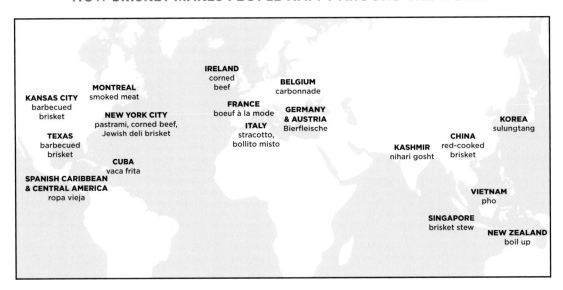

KANSAS CITY
barbecued
brisket

MONTREAL
smoked meat

TEXAS
barbecued
brisket

NEW YORK CITY
pastrami, corned beef,
Jewish deli brisket

CUBA
vaca frita

**SPANISH CARIBBEAN
& CENTRAL AMERICA**
ropa vieja

IRELAND
corned
beef

BELGIUM
carbonnade

FRANCE
boeuf à la mode

ITALY
stracotto,
bollito misto

**GERMANY
& AUSTRIA**
Bierfleische

KASHMIR
nihari gosht

CHINA
red-cooked
brisket

KOREA
sulungtang

VIETNAM
pho

SINGAPORE
brisket stew

NEW ZEALAND
boil up

It wasn't until the late 1950s that Black's BBQ in Lockhart became the first Texas barbecue joint to offer brisket as a barbecue specialty in its own right. Prior to that, pit masters would smoke the entire beef forequarter. If you wanted "lean" beef, they'd serve you shoulder clod; if you wanted "fat," you'd get brisket.

Vaughn credits brisket's ascension to barbecue Valhalla with two different technological revolutions in the meatpacking industry. The first was the publication of the Institutional Meat Purchase Specifications (IMPS) in 1958. For the first time, butchers and meat purveyors had a precise universal definition of the various beef cuts, including brisket. (In case you're curious: the IMPS number for a packer brisket is 120; the flat is 120A, the point is 120B.) Prior to this time, butchering was done at community meat markets, with scant concern for uniformity. But large customers, like the military—and eventually grocery and restaurant chains—required a consistently recognizable product, and here the IMPS provided invaluable guidance.

The second advance was the advent of boxed beef in the 1960s. "In the old days, we bought our meat as hanging beef [half carcasses]," recalls octogenarian pit mistress Tootsie Tomanetz of Snow's BBQ in Lexington, Texas (more on Tootsie on page 253). "We'd butcher it in-house and grind the brisket into hamburger." Boxed meat (cut into consumer cuts and packaged at the processing plant) brought uniform, neatly butchered briskets in vacuum-sealed plastic bags to meat markets and restaurants. Gradually (and surprisingly recently), brisket became the most revered barbecue in Texas. When Snow's opened in 2003, for example, they typically sold a half-dozen briskets on the one day of the week they're open to the public: Saturday. Today, they cook ninety briskets and can barely keep up with demand.

If there's one person responsible for the modern brisket craze, it's Aaron

BRISKET SPEAK:
AT A BARBECUE RESTAURANT OR COMPETITION

Bark: The exterior of a barbecued brisket. When a brisket is properly cooked, the bark will be dark, salty, smoky, and crusty.

Burnt ends: Traditionally, the crisp, tough, fatty brisket trimmings pared off before the meat is sliced and served. Pit masters, like the late Arthur Bryant in Kansas City, would give them away for free to the customers waiting patiently in line for the restaurant to open. In modern parlance, "burnt ends" have come to denote cubes of smoked brisket (typically brisket point) that are slathered with sweet barbecue sauce and smoked again. These are burnt ends you pay for. (See the recipe on page 74.)

Deckle: What butchers call the fatty tissue between the brisket flat and the rib cage. It's normally removed at the packing house. Note: In Jewish deli parlance, deckle is another name for the **point** (see below).

Fat cap: The thick layer of waxy white fat atop a brisket. Some of this will be removed

during trimming, but always leave at least ¼ inch. The **seam fat** is the thick layer of fat between the point and the flat.

Flat: The lean, flat, trapezoid-shaped muscle that comprises the "bottom" of a brisket (although in fact, it's anatomically located higher up on the steer, next to the rib cage—see Brisket Anatomy on page 2). This is the cut used to make lean corned beef.

Packer brisket: A whole brisket with both point and flat intact. After trimming and cooking, 40 to 50 percent remains edible meat.

Point: The fatty muscle that sits atop the brisket flat. On a steer, the point is located on top of and forward of the flat. The brisket point tends to be more tender, luscious, and fatty than the flat.

Smoke ring: A subcutaneous band of reddish pink found at the periphery of a slice of barbecued brisket. It results from a chemical reaction between the nitrogen dioxide found in wood smoke and the myoglobin found in the meat. Historically, this was the telltale mark of a properly smoked brisket, but it can be replicated by rubbing the outside of a brisket with a curing salt, like Prague Powder #1 (sodium nitrite). See the box on the smoke ring on page 36.

Franklin of Franklin Barbecue in Austin. (Read all about him on page 262.) Franklin transformed brisket from a regional Texas specialty to a cult meat prepared in places where you wouldn't necessarily expect it, including Brooklyn, Los Angeles, and even Paris. This once Texas-poor-man's beef earned Franklin highbrow acclaim in the *New York Times* and the *New Yorker* magazine, culminating in

BRISKET SPEAK: AT A DELICATESSEN

Corned beef: Brisket that has been cured in a brine with sodium nitrite and pickling spices. It is boiled, then sometimes steamed, but not smoked—at least not usually. (On page 116 you'll find a *Brisket Chronicles* first: smoked corned beef brisket.)

Montreal smoked meat: Canadian pastrami. Unlike American pastrami, it's cured with dry seasonings, not in a brine.

Pastrami: Brisket that has been cured in a garlicky brine with sodium nitrite, onions, and aromatics. Next, it's crusted with coriander, black pepper, and other spices, then smoked. The final step is steaming.

"Cold": Chilled pastrami, corned beef, or brisket. Chilling allows you to slice the

meat paper-thin, which is the way I like it. (So did the character Leo McGarry on the political drama *West Wing*.)

"Lean": Lean pastrami or corned beef sliced from the flat section of the brisket.

"Fat": Super-well-marbled pastrami or corned beef sliced from the point section of the brisket. Some people think of this as Jewish foie gras.

"Hot": Pastrami, corned beef, or brisket served hot from the steamer. Must be sliced thick or it will fall apart.

---

an unprecedented James Beard Award for best regional restaurant in 2015.

BRISKET AROUND THE WORLD

Back to our steer, Sam. His brisket will probably wind up as barbecue in Texas or Kansas City, or at a delicatessen in the form of pastrami, corned beef, or smoked meat.

- If you're Jewish, you likely grew up with brisket braised with aromatic root vegetables and/or dried fruits as the centerpiece for Rosh Hashanah and other holiday dinners. Or perhaps you ate it chilled and sliced paper-thin on rye bread slathered with mustard (or if you were a Raichlen, mayonnaise—heresy for everyone else), a deli platter classic.

- In Ireland, brisket is "pickled"—cured in a brine flavored with salt, cloves, allspice berries, mustard seeds, and bay leaves, then boiled to make an electric pink meat enjoyed the world over. Traditionally, the salt came in grains the size of barley corns, so the meat became known as corned beef.

- The French braise brisket (*poitrine de boeuf*) with onions, carrots, bacon, and red wine to make a bistro classic: *boeuf à la mode*.

- In Germany and Austria, brisket braised with caramelized onions and beer becomes a comfort dish called *Bierfleische* ("beer-meat"). The Belgians and the French have a similar dish called *carbonnade*.

- Italians also braise brisket (both beef and veal) with red or white wine to make a soulful stew called *stracotto*. In Venice and Rome, they chop it and pile it on crusty rolls to be eaten as *panini*. In the Piedmont region in northern Italy, *bollito misto* reigns supreme. Picture brisket (again, both beef and veal) simmered for hours with chicken, beef tongue, and sausage and served sliced with tangy *salsa verde* (caper herb sauce—page 170). Traditionally dished up from a special silver trolley with great ceremony, it's the world's most elegant boiled dinner.

- Brisket is also beloved in the Spanish Caribbean and Central America, where it's boiled, shredded, then simmered with cumin-scented Creole sauce to make the colorfully named dish *ropa vieja*, "old clothes." Cubans deep-fry shredded boiled brisket with onions and garlic to make the equally poetic *vaca frita*, "fried cow."
- Farther afield, brisket turns up in Kashmir, where it's stewed in a thick paste of ginger, coriander, cardamom, and other spices to make a dish equally beloved by Pakistanis and Indians, *nihari gosht*.
- Koreans simmer it with glass noodles to make a

rib-sticking soup called *sulungtang*. They also defy brisket physics by slicing it paper-thin and direct-grilling it like minute steaks (see page 89).
- Singaporeans simmer it in stews; the Chinese "red cook" it with soy sauce and fragrant star anise (page 149).
- And more than 8,000 miles away from Sam's pasture, brisket becomes another national dish and cultural treasure, *pho chin nac* (colloquially referred to as pho in the West)—the beef noodle soup eaten just about any time of day or night in Vietnam.

In other words, brisket has achieved culinary cult status around the world, and the multiplicity of dishes—soups, stews, sandwiches, and smoky slabs of meat—attests to its universal appeal.

BRISKET TODAY AND TOMORROW

Like any cult meat, brisket and how it's cooked continue to evolve. Consider that epicenter of Texas barbecue, Austin: On a recent trip there, I enjoyed brisket ramen (page 164) and brisket "hot pockets" (page 203) at the Asian-Texas fusion restaurant Kemuri Tatsu-ya.

Aaron Franklin and Tyson Cole (who is the owner of Austin's renowned Uchi restaurant) serve kettle corn with brisket bits (page 260) at their sizzling Asian smokehouse, Loro. In Austin, you could start your day with brisket breakfast tacos (page 179) at Valentina's and snack on brisket tots (page 200) at EastSide Tavern. What's next—a brisket dessert? It's already here in the form of the brisket chocolate chip cookies (page 263) served by Evan LeRoy at his LeRoy and Lewis food truck.

WHY BRISKET, WHY NOW?

So what is it about brisket that inspires such reverence and mystique, that makes it such a culinary icon and—dare I say—fetish?

Well, first there's the flavor and texture. Like all well-exercised muscles, brisket possesses an extraordinarily rich, soulful, beefy flavor. When properly prepared, it becomes tender, but even when smoked or braised for the better part of a day, it retains a satisfying chew.

Then there's its versatility. You can braise it, boil it, bake it, and, yes, even grill it. Served by itself, it dominates the meal, but it also makes a welcome addition to sandwiches, soups, stews, and stir-fries.

Price is a factor, too, and while brisket costs a *lot* more than it used to, it's still a relative bargain compared with, say, prime rib or beef tenderloin.

And there's no discounting good looks, for few food sights have the majesty of a whole, crusty, dark brisket hot out of the smoker. Or a steaming, kaleidoscopically colorful bowl of Vietnamese pho.

Finally, there's the sheer challenge of barbecuing a brisket and the unabashed sense of triumph you feel when you nail it. Aaron Franklin puts it this way: "Ribs cook in a few hours. Pork shoulder is virtually impossible to screw up. But brisket requires fifteen hours of constant attention and supervision, and, believe me, there are no shortcuts. People know what you had to go through to get it right."

This book is about brisket in all its multifarious glory. Brisket cooked outdoors in the best American barbecue tradition. Brisket cooked indoors in Dutch ovens and stockpots. Brisket cured to make corned beef, pastrami, and smoked meat. Brisket used to enhance everything from baked beans and baked potatoes to scones. Brisket may seem simple (many recipes require only the meat, plus salt, and pepper), but it isn't always easy. In the following section, you'll find everything you need to know about preparing brisket, from buying and seasoning it to cooking and serving it.

HOW TO BUY BRISKET— GRADES AND CUTS

Choice versus Prime? Grass-fed or Wagyu? Point versus flat? Brisket comes in a wide range of grades and cuts. The first step in brisket mastery is understanding them and buying the right cut for you.

CATTLE BREEDS
There are more than 250 recognized breeds of cattle in the world. Popular breeds here in the US include Angus, Hereford, Texas Longhorn, and Brahman. Farther afield, you find Jersey and Aberdeen Angus in the UK, Charolais in France, Chianina in Italy, Charbray and Brangus in Australia, and Japanese Black and Red (Akaushi) in Japan. Most North American brisket masters use Certified Angus Beef, colloquially known as CAB.

MAKING THE GRADE
Once processed, the beef is graded according to the amount of intramuscular fat (**marbling**) in the rib eye between the twelfth and thirteenth ribs. The quality of the final brisket varies with the cattle breed, how it's raised, what it eats, and how it's graded. In descending order of richness you find the following:

Prime has the most marbling (and correspondingly, the highest price), with fat ranging from "abundant" to "moderately abundant" to "slightly abundant." (Quotes indicate USDA language.) Only 3.8 percent of the beef sold in the US merits the grade Prime. Look for Prime brisket at high-end butcher shops and meat markets. A small but growing number of barbecue restaurants, like Franklin Barbecue in Austin, serve only Prime brisket.

Choice beef has a "modest" to "small amount of

marbling." This is the grade sold at most supermarkets and served at many barbecue restaurants. It may lack some of the fat of Prime, but it still has plenty of flavor.

Select beef has a "slight" amount of marbling, but costs less than Prime or Choice. Most of it goes to food service, but you sometimes find it at the supermarket. Before you dismiss it outright, know that Select is the grade served at Snow's BBQ in Lexington, Texas.

Choice Plus/Top Choice/ Upper Choice, etc.:

Many packing houses reserve their best Choice briskets for restaurants and institutional customers. They sell them under proprietary brand names, like Ranger's Reserve, Boulder Valley, Seminole Pride, and so on. You may see these referenced on restaurant menus—or occasionally sold at meat markets. Expect a brisket with a little more marbling than Choice but less than Prime.

Wagyu: Native to Japan and now raised worldwide (including in the US), Wagyu beef is prized for its exceptionally generous marbling. A great Wagyu brisket will all but ooze with

fatty goodness when you bite into it, with a buttery richness that lingers on your tongue long after you've swallowed it. But much Wagyu brisket sold in the US isn't much richer than conventional Prime beef.

American Wagyu beef is rated by its **BMS** (beef marble score), with 3 being the lowest and 12 being the highest. Sometimes you'll hear Wagyu referred to as **A5**, which designates a BMS of 8 or higher. This is extraordinary beef—some of the best on the planet. Picture white lace over a red tablecloth and you get a good idea of what A5 Wagyu looks like. Lower-ranked Wagyu is more on par with USDA Prime beef (which rates 4 to 5 BMS). This fatty goodness does not come cheap: Wagyu brisket typically costs two to four times as much as Choice brisket. Two good sources are Mister Brisket (misterbrisket.com) in Cleveland Heights, Ohio, and Idaho-based Snake River Farms (snakeriverfarms.com).

Wagyu brisket. Now *that's* what you call marbling!

Kobe: Refers to Kuroge Washu and Tajima breed steers raised according to strict guidelines in Japan's Hyogo Prefecture. Only a handful of restaurants are allowed to import and serve it in the US. Be very wary of brisket labeled "Kobe" in this country. I can almost guarantee you it's not the real McCoy.

Grass-fed: *Bos taurus* (the domesticated cow) evolved as a grass eater. Grass-fed brisket has a distinctive flavor that ranges from herbaceous to minerally. Here in America, most grass-fed beef tends to be pasture-raised on small family farms. So if you're concerned about eating humanely raised beef that's free of antibiotics and growth hormones, grass-fed brisket is your ticket. (Food activist Michael Pollan would approve.) On the downside, grass-fed brisket tends to be leaner and tougher than grain-fed, making it more challenging to cook. One good source for superlative grass-fed brisket is Strauss Meats (straussdirect.com). Note: If you happen to live near or visit Charlotte, North Carolina, Vance Lin and Lindsay Williamson of the Farmhouse BBQ catering company (goodforyou.com)

Grass-fed brisket: lean meat, great flavor

serve excellent grass-fed barbecued brisket at local fairs and farmers' markets.

Craft beef: A new term coined by the online beef marketing company Crowd Cow to refer to "beef produced by small-scale, independent farms with an emphasis on unique flavors and high ethical standards." In other words, it's the opposite of the feedlot commodity beef found in most American supermarkets. I can tell you firsthand, it's great meat. For more information and ordering, visit crowdcow.com.

Grain-fed: Corn-fed cattle grow faster and bigger than grass-fed, and their meat has a rich, appealing mouthfeel. Virtually all industrially raised beef is corn-fed—a diet that often requires treating the steers with antibiotics to keep them healthy in the feedlot. From a strictly taste-centered point of view, most Americans prefer grain-fed beef. One compromise is to buy grass-fed, grain-finished beef—ideally from a local or family farm that raises its cattle humanely. Remember: How your meat is raised matters as much as how you cook it.

Wet-aged beef/dry-aged beef: Freshness matters for seafood, but if you were to try to cook meat from a freshly slaughtered steer, you'd be surprised by how tough and dry it tastes. Aging improves the texture and flavor of all beef, and that aging can last anywhere from a few days in a vacuum-sealed plastic bag (**wet aging**) for typical supermarket beef to four to six weeks or even more unwrapped in a meat locker (**dry aging**). Aging produces the most dramatic results in the tender muscles that give us steak. According to Dr. Jeffrey Savell, Distinguished Professor of Meat Science at Texas A&M University, aging does not significantly improve a tough muscle like brisket. I can't recall experiencing a single dry-aged brisket on my travels around Planet Barbecue.

Veal brisket: Nearly all of the brisket cooked in North America comes from steers, but in Italy, people love veal brisket. On page 139 you'll find a recipe for Venetian braised veal brisket. The *bollito misto* on page 167 contains both veal and beef brisket. You'll probably need to special-order veal brisket from a butcher. One good mail order source is straussdirect.com.

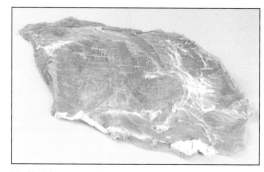
Veal brisket: Note the lighter color of the meat.

A 4-pound section of brisket comprising both the flat and the point

THE CUT

As we have seen (page 2), brisket is comprised of two muscles: the *pectoralis profundus* (the lean flat) and the *pectoralis superficialis* (the fatty point). Together they comprise a **packer brisket**. This is a full brisket—12 to 18 pounds—and it's what the pros smoke at the great barbecue restaurants in Texas, Brooklyn, and beyond. Supermarkets rarely display full packer briskets in the meat case (unless you live in Texas), so you'll likely need

A whole packer brisket

The brisket flat

to order one ahead of time from the meat manager or your local butcher. Note: Sometimes meat markets sell partially trimmed packer briskets typically weighing more in the neighborhood of 10 pounds.

More often, what you will find at the supermarket are **brisket flats**, often cut into 3- or 4-pound sections, or on rarer occasions, fatty **brisket points**. The markets where I shop typically sell 4- to 8-pound sections of packer briskets that include both flat and point. Use these sectioned packer briskets or whole points for barbecuing. Four to 6 pounds is ideal— unless you're up to smoking a whole packer brisket, which is even better. (It's difficult to barbecue a brisket section weighing less than 3 pounds—it dries out before you get it fully cooked.)

Use brisket flats or smaller sections for boiling, braising, and stewing—or barbecuing draped with bacon (as described on page

The brisket point

44) or in the style of Kansas City (page 56).

Curiously, brisket changes shape slightly from season to season, depending on market conditions. When brisket flats are at a premium, a packer brisket may come with more point and less flat. Brisket points are in high demand in Korea, so often this part gets exported, with the lean flat remaining in the US. Brisket prices tend to spike just before St. Patrick's Day, Rosh Hashanah, and other holidays at which brisket is traditionally served.

Bottom line: Buy Prime brisket when you can; Choice or Choice Plus when you're on a budget; and Wagyu when you're feeling really extravagant. Look for **NHTC** (non-hormone-treated cattle) and avoid beef treated with antibiotics or **HGPs** (slow-release hormone growth promotants). Ask questions—you'll get better brisket and your butcher will respect you more.

TRIMMING BRISKET

You can imagine that there are many opinions on the proper way to trim a brisket. Some restaurants, like Snow's BBQ, trim quite radically (a 14-pound packer gets trimmed down to 6 to 8 pounds). Other restaurants hardly trim at all. In Kansas City, they routinely separate the point from the flat and smoke them separately, serving the point as burnt ends and the flat thinly sliced for sandwiches.

Aaron Franklin of Franklin Barbecue in Austin has turned trimming into high art. He starts by squaring off the long sides, then trimming the fat on the top and bottom. He cuts off the thin edges, which would burn in the smoker. (Some restaurants turn these flap pieces into chicken fried steak.) His briskets have rounded edges—the beef equivalent of an Airstream trailer. "Smoke and air don't move in a linear fashion," explains Franklin. "An aerodynamic brisket just cooks better."

My own trim style loosely follows the Aaron Franklin method, but with a little more fat removed from the seam between the point and the

1. Trim one slender edge off the flat section of the brisket.

2. Trim the slender edge off the other side of the brisket flat.

3. Trim the excess fat off the top of the brisket, but leave at least ¼ inch of the fat.

4. Cut out some of the seam fat between the point and the flat.

5. Cut out most of the hard lump of fat at the top and end of the point, again leaving a ¼-inch layer of fat.

6. Trim off the hard pocket of fat on the underside of the brisket under the point.

7. You can see how lean the underside is, and you can see the tight grain of the brisket flat.

8. Hang on to the fat trimmings—you can use them to grease the grill grate or to make Brisket Butter (page 259).

flat. See step-by-step photos for details.

But however you trim, always leave *at least a ¼-inch-thick layer of fat* on the meat to keep it from drying out. When in doubt, err on the side of more fat.

> **BRISKET HACK:** Brisket is easier to trim when it's cold. Place it in the freezer for 30 minutes before trimming.

COOKING BRISKET— THE OVERVIEW

Brisket is a tough, flavorful cut loaded with a chewy connective tissue called collagen. Over the centuries and around the world, brisket lovers have relied on moist, low-heat cooking methods to make it tender. If you live in Texas or Kansas City (or elsewhere in America's barbecue belt), for example, you likely cook your brisket outdoors in a smoker or barbecue pit. If you live in Latin America, Europe, or Asia, you probably use a Dutch oven, stockpot, or wok. Here are the traditional ways to cook brisket, plus one that proves the exception to the rule.

Barbecuing/smoking: For many Americans (and Raichlen readers and viewers, of course), this is the *only* way to cook brisket. You fire up your smoker (offset, water, drum, pellet, electric, what have you—see pages 16 to 22). You burn wood or charcoal (or a combination of both), working at a temperature between 225° and 275°F for a cooking time that typically runs 12 to 14 hours for a whole packer brisket (somewhat less for flats). You wrap the brisket in butcher paper two-thirds of the way through the cook. Once it's cooked, you rest the brisket in an insulated cooler for 1 to 2 hours before carving. The result? Crusty bark and luscious meat, with smoke, salt, and spice in perfect equipoise.

Texas-style brisket—barbecued

Braising: If you grew up in a Jewish family like I did, this was probably the first way you experienced brisket: braised in a covered pot with aromatic vegetables or dried fruit (or both) in a generous amount of liquid (ranging from water to wine to Coca-Cola). Braising takes its name from the French word for embers (*braises*). In the old days, you'd braise in a Dutch oven in your fireplace, the pot nestled in the embers, with more embers on the lid. Today, most of us braise in the oven, but the fiber-penetrating steam and low, moist heat still render the toughest brisket fork-tender.

Added advantage: You make a sauce right in the pot.

Holiday brisket—braised

Stewing: Cut the brisket into smaller pieces and simmer it in considerably more liquid and you have another popular method for cooking brisket: stewing. Spanish Caribbean and Central American cooks stew shredded brisket in a cumin-scented tomato sauce to make the colorfully named *ropa vieja* (page 171). Stewing is generally done in a deep pot on the stove.

Ropa vieja—stewed

Boiling: This is the simplest method of all for cooking brisket: You place it in a pot of water (usually flavored with aromatic vegetables, fragrant herbs, and pungent spices) and boil it into submission. It sounds simple-minded—even boring—until you pause to remember that boiling produces three of the world's most revered brisket dishes: Italian *bollito misto* (mixed boiled meats; page 167), Vietnamese pho (beef and rice noodle soup; page 155), and Korean *sulungtang* (brisket glass noodle soup). Nor should we forget New Zealand's "boil up" (brisket or pork boiled with aromatic vegetables). Boiling is often done in two stages, starting with an initial boil called blanching, which removes the surface impurities. (Blanching typically takes 3 minutes of boiling, after which you rinse the meat, discard the boiling liquid, and wipe the pot clean.) A second boil (or more accurately, simmer) in fresh water does the cooking. Boiling actually serves two purposes. It cooks and tenderizes the meat, of course. But it also transfers the rich beefy flavor of the brisket to the broth. Note: In Cuba, boiling is combined with deep-frying to make a

Pho—boiled

crispy shredded brisket dish called *vaca frita* ("fried cow"; page 174).

Grilling: Normally, direct grilling a tough cut like brisket would be a recipe for disaster. Well, here's a shocker: At Korean grill parlors, they routinely direct grill brisket on tabletop braziers. The secret is to freeze the brisket, then slice it paper-thin on a meat slicer (or in a food processor). Grilled brisket has a completely different texture and flavor than smoked brisket. I love its crisp, fatty, beefy richness. (Try the recipe on page 83.)

Korean brisket—grilled

BRISKET COOKERS AND GEAR

Here in North America, the most popular way to cook brisket, of course, is barbecuing. You do it outdoors in a barbecue pit, smoker, or grill (set up for indirect grilling—or direct grilling in the case of the Brisket "Steaks" and Korean Grilled Brisket in chapter 2). But while barbecued brisket is king in the US, much of the world's brisket is cooked indoors on the stove or in the oven. Indoor brisket includes Irish corned beef, Spanish Caribbean *ropa vieja*, Jewish braised brisket, Italian *bollito misto*, and Vietnamese pho.

Here's what you need to cook brisket indoors and out.

INDOOR COOKERS

Dutch oven: Thick-walled and heavy-lidded, and twice as wide as it is tall, this is the quintessential pot for braising a brisket. A tight-fitting lid is essential for holding in the steam, which in turn is essential to cooking and tenderizing the meat. Three good brands are Staub, Lodge, and Le Creuset.

Stockpot: A waist-high stockpot dominates the kitchen at Pho Hoa Pasteur in Ho Chi Minh City, Vietnam, where brisket, oxtails, and aromatic vegetables simmer for

the better part of a day to make pho. You won't need a stockpot quite that big, but choose one that holds at least 3 to 4 gallons, with thick walls to distribute the heat. It's also useful for making Italian *bollito misto* (page 167) and boiling the brisket for *ropa vieja* (page 171).

Pressure cooker, programmable electric cooker, slow cooker: These devices use pressure and/or electricity to cook your brisket. A **pressure cooker** shaves hours off the process of boiling or braising a brisket. (Choose one large enough to hold the size brisket you plan to cook.) A **programmable electric cooker** lets you sauté, simmer, boil, steam, and pressure-cook in a single device. It works well for any of the braises or soups in this book. Instant Pot is the industry standard. A **slow cooker** uses low moist heat and an extended cooking time—the time-honored method for cooking brisket. Crock-Pot is the industry standard. Follow the

manufacturer's instructions on how to use these appliances.

OUTDOOR COOKERS

And now to the subject that generates, er, heated debate: the best smoker, grill, or barbecue pit in which to barbecue your brisket. Smokers vary widely in terms of function, capacity, and price. Each has its advantages and disadvantages. Here's an overview. For a more in-depth discussion of how to use the various smokers, see my book *Project Smoke* and, of course, the manufacturer's instructions.

Water smoker: This is a great all-purpose smoker—affordably priced and easy to use. Thanks to its simple design, it turns out excellent barbecued brisket every time. The fuel (charcoal, with wood chunks or chips added to generate wood smoke) goes in the bottom. A wide bowl of water sits in the center, shielding the brisket from direct heat. The brisket goes on a circular grate toward the top. You control the heat by opening or closing the vents at the top and bottom. Good brands include the Weber Smokey Mountain and Napoleon.

Advantages: Inexpensive (usually under $300) and easy to operate. The water in the pan creates a humid environment, which keeps the brisket moist and helps it absorb the wood smoke. Easy to maintain a consistent smoking temperature. Good for neophyte smokers, and its small footprint makes it ideal for people with limited space.

KEY TEMPERATURES FOR COOKING AND SERVING BRISKET

Brisket's high collagen content and unique muscular structure (two separate muscles whose fibers run almost perpendicular to one another) require a series of precise storing, cooking, and serving temperatures to maximize tenderness. Here are the key temperatures.

STORING UNCOOKED BRISKET

Below 40°F: The temperature at which brisket should be stored until you're ready to cook it.

SMOKER, OVEN, AND STOVE TEMPERATURES

212°F: The temperature at which you boil brisket at sea level.

225° to 275°F (with 250°F being your target temperature): The proper temperature for your smoker or cooker.

300°F: The proper temperature for braising a brisket in the oven.

INTERNAL TEMPERATURE

150° to 170°F: The temperature at which the stall (see page 30) takes place when barbecuing brisket. This typically occurs 6 to 8 hours into the cooking.

140° to 160°F: Brisket fat starts to render and its collagen starts to convert to gelatin.

165°F: The temperature at which you should wrap a barbecued brisket. Typically, you do this between 8 and 10 hours into the cook. (See The Wrap, page 31.)

175°F: The temperature to which you cook pastrami or smoked meat before steaming it.

185°F: If you live in Kansas City and you like your meat thinly sliced, cook your barbecued brisket to this temperature. This is also the temperature to aim for when boiling brisket to slice for pho.

203° to 208°F (with 205°F being your target temperature): If you live in Texas, Brooklyn, and elsewhere on Planet Barbecue, smoke a packer brisket to this temperature. Typically, the brisket reaches this temperature in 10 to 15 hours.

RESTING AND SERVING BRISKET

140° to 160°F: Once your brisket has rested, this is the temperature at which to slice and serve it.

Drawbacks: Like all charcoal smokers, it requires some attention every hour.

BRISKET HACK: Use the **top-down burn** technique to run your smoker for 4 to 6 hours or even longer without refueling. Pile unlit charcoal in the firebox (the bottom section with the perforated metal ring). Intersperse the charcoal with wood chunks or chips. Just before smoking, pour a third- to a half-chimney of hot embers on and in the center of the unlit coals. The fire will burn down gradually, giving you a long, slow, steady burn.

Kevin Kolman (of Weber) recommends placing two logs at the bottom of your smoker, with a chimney of unlit coals on top, then a chimney of lit coals on top of that. Run the smoker for at least 30 minutes to equalize the temperature before you add the brisket.

Drum smoker: Picture an upright metal drum with vents at the top and bottom. The brisket rests on a wire rack toward the top. You fill the coal basket with unlit charcoal, then pour lit coals on top for a classic top-down burn. Intersperse the coals with wood chunks or chips to generate

wood smoke. The gold standard is the Pit Barrel Cooker.

Advantages: Another affordable smoker ($300) that's easy to use and space efficient. Its compact size and light weight make it quite portable (tailgaters take note).

Drawbacks: Relatively limited capacity (two flats or points or one full packer brisket).

BRISKET HACK: On a Pit Barrel Cooker and other models, the vents come preset. At high altitudes, you'll want to open the bottom vent a little wider to let in more air to boost the heat.

Kamado-style cooker: Epitomized by the Big Green Egg, these ovoid cookers have thick ceramic walls to hold in and maintain the heat, with a highly efficient vent system to help you regulate the temperature. (Newer models, like the Weber Summit charcoal grill and Char-Griller Akorn, use double-walled stainless steel.) When indirect grilling and smoking, a ceramic or metal plate (aka heat diffuser) goes between the fire and the grate to shield the brisket from the fire. As in the previous smokers,

use a top-down burn to obtain a slow steady heat, interspersing wood chips or chunks throughout the charcoal to generate smoke. This huge and growing category includes the Big Green Egg, Komodo Kamado, Primo, Char-Griller Akorn, Monolith, Kamado Joe, Char-Broil, and others.

Advantages: The thick walls ensure a consistent temperature—even in winter. The tight felt or silicone gasket holds in moisture. Thanks to the efficient venting, a single load of charcoal burns many hours.

Disadvantages: Kamado cookers can be quite expensive. Depending on the model, your cook space is limited to one or two briskets. You don't need to refuel often, but when you do, you have to remove the brisket, grates, and hot heat diffuser to add more charcoal.

Offset smoker: This brings us into professional territory, for these massive steel cookers are what the pros use at barbecue competitions and restaurants. Picture a large horizontal metal cylinder with a hinged lid (the cook chamber), with a smaller cylinder with a hinged lid (the firebox) mounted slightly lower at one end, and a chimney pipe at the other. (Some models feature metal boxes instead of cylinders. On other models—called reverse flow smokers—the chimney is next to the firebox.) "Stick burners," as these smokers are often called, burn logs or a combination of logs and charcoal. Respected brands include Horizon, Yoder, Pitts

and Spitts, David Klose, Oklahoma Joe's, and so on.

Advantages: If you love the process of splitting wood, building and maintaining a fire, and cooking like a barbecue pro, the stick burner is for you. It burns logs—the traditional way to barbecue brisket. Even small models can hold two or three packer briskets—professional scale models might hold thirty to fifty.

Disadvantages: Stick burners—especially those with thick metal walls (and you want thick metal walls, especially if you live in a cold climate)—can be quite expensive. They take up more real estate than water smokers or kettle grills and aren't very portable—unless you attach one to a trailer. They also require hourly attention.

Gravity smoker: A relative newcomer to the world of barbecue, but its simplicity and efficiency make up for lost time. In most smokers the wood goes on top of a bed of burning charcoal. In a gravity smoker, the hot coals drop from an overhead chute onto the wood, from whence the resulting smoke passes into the smoke chamber. State-of-the-art brands include Kalamazoo Outdoor Gourmet, T&K Smokers, and Deep South Smokers.

Advantages: Extremely fuel efficient and easy to refuel. They deliver smoke slowly and steadily for long cooks.

Disadvantages: They can be expensive.

Kettle grill: Yes, you can use a kettle grill or other charcoal grill as a smoker (provided it has a high lid for clearance). Set it up for indirect grilling, adding wood chunks or soaked wood chips to the coals  to produce wood smoke. The same holds true for a frontloading charcoal grill, like the Char-Broil 940X.

Advantages: Affordable and easy to use. You may well own one already. The small footprint makes it ideal for people with limited space.

Disadvantages: Capacity is limited to a single brisket. Requires frequent refueling.

> **BRISKET HACK:** Use only half as much charcoal as you normally would to keep the temperature low.

Pellet grill: If you like the convenience of push-button ignition and turn-of-the-knob heat control, a pellet grill may be for you. The fuel (hardwood sawdust pellets) goes into a hopper, whence it's fed by an auger into the burn chamber. This is another high-growth cooker

category; good brands include Green Mountain Grills, Yoder, Memphis Wood Fire Grills, REC TEC, Traeger, and MAK.

Advantages: Pellet grills are exceedingly easy to operate, with a steady temperature control and smoke output. They truly are set-it-and-forget-it smokers.

Disadvantages: Like any machine with moving parts and electronics, they can break, requiring professional repair.

> **BRISKET HACK:** The lower the temperature, the greater the smoke output, which works out nicely for brisket.

Electric smoker/gas smoker: Like pellet grills, electric smokers fall into the set-it-and-forget-it category, with digital thermostats to control the temperature and wood dispensers to deliver the smoke. One well-known brand,

Masterbuilt, burns hardwood chips. Another, Bradley, burns compressed sawdust disks, called bisquettes. Gas smokers run on propane instead of electricity, using wood chips to generate smoke. Other popular brands include Smoke Hollow, Char-Broil, Dyna-Glo, and Smoke Vault.

Advantages: In two words, convenience and consistency. Electric smokers take the guesswork out of barbecue.

Disadvantages: Like any machine with moving parts and electronics, electric smokers can break, requiring professional repair.

> **BRISKET HACK:** Some models are too narrow to accommodate a full packer brisket. Cut the meat in half widthwise and smoke it on two separate racks.

Gas grill: I list gas grills reluctantly. It's challenging to run a gas grill at a consistently low temperature (250°F) for the extended time it takes to cook a whole brisket. And even if your gas grill has a built-in smoker box, it's hard to keep enough smoke under the hood to put significant flavor to the meat. (Most of the smoke escapes through the gap between the

SETTING UP YOUR GRILL FOR INDIRECT GRILLING AND SMOKING

To set up a kettle grill or other charcoal grill for indirect grilling, light the coals in a chimney starter, then rake the embers into two piles at opposite sides of the bottom (coal) grate. Or if your grill has side baskets, place the coals in them. Place a foil drip pan in the center, between the mounds of coals. Add wood chunks or chips to generate smoke. (For prolonged smoke sessions, soak the chips in water for 30 minutes, then drain. This slows the rate of combustion.) Place the brisket or other food to be smoked over the drip pan between the mounds of coals.

To smoke low and slow on a charcoal grill, use only half as much charcoal as you normally would.

To indirect grill on a two-burner gas grill, light one side and cook the brisket on the other (unlit) side. On a three-, four-, five-, or six-burner gas grill, light the outside or front and rear burners and leave the center burner(s) off. To generate wood smoke, use a smoking box, smoking puck, or foil smoking pouch (wood chips wrapped in heavy duty foil, which you then perforate with a sharp point), or place hardwood chunks under the grate over the burners. *Not* that I recommend cooking brisket on a gas grill, but that's how you would do it.

firebox and the lid in the back.) It helps to have a gas grill with multiple burners—the more burners, the more likely you'll be able to maintain a low temperature.

Advantages: Push-button ignition and turn-of-a-knob temperature control. Okay for grilling brisket burgers, brisket steaks, and Korean grilled brisket.

Disadvantages: It's very difficult to obtain a meaningful smoke flavor with a gas grill.

> **BRISKET HACK:** Set up the grill for indirect grilling. Place the brisket fat side up, away from the lit burner(s). Use an under-the-grate smoking pouch or use a grate-top smoker, like a smoking puck. Just don't expect miracles.

Hibachi: Use this small charcoal-burning brazier to direct grill paper-thin shavings of frozen brisket (see page 83).

Advantages: Inexpensive, portable, and small enough for tabletop grilling.

Disadvantages: Good only for direct grilling, so this is a one-trick pony. (But, oh, what a trick.)

> **BRISKET HACK:** Place the hibachi on an inverted sheet pan or other heatproof surface in the center of your table. Have each guest grill his or her own brisket.

THE GEAR

You don't need a lot of fancy equipment to cook brisket, but the following tools definitely make the work easier and more efficient.

Airflow controller: A barbecued brisket can take up to 15 hours of smoking, and this ingenious device keeps your cooker burning at a consistent temperature for the duration of the cook. It does so by controlling the airflow, adding more air when the temperature drops, and cutting the airflow if the temperature rises too much. A motorized fan over the intake air vent at the bottom moderates the airflow, while a thermocouple clipped to the grate monitors the temperature inside the smoke chamber. The CyberQ by BBQ Guru is the industry standard, with controllers that fit Big Green Egg and other kamado-style cookers, the Weber Smokey Mountain and other water smokers, and so on. To control the heat and

Perfect Draft BBQ Blower (top) and CyberQ (bottom)

airflow in an offset barrel smoker, use the Perfect Draft BBQ Blower.

Aluminum foil pans: Sometimes called drip pans, these are indispensable for indirect grilling, smoking burnt ends, and generally holding and moving ingredients. You'll want several dozen 9-by-13-inch pans. While you're at it, get some smaller 6-by-8½-inch pans.

Barbecue mop: A miniature cotton mop (some versions come in silicone) for swabbing mop sauces and bastes on the brisket. Look for a removable head so you can clean the mop in the dishwasher.

Cutting boards: Use for trimming and slicing (not the same board unless you wash it thoroughly with soapy water between uses). For serving brisket, you need a large board with a deep

well (a groove around the perimeter) for catching the juices.

Gloves: Most pit masters check brisket for doneness by feel, not solely by internal temperature. How it bends when you lift it. Or how the fat jiggles when you poke it. You need to protect your hands with **insulated gloves** (usually rubber or silicone). They're also useful for transferring hot cooked briskets from the smoker to the insulated cooler for resting, then to the cutting board for carving. Note: Some old-timers prefer the dexterity of wearing wool gloves with plastic or latex gloves over them to seal out the grease. **Latex or rubber gloves** are useful for keeping your hands clean while handling raw meat and applying rubs.

Injector: Used on the competition circuit to inject beef broth and other flavorings into the lean brisket flat to make it extra moist and flavorful.

Insulated cooler: One of the secrets to moist, tender barbecued brisket is to rest it for 1 to 2 hours after it comes out of the smoker (see page 33). The best place to rest it is in an insulated cooler, which keeps the brisket hot.

Jumbo (2.5-gallon capacity) resealable plastic bags: These are handy for brining brisket when making corned beef and pastrami. Use heavy-duty bags and double them up. I like to place them in a bowl or baking dish in the unlikely event that the bag leaks.

Knives: Unlike steak, brisket requires extensive trimming before cooking and careful carving for serving. So a good set of knives is essential. At a minimum, you'll need:

A **chef's knife** for cutting the brisket into pieces.

A **boning knife** with a curved slender blade for trimming the fat.

A **paring knife** for fine trimming and cutting the vegetables to add to brisket soups and stews.

A **slicing knife** for serving the brisket. Many pit masters slice with a **serrated knife**. Others use hollow-ground slicing knives, like the Shun brisket knife.

Meat slicer: Yes, I know this sounds like a formidable piece of equipment for a home kitchen, but without a meat slicer, it's hard to cut those even, paper-thin slices of corned beef (page 111) and pastrami (page 93) that are the glory of a deli sandwich. It is also used to slice the boiled brisket for Vietnamese pho (page 155) and the frozen meat for Korean Grilled Brisket (page 83).

And this is the tool Kansas City pit masters use to make those thin, tender slices of smoked brisket flat that go on a Kansas City barbecue sandwich. Meat slicers are available both motorized and hand-cranked. Two good brands are Chef'sChoice and Kitchener.

Pink paper/butcher paper: Wrapping is an indispensable step in the process of smoking a brisket (see page 31). The wrap preferred by most pit masters is unlined butcher paper, often called pink paper (the color of leading brands, such as Bryco Goods). It's important to use unlined butcher paper, which seals in moisture but releases the steam. Note: The butcher paper you get at a supermarket, like Whole Foods or Fresh Market, comes lined with plastic—not what you want for wrapping brisket.

Plastic buckets: Useful for brining briskets (and soaking and rinsing them when the brisket is cured). YETI makes cool plastic buckets.

Sprayer: Useful for spraying cider, vinegar, or other flavorful liquids on the brisket.

Thermometers: Essential for monitoring the internal temperature of a brisket as it cooks. At the very least, you'll want a **stick thermometer** with a slender probe you insert in the meat. For long slow cooks, you'll want a **remote digital thermometer** that has a probe for the meat and an external monitor that displays the temperature outside the smoker. Higher-end models have multiple probes (one for the meat, for example, and one to measure the temperature of the cook chamber at grate level). Some remote thermometers send the information directly to your smartphone. The industry leaders are Maverick and ThermoWorks.

Thermometers for checking doneness

THE 11 STEPS TO BARBECUED BRISKET NIRVANA

I've said it before; I'll say it again: Brisket is simultaneously the easiest and most difficult meat there is to barbecue. Easy, because all you do is season it with salt and pepper and smoke it low and slow until it's tender enough to cut with the side of a fork. Difficult, because every brisket is different and there are dozens of variables—and if you don't get them right, your rich, luscious, meltingly tender slab of meat may come out more like beefy shoe leather. But you can break the process into easy, manageable steps, which will help you achieve brisket nirvana every time.

STEP 1: THE MEAT

Brisket comes in a wide range of grades from a variety of cattle breeds—each with its own flavor, texture, and cooking properties. Grass-fed brisket cooks and tastes different than grain-fed; Wagyu has a remarkably different fat structure and content than Angus. I'm not saying one is better than the other—just different. On pages 10 to 16, you'll find a complete description of the various types of brisket and the best methods for cooking them.

A whole brisket (also known as a packer brisket) is comprised of two separate muscles: the fatty point and the lean flat. Most professionals cook them together as one. Your supermarket may sell them in sections or as separate cuts—especially the brisket flat. On page 41 you'll find instructions for smoking a whole packer brisket; on page 49, a brisket point; and on page 44, a brisket flat.

Regardless of cut, brisket comes with a thick cap of fat and a hard waxy stratum of fat between the point and flat, both of which you'll need to trim. The purpose of trimming is to remove excess fat, which takes time, fuel, and energy to cook (only to be discarded before serving). But you have to leave enough fat to melt and baste the brisket as it cooks, keeping it rich-tasting and moist. On page 14, you'll find step-by-step trimming instructions and photos.

STEP 2: THE SEASONING

Pit masters are divided on how simple or complex to make the seasonings. I like a "newspaper rub": black (pepper), white (sea salt), and "read" (red—hot pepper flakes) all over. Wayne Mueller of Louie Mueller Barbecue in Taylor, Texas, seasons solely with salt

3. To make a newspaper rub, mix in hot red pepper flakes.

1. To make a Dalmatian rub, combine equal parts coarse salt and pepper in a bowl.

2. Mix the seasonings with your fingers.

4. Season the top of the brisket, working several inches above the brisket so the spices go on evenly.

5. Don't forget to season the sides and underside of the brisket, too.

and pepper (often called a "Dalmatian rub" on account of being white with black speckles). Conversely, Joe Carroll of Fette Sau in Brooklyn and Philadelphia uses a complex blend of coffee, brown sugar, cumin, and other spices (see page 51). John Lewis of Lewis Barbecue in Charleston slathers his brisket with mustard before applying the seasonings.

Other techniques—often practiced on the competition barbecue circuit—add additional layers of flavor. Some pit masters inject their briskets with a mixture of beef broth, melted butter, and spices. (You'll find the recipe for a great injector sauce on page 252.) Others swab their briskets with a mop sauce (see page 251) or spray the meat with vinegar, wine, or apple cider.

But remember: The purpose of the seasoning is to flavor the brisket *without* camouflaging its primal smoky beef taste.

STEP 3: THE COOKER

You can barbecue an excellent brisket in a stick burner (offset smoker), water smoker, barrel cooker, ceramic cooker, electric or gas smoker, pellet grill, and, of course, in a charcoal kettle grill. What's important is to use a cooker that runs at a consistent temperature and provides a steady stream of wood smoke during the cook. Remember: The smoker both smokes and cooks your brisket. Every model operates differently and has its own advantages and disadvantages: See the guide to the various smokers and grills on pages 16 to 22.

STEP 4: THE FUEL

To barbecue your brisket, you'll need fuel, and that means wood, or a combination of wood and charcoal. (Electric and gas smokers use those heat sources respectively for igniting the wood or wood pellets.) Wood comes in several forms, starting with the most elemental—hardwood logs.

Hardwood logs: The fuel of choice for professional pit masters. Texans burn oak; Kansas Citians burn hickory and apple. Other popular woods for brisket include pecan, cherry, and mesquite. (I suspect that regional preferences

have less to do with flavor profile than with what wood traditionally grew abundantly in a particular area.) The variety matters less than using logs that are split and seasoned (dried). Twelve to 16 inches in length is ideal. Avoid green wood: The smoke will be bitter and it takes a ton of BTUs just to evaporate the water.

> **BRISKET HACK:** If you have green or damp logs, place them on top of your smoker to dry them out before adding them to the fire.

Wood chunks: Most home cooks use a combination of **charcoal** and **hardwood chunks** or **chips**. The charcoal provides the heat; the wood generates the smoke. Look for wood chunks at hardware stores and supermarkets. See above for common varieties. Soaking is optional (see below). Add fresh wood chunks every hour (or as needed) to generate a continuous stream of smoke.

Wood chips: The most common form of smoking wood is the wood chips available in supermarkets

and hardware stores everywhere. I like to soak chips in water to cover for 30 minutes, then drain them before adding them to the coals. Soaking slows the rate of combustion, giving you a longer, steadier smoke. Add soaked wood chips every 30 to 45 minutes (or as needed).

Pellets: Pellet grills use tiny cylinders of compressed hardwood sawdust to generate heat and smoke; the pellets come in a variety of flavors. Look for food-safe pellets made without fillers. Avoid pellets held together with cheap vegetable oil, plus bags with a lot of dust in the bottom, or pellets that have been stored outside. Moisture compromises their integrity.

Bisquettes and other sawdust disks: Made of compressed hardwood sawdust, these disks generate smoke in Bradley electric smokers.

WHAT YOU NEED TO KNOW ABOUT WOOD

Smoke is the soul of barbecue—especially barbecued brisket—and it's also one of the defining flavors of pastrami and Montreal smoked meat. So as you become a brisket master, you need to understand smoke—how to generate it, which woods produce the best smoke, and how to harness its flavor-producing properties to take *your* brisket over the top.

All burning wood, and many other burning plants, like straw and hay, produce smoke. Softwoods, such as spruce and pine, produce an unpleasantly resinous smoke. The best smoke comes from hardwoods (deciduous trees, which shed their leaves each year). Hardwoods come in two main categories: fruitwoods, such as apple, cherry, and peach, and nut woods, such as hickory, pecan, and oak.

A lot of ink has been spilled about the best wood for smoking, so I'm about to make a controversial statement: While apple, cherry, oak, and hickory smokes differ *slightly* in their flavor profile, by the time you've smoked a brisket for 12 hours, they're pretty interchangeable. The one exception here is mesquite, whose smoke is noticeably stronger and more bitter. For the record, the wood burned by most American pit masters, from Wayne Mueller at Louie Mueller Barbecue in Taylor, Texas, to Billy Durney (page 225) in Brooklyn, New York, is oak.

Use the hardwood that grows in your area—that's what the original pit masters did, and what experienced pit masters still do

today. As for mixing woods (cherry for the first 4 hours, apple thereafter), it makes for good storytelling on the competition circuit, but I'm not sure you can really taste the difference. Stick with one wood and focus on burning it right.

Far more important than the species of the wood is its overall condition and moisture content. Green wood (from freshly cut trees) contains up to four times as much moisture as seasoned (aged and dried) wood. It takes longer to light and is slower to burn, delivering less heat and more bitter creosote. Fully seasoned wood contains less than 20 percent moisture, which makes it easier to light and burn. There are two ways to season wood: in a kiln or by leaving it outdoors in a dry place for months or even years. Seasoned wood has a silvery-gray appearance. It burns efficiently and clean: That's what you want for your brisket.

When you burn wood, it goes through three stages: desiccation (drying out), pyrolysis (decomposition by fire), and combustion. Smoke production takes place during the pyrolysis stage between 340° and 800°F. This is your barbecue sweet spot. Beyond that, the wood catches fire, producing heat but no smoke. This is useful for grilling, which you don't normally do with a tough meat like brisket, unless you're cooking the brisket burgers on page 211 or the brisket "steaks" on page 79. When it comes to barbecued brisket, low and slow wins the race.

Charcoal: Supplies the heat in water smokers, kamado cookers, drum cookers, kettle grills, and other charcoal-fueled cookers. I prefer **lump charcoal**, which contains only wood. But **charcoal briquettes** (a composite of wood, coal dust, borax, and petroleum or starch binders) are the fuel used at the big barbecue competitions, like the Jack Daniel's and the American Royal. Just make sure the briquettes are lit completely (glowing red with a light dusting of gray ash) before you put the brisket in the smoker.

STEP 5: THE SMOKE

Wood smoke is an incredibly complex substance comprised of solids (such as soot), liquids (in the form of water and tars), and gases (of which there are hundreds, ranging from aldehydes to phenyls). Each contributes to the appearance, aroma, and ultimate flavor of your barbecued brisket.

The soot and tars, for example, help color your brisket, producing the appetizing dark, savory crust we call bark. Gases include acids, such as formic and acetic acids, which give the smoke a pleasant tartness. Carbonyls (produced around 390°F) have antimicrobial and preservative properties. (Remember, throughout most of human history, the main purpose of smoking foods was to keep them from spoiling.)

But it's the phenyls (which start forming around 570°F) that give us the complex micro-flavors we associate with the best barbecued brisket. One such phenyl, syringol, produces the textbook smoke flavor. Creosol delivers a peat-like taste that may remind you of Scotch whisky. Guaiacol is responsible for clove-like spice flavors, while vanillin adds a musky sweetness we associate with dessert.

Just as important as what's *in* smoke is how you produce and deliver it. Add too much smoke too fast and your brisket will taste bitter. Add too little smoke (a chronic problem with gas grills) and your brisket will taste like cooked beef—but not barbecue. Dose the smoke slowly and steadily for half a day and you'll experience that quasi-religious state I like to call brisket nirvana.

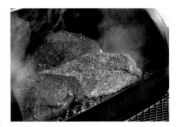

A steady stream of blue smoke is essential for great brisket.

Slow and steady means a clean-burning fire to which you add a couple of logs every hour. Or if you're cooking on a charcoal smoker, add the wood chunks or chips gradually. Two handfuls of wood chips every hour is good. Too much wood at the start of the smoke will make your brisket taste like an ashtray.

The color of your smoke tells you whether you're doing it right. Black smoke indicates a dirty fire full of the bitter creosote. White smoke indicates a fire that's starved for oxygen. You're looking for what pit masters call "blue smoke"—a pale wispy smoke with a faint bluish tinge. Or in the words of one Texas pit master, "You want the smoke to kiss the brisket, not overpower it."

STEP 6: THE FIRST COOK

The first cook takes your brisket to an internal temperature of 165° to 170°F. It browns the exterior, forming

HOW TO MAKE A CARDBOARD SMOKING PLATFORM

Ever notice how the bottom of the brisket flat tends to dry out and sometimes burn during long smoke sessions?

Billy Durney of Hometown Bar-B-Que in Brooklyn (see page 225) has an ingenious hack for preventing this, and it also makes your cooked brisket easier to handle.

Place the raw brisket on a piece of cardboard (clean, obviously) and trace its outline on top. Cut the cardboard into this shape, then wrap it tightly with heavy-duty aluminum foil.

Using an ice-pick, Phillips-head screwdriver, or other sharp implement, poke holes in the foil-wrapped cardboard every inch or so. This allows the smoke to penetrate the smoking platform and flavor the meat.

1. Trace around the brisket, then cut the cardboard to shape.

2. Poke holes in the foil-wrapped cardboard.

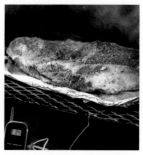

3. The platform prevents the bottom of the brisket from drying out.

a salty, smoky crust known as **the bark**. It perfumes the meat with wood smoke, renders out some of the fat, and starts to convert the tough collagen into tender gelatin.

A foil cap protects the narrow end of the brisket.

(See page 3.) The first cook of a packer brisket normally takes 8 to 10 hours. Protect the end of the flat with an aluminum foil cap and the bottom with a cardboard platform (see above) to keep them from drying out.

At some point during the cooking process, the internal temperature rise will slow down, stop, or even drop. This is called **the stall** and although it causes anxiety, it's a normal part of cooking a brisket. The stall typically takes place around

6 to 8 hours into the cooking process, when the internal temperature of the brisket is in the range of 150° to 170°F. You watch your remote thermometer with growing disbelief. You add more fuel to the fire in an attempt to reverse the stall. But the temperature stays steady or even drops.

What's actually happening is simple: As the brisket cooks, moisture pools on its surface. As that moisture evaporates, it cools off the brisket, much as perspiration cools you off—even on a hot day.

The stall normally lasts for 2 to 3 hours. Once all the moisture has evaporated, the internal temperature will start to rise again.

So what should you do when *your* brisket stalls? Don't panic. Don't add more fuel to the fire. Be patient and power through it. Sure as night turns into day, the temperature will rise and finish cooking your brisket.

STEP 7:
THE WRAP

You've stoked your smoker and powered through the stall. The meat's exterior has darkened to a handsome, espresso-hued crust, and the internal temperature has reached 165°F.

It's time for one of the most essential, if paradoxical, steps in barbecuing a perfect brisket: the wrap.

Paradoxical, because in effect, you're segregating the brisket from the one ingredient that defines it as barbecue: wood smoke.

Essential, because it seals in moistness and keeps your brisket from drying out.

And every serious pit master does it, although debate rages as to whether you should wrap in butcher

paper, aluminum foil, plastic wrap, a bath towel, or some combination of the four.

Aaron Franklin of Austin's Franklin Barbecue wraps in butcher paper. Tootsie Tomanetz of Snow's BBQ in Lexington, Texas, wraps in foil. Quinn Hatfield of Mighty Quinn's Barbeque (with locations around New York, New Jersey, and abroad) wraps in plastic. Wayne Mueller of Louie Mueller Barbecue in Taylor, Texas, takes a one-two approach, wrapping first in plastic, then in butcher paper, and rewrapping each piece after slicing off a serving.

Wrapping serves several purposes. It seals in moisture during the final stage of the cook. It makes it easier to handle the cooked brisket. And it swaddles the brisket during the all-important resting period, allowing the juices to redistribute and the meat to relax.

I used to wrap brisket in aluminum foil—a practice that led me into a Twitter war with the late Anthony Bourdain. It's true that foil delivers a fork-tender brisket every time. It does so by converting the moisture to steam, which tenderizes the brisket (much the way you steam pastrami to finish cooking it). The problem is that with supernatural tenderness comes a pot

roast–like consistency. So eventually, I switched to wrapping in butcher paper, and I've never looked back. The advantage of butcher paper is that it "breathes," releasing the steam while keeping the moisture in the meat.

So here, step-by-step, is how to wrap your brisket. Dimensions are for a full packer brisket; use smaller sheets to wrap brisket flats or points.

1. Lay two sheets of butcher paper, each about 3 feet long, on your work surface so they overlap in the center to form a 3-foot square. Wearing heatproof gloves, transfer the brisket to the center of the paper square so the long side of the meat runs parallel to your shoulders.

2. Lift the back of the paper square (the side closest to you) and fold it over the brisket.

3. Tuck and fold in the sides of the paper as though you're making a blintz or an eggroll.

4. Roll the brisket over to enclose it completely in the pink paper. Note the orientation: You want the point (the fatty part) of the brisket to remain on top.

5. Tuck any overlapping paper into the seam, which, ideally, will be at the bottom. Return the wrapped brisket to the cooker.

STEP 8:
THE SECOND COOK

During the second cook, you'll take the brisket to an internal temperature of around 205°F. The purpose of the second cook is to finish rendering the fat and converting the tough collagen into tender gelatin. This will require an additional 2 to 5 hours, bringing your total cooking time to 10 to 14 hours, depending on the size of your brisket.

STEP 9:
THE DONENESS TEST

You've spent $50 to $100 buying your brisket, plus up to 14 hours cooking it to smoky perfection. The last thing you want to do is over- or undercook it. So how do you know it's done? Internal temperature is a useful indicator. So are visual tests, such as the jiggle, bend, and chopstick tests. Good pit masters use several tests at once. Here are the ones I use:

Internal temperature test:
185°F: The temperature to which Kansas City pit masters cook their brisket flats. At this stage the brisket is still firm enough to slice on an electric meat slicer.

Check the internal temperature using an instant-read meat thermometer. You're looking for around 205°F.

203° to 208°F: The temperature to which Texas pit masters cook packer briskets. At this stage the collagen is fully gelatinized and the fat fully rendered. The brisket will be so tender that you need to hand-carve it with a knife. All the following tests apply to a well-done brisket cooked to this stage.

Jiggle test: Grab the brisket from the fat end and poke/shake it. The meat will seem to jiggle a bit like Jell-O.

Bend test: Grab the brisket at both ends and lift. It should bend easily in the middle. Alternatively, slide your hand under the brisket in the center. The ends will droop like a forlorn mustache.

STEP 10: THE REST

You can certainly eat the brisket following the second cook, and after 10 to 14 hours of cooking, I won't blame you if you want to do so. But there's one more step that will take your barbecued brisket from excellent to sublime: the rest. In a nutshell, you rest the wrapped brisket in an insulated cooler for 1 to 2 hours. This allows the meat to "relax" and the juices to

1. Place the wrapped brisket, flat side down, in an insulated cooler to rest it.

Note the use of insulated food gloves during the jiggle test—the brisket will be hot!

The chopstick test: Insert the slender end of a chopstick through the brisket from top to bottom. It will pierce the brisket easily.

Chopstick test: Insert the slender end of a chopstick or the handle of a wooden spoon through the top. It should pierce the meat easily.

Bottom line: Your brisket is done when the meat is

crusty and darkly browned on the outside, and smoky and tender (but not mushy) on the inside. Each bite should be meaty, fatty, and rich, and each slice should pull apart, not fall apart.

2. Let the wrapped brisket rest for 1 to 2 hours in the cooler.

redistribute. This makes your brisket juicier and more tender. It also allows you to control the precise moment when you serve it.

STEP 11:
FINALLY, THE CARVE

In a process as idiosyncratic as cooking a brisket, there are lots of theories on the best way to carve it. Over the years, I've come to adopt the Aaron Franklin method (more on Franklin on page 262), in which you cut the brisket in half widthwise (roughly where the bulge of the point starts), then slice the flat section on the diagonal across the grain, and the point section perpendicular to the edge— again, so you wind up slicing the meat across the grain. (See photos on page 35.) An alternative method was proposed by Ohio pit master and restaurateur Jim Budros: separating the point and the flat (removing the fat between them) and realigning them, giving the point a 60-degree turn, so the meat fibers all run the same way. This way you can slice the meat from top to bottom, across the grain.

So, what's the best way to serve barbecued brisket? To my mind, as simply as possible. Texas tradition calls for slices of factory white bread. In Brooklyn, you might get brisket with brioche rolls. In Tex-Mex circles, you serve it on tortillas (page 179). In Los Angeles, you might eat it *banh mi* style, with Vietnamese condiments on a crusty baguette (page 223).

Sauce? If you've smoked your brisket correctly, you won't need it. (For more than half a century, the historic Kreuz Market in Lockhart, Texas, didn't even serve it.) If you insist on sauce (find some of my favorites on pages 248 to 257), serve it on the side and first taste the brisket without it. That way, you can enjoy the smoky awesomeness of the meat before you add what for some people (me among them) are the dissonant notes of sugar, molasses, or tomatoes. Remember, the accompaniments should support—not camouflage— the meat.

A pitch-perfect barbecued brisket after it's gotten its beauty rest

1. Cut the brisket crosswise into 2 sections: the flat section and the point section.

4. Slice the brisket flat. Note how you cut across the grain.

7. A proper slice of Texas-style barbecued brisket will be about the thickness of a No. 2 pencil.

2. Trim any excess fat off the top of the brisket.

5. Cut the brisket point section in half widthwise.

3. Cut off the hard, dry tip and dice it to serve as burnt ends.

6. Slice the brisket point pieces against the grain.

THE SMOKE RING

Examine a slice of properly smoked brisket (the sort you get at a great barbecue joint). Just below the surface, you'll notice a band of crimson extending ⅛ to ⅜ inch into the meat. Aficionados call this the smoke ring, and it's a chemical reaction that occurs naturally whenever you expose brisket to wood smoke. It doesn't automatically indicate competition-worthy brisket (more on that in a minute), but you seldom find world-class barbecued brisket without it.

Like all beef, raw brisket owes its bright red color to a protein called myoglobin. Cooking turns that into metmyoglobin, darkening the carnivorous red into the brownish-gray of well-done meat.

Enter nitrogen dioxide, a gas found in wood smoke that binds with the myoglobin, preventing it from browning. Since the gas is absorbed from the outside in, the smoke ring appears only at the edge of the meat. And since it only acts on raw meat, the smoke ring forms in the first few hours of smoking.

A smoke ring develops best when the smoke chamber is humid and the wood smoke circulates freely. Any wood-burning

smoker will produce a smoke ring—especially a water smoker or a stick burner (offset smoker).

Here are some other means of maximizing your smoke ring:

- Start with a cold, moist brisket.

- Place a metal bowl or aluminum foil pan of warm water in the smoker. (The water bowl is an integral part of the setup in a water smoker or an electric smoker.) This helps create a humid smoking environment.

- Spray the brisket with a liquid, like apple cider (see the burnt ends on page 74) or swab it with a mop sauce (see page 251).

There's another way to form a "smoke ring"—sometimes used by unscrupulous competitors, and you don't even need wood smoke. Rub the outside of the brisket with a curing salt, like Prague Powder #1 or InstaCure #1. The sodium nitrite in the curing salt turns the periphery of the meat pink—exactly as it does corned beef or pastrami.

Mindful of this subterfuge, the Kansas City Barbecue Society and organizers of other major barbecue contests instruct their certified judges to disregard the presence or absence of a smoke ring when evaluating competition brisket.

The smoke ring has no effect on a brisket's taste or tenderness, but it impacts the experience of eating barbecue big-time nonetheless. When done the right way, it's a sign that someone took the time and care to smoke a brisket properly. And that's not just aesthetics.

A gorgeous smoke ring

Properly sliced barbecued brisket is a thing to behold. Brisket flat slices fill the top half of the cutting board, while brisket point slices (and a whole chunk of point) sit at the bottom. The burnt ends are at the top right.

Chapter 2

BRISKET BARBECUED AND GRILLED

To many Americans, virtually all Texans, and no small number of Raichlen readers and viewers, brisket means one thing: barbecue. Thick slabs of beef slow-smoked over oak or hickory until the exterior is as dark as espresso, as smoky as a fire pit, and as salty-peppery as a pork crackling channeling beef jerky. So, it's only fitting that the first recipe chapter of this book focuses on barbecued brisket. In the following pages, you'll learn how to barbecue every imaginable cut, from massive packers to fat-laced points, from bacon-wrapped brisket flats to insanely rich Wagyu briskets. You'll master the Texas Hill Country and Kansas City styles, not to mention Jamaican jerk brisket and burnt ends. I'll even show you how to direct grill brisket (I'm not kidding) like they do it in Korea.

THE BIG KAHUNA
BARBECUED PACKER BRISKET

Admit it: Here's why you bought this book—to learn how to barbecue a real deal Texas-style brisket. Well, here's the big kahuna: fourteen pounds of pure proteinaceous awesomeness. The brisket that makes reputations—and fortunes. I speak, of course, of a full packer brisket (so named because that's how it's shipped from the packing house), seasoned with nothing more than salt and pepper and maybe some hot red pepper flakes, then slow-smoked Texas Hill Country–style for the better part of a day or night. The sort of glorious slab of meat—all smoke, spice, and rich, fatty beef—you line up for at Franklin Barbecue in Austin (see page 262), or at Louie Mueller Barbecue in Taylor, Texas. But can you *really* cook a Hill Country brisket at home? I'm pleased to say you can, and it's not even all that difficult. It does require the right cut of meat—a full brisket with both point and flat (see page 13)—and a smoker, cooker, or grill capable of maintaining a low, even cooking temperature for a 10- to 14-hour stretch. Above all, it requires patience. Follow the 11 Steps to Barbecued Brisket Nirvana (page 25) and this recipe and you'll turn out a brisket that would do a Texan proud every time.

You will have worked long and hard to prepare the perfect brisket—I suggest serving it unadorned so you can appreciate the complex interplay of salt, spice, smoke, meat, and fat. Texas tradition calls for a loaf of spongy factory-made white bread. Or up the ante and serve it with garlicky Lone Star Toast (page 242). A lot of ink has been spilled about which sauce—if any—you should serve with brisket. Personally, I'm a no-sauce guy—I like to let meat and smoke speak for themselves. But if you like sauce, you'll find several options in chapter 10.

YIELD: Serves 12 to 14 (with leftovers)

METHOD: Barbecuing

PREP TIME: 15 minutes

COOKING TIME: Could be as short as 10 hours or as long as 14 hours, depending on the size of your brisket, the efficiency of your smoker, and even the weather. Plus 1 to 2 hours for resting.

HEAT SOURCE: Smoker or charcoal grill

YOU'LL ALSO NEED: A rimmed sheet pan; a perforated, foil-wrapped cardboard smoking platform (optional; see page 30); wood logs, chunks, or soaked, drained hardwood chips; a metal bowl or aluminum foil pan; pink butcher paper (unlined); insulated gloves; a digital instant-read thermometer (preferably remote); an insulated cooler; a welled cutting board

Tradition
calls for a stick burner
(an offset barrel smoker—
the home version of the
monster pits used by
Texas pros). But you can
cook a respectable brisket
in a water smoker, barrel
smoker, ceramic cooker,
charcoal grill, pellet grill,
or an electric smoker.
Sorry, gas grillers: You'll
need to buy a smoker or
charcoal grill for this one.
If by some misalignment
of the fates your brisket
has come out tough,
slice it paper-thin so you
shorten the meat fibers.

INGREDIENTS

1 large packer brisket
  (12 to 14 pounds)

Coarse sea salt

Cracked black peppercorns
  or freshly ground black
  peppercorns

Hot red pepper flakes (optional)

Sliced white bread or Lone Star
  Toast (page 242), for serving
  (optional)

1. Using a sharp knife, trim the brisket, leaving a layer of fat at least ¼ inch thick (see page 14). Be careful not to over-trim. It's better to err on the side of too much fat than too little.

2. Place the brisket on a rimmed sheet pan and *generously* season the top, bottom, and sides with salt, black pepper, and, if you like your brisket spicy, hot red pepper flakes. Some people combine these ingredients ahead in a rub.

3. If using a cardboard platform (see You'll Also Need), arrange the brisket fat side up on top of it. The platform is optional, but it keeps the bottom of the brisket from drying out and burning.

4. Fire up your smoker, cooker, or grill following the manufacturer's instructions and heat to 250°F. Add the wood as specified by the manufacturer. Place a metal bowl or aluminum foil pan with 1 quart of warm water in the smoker—this creates a humid environment that will help the smoke adhere to the meat and keep your brisket moist.

5. Transfer the brisket (on its cardboard platform, if using) to the smoker. If using an offset smoker, position the thicker end of the brisket toward the firebox. Cook the brisket until the outside is darkly browned and the internal temperature registers around 165°F on an instant-read thermometer, about 8 hours. If the end of the flat starts to dry out or burn, cover it with an aluminum foil cap (see page 30). Refuel your cooker as needed, following the manufacturer's instructions.

6. Remove the brisket from the smoker and tightly wrap it in butcher paper (see page 31). Return it to the cooker.

7. Continue cooking the brisket until the internal temperature reaches 205°F and the meat is very tender when tested (see pages 32 to 33), another 2 to 4 hours, or as needed.

8. Place the wrapped brisket in an insulated cooler and let it rest for 1 to 2 hours. (This allows the meat to relax and the juices to redistribute.)

9. Unwrap the brisket and transfer it to a welled cutting board. Pour any juices that accumulated in the butcher paper into a bowl.

10. Trim off any large lumps of fat. Cut the brisket in half widthwise (long side to long side) to obtain a flat section and a point section; set the point section aside. Make a diagonal cut to remove the thinnest corner of the flat, which will likely be tougher and drier than the rest of the brisket. (Dice it and serve as burnt ends—see page 74.) Slice the brisket across the grain into ¼-inch-thick slices or as desired (see page 34).

11. Transfer the sliced brisket to a platter. Add any juices from the cutting board to the reserved juices in the bowl, spoon them over the sliced brisket. Serve the brisket by itself or with bread and/or sauce on the side. (You know where I stand on the matter.)

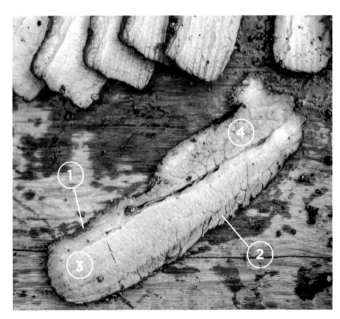

Anatomy of a perfectly barbecued brisket: 1. the bark; 2. the smoke ring; 3. the flat section; 4. the point section

BACON-SMOKED BRISKET FLAT

YIELD: Serves 6 to 8

METHOD: Barbecuing

PREP TIME: 15 minutes

COOKING TIME: 6 to 8 hours, plus 1 to 2 hours for resting

HEAT SOURCE: Smoker or charcoal grill

YOU'LL ALSO NEED: A large (13-by-9-inch) aluminum foil pan; wood logs, chunks, or soaked, drained hardwood chips; a metal bowl or aluminum foil pan; tongs; a digital instant-read thermometer (preferably remote); an insulated cooler (optional); a welled cutting board

WHAT ELSE: Yes, you can cook a lean brisket flat without drying it out like beef jerky. Draping the top with bacon serves a dual purpose: The bacon keeps the top from drying out, and the melting bacon fat humidifies the lean meat on the bottom.

True barbecued brisket fanatics have ambivalent feelings about brisket flats. On the plus side, flats are widely available and they cook in a manageable 6 to 8 hours. They're easy to slice, rewarding you with lean, clean, even, smoky slices of beef. On the minus side, they lack the intramuscular marbling and intermuscular fat of a whole packer brisket or brisket point, and their tough, stringy meat fibers have a tendency to dry out. Well, flats are what you're most likely to find at your local supermarket, so it behooves you to know how to cook one. The secret: Cook the flat in a foil pan (to shield the bottom) draped in bacon (to protect and baste the top). Follow the techniques outlined here and your brisket flat will always be tender and moist.

INGREDIENTS

1 brisket flat (4 to 5 pounds)

Coarse sea salt

Cracked black peppercorns or freshly ground black peppercorns

Hot red pepper flakes (optional)

16 thick-cut strips artisanal bacon, such as Nueske's

1. Place the brisket in an aluminum foil pan and *generously* season the top, bottom, and sides with salt, black pepper, and, if you like your brisket spicy, hot red pepper flakes. Finish with the lean (fatless) side up.

2. Set up your smoker, cooker, or grill following the manufacturer's instructions and heat to 250°F. Add the wood as specified by the manufacturer. Place a metal bowl or aluminum foil pan with 1 quart of warm water in the smoker—this creates a humid environment that will help the smoke adhere to the meat and keep your brisket moist.

3. Place the brisket (still lean side up) in its pan in the smoker. Smoke for 1 hour. (This gets smoke into the lean side of the meat.)

4. Using tongs, invert the brisket so the fat side is up. Neatly drape the top with half of the bacon strips. Cook the brisket until the bacon on top is darkly browned, 2 to 3 hours. Remove the bacon, dice, and eat it as a reward for your patience.

5. Lay the remaining uncooked bacon strips atop the brisket. Continue cooking until these new bacon strips are darkly browned and the internal temperature of the brisket registers 205°F on an instant-read thermometer. There should be a nice pool of bacon and brisket fat in the bottom of the pan. This will take another 3 to 4 hours, for a total of 6 to 8 hours in all. Refuel your cooker as needed, following the manufacturer's instructions. Note: There is no need to wrap the brisket in butcher paper or aluminum foil—the foil pan covers the bottom; the bacon strips cover the top.

6. You can eat the brisket immediately, but it will be moister and more tender if you rest it, covered with aluminum foil in an insulated cooler for 1 to 2 hours. (This allows the meat to relax and the juices to redistribute.)

7. To serve, uncover the brisket and transfer it to a welled cutting board. Remove the bacon or slice it along with the brisket. Slice the brisket across the grain into ¼-inch-thick slices, or as desired (see page 34). Spoon any juices from the cutting board on top and serve with any condiments or accompaniments you like.

BRISKET SOUS VIDE

Suppose there was a cooking method that guaranteed a perfectly cooked, textbook-tender brisket every time. A brisket with a savory bark and pronounced scent of wood smoke. All this without the customary 12 to 14 hours of babysitting a smoker.

It would sound like the answer to every brisket lover's prayer.

Well, there is such a method—firmly established in the fine-dining realm of molecular cuisine—and it's gaining a foothold in the barbecue world: sous vide.

Sous vide (literally "under vacuum") involves poaching food in a vacuum-sealed plastic pouch for a period that can last 72 hours. The bag seals in flavor and moisture. The low temperature (typically 140°F) makes it virtually impossible to overcook the brisket.

The basic sous vide setup consists of a vacuum sealer for the pouch and an immersion circulator (a water tank with a heating element) to do the cooking. Once the province of restaurant kitchens, sous vide machines are now available for home use. Two popular brands are Sous Vide Professional and Anova.

Sous vide produces moist, tender meat, but it doesn't resemble barbecue until you give the meat a wood smoke flavor and crust. To do the former, you unwrap the brisket and smoke it with oak, hickory, or other favorite wood in your smoker. Because the brisket is cooked already, you can accomplish this in 2 to 3 hours.

To lay on a crust (bark), you then direct grill the brisket briefly over medium-high heat (6 to 8 minutes per side will do it), or indirect grill it at 300°F for 1½ to 2 hours.

Sounds easy and failproof, right? So why doesn't everyone cook brisket sous vide? In a nutshell, because it's *too* easy and *too* failproof. Yes, sous vide brisket is tender—you might say supernaturally tender. But a truly great brisket isn't uniformly tender. It's supposed to offer a contrast of tender parts and less tender parts—in other words, it's supposed to retain some chew.

Similarly, you taste smoke in sous vide brisket, but not the deep, lingering smoke flavor you get in traditional barbecue.

Cooking brisket involves struggle—man against meat, as it were. Struggle in rendering the fat, converting the collagen into gelatin, in caramelizing, even in controlled-burning the animal proteins into a crust. In a very real sense, that struggle comes through in the taste.

And *that's* why, in my opinion, sous vide brisket will never trump the real McCoy.

BARBECUED WAGYU BRISKET POINT

Want to make your life easier? Smoke a Wagyu brisket point. The point (aka the deckle) refers to the fattier of the two muscles—the *pectoralis superficialis*—that comprise a brisket. A Wagyu brisket point is simply one of the most luscious, luxurious cuts money can buy. Wagyu is that stocky, gentle breed of steer originally from Japan, of course, whose meat comes generously marbled with buttery, sweet white fat. (More on Wagyu on page 11.) The drawback? A Wagyu brisket can set you back $180. Happily, even a USDA Choice or Prime Angus brisket point delivers the luscious mouthfeel and moistness that makes this part of the brisket the morsel I instinctively reach for first. Points are easier to cook than whole briskets and are always richly rewarding to eat.

YIELD: Serves 6 to 8

METHOD: Barbecuing

PREP TIME: 15 minutes

COOKING TIME: 6 to 8 hours, plus 1 to 2 hours for resting (optional)

HEAT SOURCE: Smoker or charcoal grill

YOU'LL ALSO NEED: A rimmed sheet pan; perforated, foil-wrapped cardboard smoking platform (optional; see page 30); wood logs, chunks, or soaked, drained hardwood chips; a metal bowl or aluminum foil pan (for the smoker); a digital instant-read thermometer (preferably remote); heatproof gloves; pink butcher paper (unlined); an insulated cooler (optional); a welled cutting board; a Microplane or box grater (optional)

WHAT ELSE: Brisket points are rarely sold at supermarkets. You'll need to special-order one from your butcher or buy one online (one good source is misterbrisket.com).

INGREDIENTS

1 brisket point, preferably Wagyu (3½ to 4 pounds)

Coarse sea salt

Cracked black peppercorns or freshly ground black peppercorns

Hot red pepper flakes (optional)

1 piece (3 inches) fresh horseradish root, peeled (optional)

1. Using a sharp knife, trim the brisket, leaving a layer of fat at least ¼ inch thick (see page 14). Be careful not to over-trim. It's better to err on the side of too much fat than too little.

2. Place the point on a rimmed sheet pan and *generously* season the top, bottom, and sides with salt, black pepper, and, if you like your brisket spicy, hot red pepper flakes.

3. If using a cardboard platform (see You'll Also Need), arrange the brisket fat side up on top of it. This is optional, but it keeps the bottom of the brisket from drying out and burning.

4. Fire up your smoker, cooker, or grill following the manufacturer's instructions and heat to 250°F. Add the wood as specified by the manufacturer. Place a metal bowl or aluminum foil pan with 1 quart of warm water in the smoker—this creates a humid environment that will help the smoke adhere to the meat and keep your brisket moist.

5. Place the point (on its cardboard platform, if using) fat side up in the smoker. If using an offset smoker, place the thicker end toward the firebox. Cook until the outside is darkly browned and the internal temperature registers 165°F on an instant-read thermometer, 5 to 6 hours, or as needed. Refuel your cooker as needed, following the manufacturer's instructions, to obtain a clean steady stream of smoke.

6. Remove the brisket from the smoker and tightly wrap it in butcher paper (see page 31). Return it to the cooker.

7. Continue cooking the point until the internal temperature reaches about 205°F and the meat is very tender when tested (see page 18), another 1 to 2 hours.

8. You can certainly eat the point now, but for an even moister, more tender point, rest the wrapped brisket in an insulated cooler for 1 to 2 hours. (This allows the meat to relax and the juices to redistribute.)

9. To serve, unwrap the brisket point and transfer it to a welled cutting board. Pour any juices that accumulated in the butcher paper into a bowl. Slice the brisket across the grain into ¼-inch-thick slices (see page 34). Arrange the sliced brisket on a platter and add any juices from the cutting board to the reserved juices in the bowl. Spoon the cooking juices over the brisket slices, then finely or coarsely grate fresh horseradish, if desired, over the top using a Microplane or a box grater.

Wagyu brisket: The marbling looks like lace.

FETTE SAU'S COFFEE-RUBBED BRISKET
WITH CIDER BEER BARBECUE SAUCE

Think of America's great barbecue regions: Kansas City. Memphis. Texas. North Carolina. Brooklyn. Brooklyn? Yes, New York City's most populous borough now boasts some of the best barbecue around (think Hometown Bar-B-Que, Arrogant Swine, Fletcher's Brooklyn Barbecue, and so on). And it all started when Joe Carroll opened Fette Sau in a run-down garage in Williamsburg in 2007. The musicologist-turned-restaurateur turned heads with his pitch-perfect brisket, pork shoulders, ribs, and pastrami. In this age of salt-and-pepper minimalism (the preferred seasoning in Texas Hill Country), Carroll seasons his meat with a complex amalgam of cinnamon, cumin, garlic, and ground espresso beans. If this were winespeak, I'd tell you to look for spice and coffee notes overlaid with the perfume of wood smoke. Since it's brisket, I'll simply tell you to fire up your smoker and get ready for some of the awesomest barbecued meat east of the Mississippi.

YIELD: Serves 12 to 14

METHOD: Barbecuing

PREP TIME: 15 minutes, plus 10 minutes for the sauce

COOKING TIME: 10 to 14 hours, plus 1 to 2 hours for resting

HEAT SOURCE: Smoker or charcoal grill

YOU'LL ALSO NEED: A rimmed sheet pan; a perforated, foil-wrapped cardboard smoking platform (optional; see page 30); wood logs, chunks, or soaked, drained hardwood chips; metal bowl or aluminum foil pan; spray bottle (optional); pink butcher paper (unlined); heatproof gloves; a digital instant-read thermometer (preferably remote); an insulated cooler; a welled cutting board

INGREDIENTS

¾ cup packed dark brown sugar

½ cup ground espresso coffee beans (medium grind)

½ cup kosher salt

2 tablespoons freshly ground black pepper

2 tablespoons granulated garlic

1 tablespoon ground cinnamon

1 tablespoon ground cumin

1 tablespoon cayenne pepper

1 packer brisket (12 to 14 pounds)

1 cup hard cider or apple cider, in a spray bottle, for spritzing (optional)

Cider Beer Barbecue Sauce, for serving (recipe follows; optional)

1. Make the rub: Place the sugar, coffee, salt, pepper, garlic, cinnamon, cumin, and cayenne in a mixing bowl and mix well, breaking up any lumps in the sugar with your fingers. You'll need ½ to ¾ cup of rub for this recipe—enough to coat the

WHAT ELSE: "Brisket is the most difficult meat to get just right," writes Joe Carroll in his illuminating book *Feeding the Fire*. "There is a narrow window between the time when this tough, lean cut turns moist and tender and when it starts to dry out." Joe cooks his brisket at a slightly lower temperature than I do—between 210° and 225°F—and he uses the most compelling doneness test of all: "Tear off a piece and taste it." Like most serious barbecue guys, Carroll serves his brisket naked (sans sauce), making the latter available on the side for people who want it. His Cider Beer Barbecue Sauce (see page 53) offsets the inevitable sweetness of ketchup with Worcestershire sauce, beer, and hard cider. If you choose to make it, you can pull the sauce together while the meat rests.

brisket. (Store the remainder in a sealed jar away from heat and light. It will keep for several weeks.)

2. Using a sharp knife, trim the brisket, leaving a layer of fat at least ¼ inch thick (see page 14). Be careful not to over-trim. It's better to err on the side of too much fat than too little.

3. Place the brisket on a rimmed sheet pan. Sprinkle the rub on all sides, massaging it into the meat with your fingertips. If using a cardboard platform (see page 30), arrange the brisket fat side up on top of it. This is optional, but it keeps the bottom of the brisket from drying out and burning.

4. Fire up your smoker, cooker, or grill following the manufacturer's instructions and heat to 250°F. Add the wood as specified by the manufacturer. Place a metal bowl or aluminum foil pan with 1 quart of warm water in the smoker—this creates a humid environment that will help the smoke adhere to the meat and keep your brisket moist.

5. Place the brisket (on its cardboard platform, if using) fat side up in the smoker. If using an offset smoker, position the thicker end toward the firebox. Cook the brisket until the outside is darkly browned

and the internal temperature registers about 165°F on an instant-read thermometer, about 8 hours. (If using the cider, spray the brisket after 1 hour and then every hour thereafter.) Refuel your cooker as needed following the manufacturer's instructions.

6. Remove the brisket from the smoker and tightly wrap it in butcher paper (see page 31). Return it to the cooker.

7. Continue cooking until the internal temperature reaches about 205°F and the meat is very tender when tested (see page 32), another 2 to 4 hours, or as needed.

8. Place the wrapped brisket in an insulated cooler and let it rest for 1 to 2 hours. (This allows the meat to relax and its juices to redistribute.)

9. To serve, unwrap the brisket and transfer it to a welled cutting board. Pour 3 to 4 tablespoons of the meat juices that accumulated in the butcher paper into the barbecue sauce, if using, and whisk to mix (reserve the remaining juices in a bowl). Slice the brisket across the grain into ¼-inch-thick slices (see page 34). Serve with the juices spooned over and the Cider Beer Barbecue Sauce on the side, if desired.

CIDER BEER BARBECUE SAUCE

YIELD: Makes about 2½ cups

Joe starts with the basic tomato-based barbecue sauce, balancing the brown sugar sweetness with hard cider and beer and enriching the sauce with brisket drippings at the end. Gather the latter in your smoker's drip pan and from the meat juices that accumulate in the butcher paper when you unwrap the brisket for slicing.

INGREDIENTS

2 cups ketchup

⅓ cup hard cider

⅓ cup dark beer

3 tablespoons Worcestershire sauce (preferably Lea & Perrins)

3 tablespoons apple cider vinegar, or to taste

2 tablespoons brown sugar (light or dark), or to taste

2 teaspoons dry mustard powder, such as Colman's

1 teaspoon kosher salt, plus extra as needed

½ teaspoon garlic powder

½ teaspoon freshly ground black pepper, plus extra as needed

3 to 4 tablespoons brisket juices and drippings (or melted butter)

1. Combine the ketchup, cider, beer, Worcestershire sauce, vinegar, brown sugar, dry mustard, salt, garlic powder, and pepper in a large, heavy saucepan. Gradually bring to a boil, whisking to mix, over medium-high heat.

2. Reduce the heat to low and gently simmer the sauce, uncovered and whisking occasionally, until it is mahogany-colored and concentrated, 20 to 30 minutes.

(Yes, I know this is longer than you normally simmer barbecue sauce, but you need the prolonged cooking to caramelize the ingredients properly.)

3. Just before serving, whisk in the brisket juices and drippings. Correct the seasoning, adding salt and pepper to taste.

Cider Beer Barbecue Sauce will keep, in a sealed container in the refrigerator, for at least a week.

CAMP BRISKET

They came from as far away as California, Miami, and Ontario, Canada. They debated the fine points of smoke rings, stalls, collagen conversion, and reverse-flow smoke engineering like medieval theologians arguing the number of angels that fit on the head of a pin. When the professor wheeled out an enormous hanging steer carcass, the sixty men and women assembled at the Rosenthal Meat Science and Technology Center did not recoil with horror but licked their chops in anticipation.

Welcome to Camp Brisket, a two-day seminar and crash course on the Lone Star State's gift to the world of barbecue, staged by Foodways Texas and Texas A&M University in College Station, Texas.

"Our goal is to explore the culture, science, business, and practical culinary how-tos of the best barbecue in the world—Texas brisket," explains Distinguished Professor of Meat Science Dr. Jeffrey Savell. Dean and head counselor of Camp Brisket, Savell lectured on the anatomy of beef, the chemistry of smoke, and the physics of cooking to an audience enraptured only slightly more by the prospect of sampling the brisket.

The faculty includes some of the biggest names in Texas barbecue, from Kerry Bexley and Tootsie Tomanetz of Snow's BBQ in Lexington, Texas (ranked the state's top barbecue spot by *Texas Monthly* magazine), to the irrepressible Aaron Franklin of Franklin Barbecue in Austin.

So what does one actually learn at Camp Brisket? The short list of topics at the session I attended included the following:

- Brisket anatomy

- Brisket grades (Select, Choice, Prime, Wagyu, and so on)

- Brisket trimming and carving (demonstrated by Aaron Franklin)

- The difference between restaurant brisket and competition brisket (see page 64)

- Wood selection and fire management

- Smoking techniques, from top-down burns to reverse-flow smoking

- The origin of the term *barbecue pit* (the first Texas barbecue was cooked over ember-filled trenches—hence the word *pit*)

Equally fascinating were the blind taste tests designed to challenge our preconceived notions. In one such test, we sampled Select, Choice, Prime, and Wagyu briskets—all seasoned and cooked the same way. Surprisingly, the Select received the highest rating.

In another blind test, we compared the smoke flavor of popular woods, such as hickory, pecan, oak, smoking pellets, and mesquite. Not surprisingly, mesquite delivered the strongest smoke flavor. What was surprising is how little the flavor varied from wood to wood.

The last panel discussion—Life as a Pit Master—was aimed at the not inconsiderable number of participants who nurse fantasies of leaving their day jobs as lawyers and IT experts (the two professions most highly represented in the audience) to open barbecue restaurants of their own.

But lest anyone take themselves *too* seriously, Wayne Mueller of the legendary Louie Mueller Barbecue in Taylor, Texas, summed it up this way: "My dad [Louie Mueller] wasn't interested in becoming a barbecue celebrity. He was just trying to keep the lights on."

About the only downside to Camp Brisket is the difficulty of getting in. Demand for the program far exceeds the sixty slots, necessitating a lottery for admission. To participate, first become a member of Texas Foodways (foodwaystexas.com) and sign up for their newsletter. (It's a worthy organization, and you'll learn a lot about Texas food culture.) In July, you'll receive instructions for submitting an application. Winners are chosen randomly (but a multiplier is assigned to your application if you've been a member for more than one year) and are notified in August.

Dr. Jeffrey Savell gives a lesson in brisket anatomy.

JOE'S KANSAS CITY–STYLE BRISKET

YIELD: Serves 10 to 12

METHOD: Barbecuing

PREP TIME: 20 minutes

COOKING TIME: 8 to 10 hours, plus 1 to 2 hours for resting

HEAT SOURCE: Smoker (ideally, an offset barrel smoker)

YOU'LL ALSO NEED: A large (13-by-9-inch) aluminum foil pan; wood logs, chunks, or soaked, drained hardwood chips; a metal bowl or aluminum foil pan (for the smoker); a digital instant-read thermometer (preferably remote); spray bottle; heavy-duty aluminum foil; an insulated cooler; a rimmed sheet pan; a deli-style meat slicer or electric knife

In a city as barbecue-obsessed as Kansas City, there are many styles of brisket. None is quite as distinctive as the brisket at Joe's Kansas City Bar-B-Que, founded by Jeff Stehney, head pit master of the much-decorated Slaughterhouse Five championship barbecue team and a 2017 inductee in the Barbecue Hall of Fame. Stehney starts not with whole packers, as is the practice in Texas, but with brisket flats. He gives them the usual rub and smoke treatment, but what really sets them apart is the way they are carved—into paper-thin slices on a deli-style meat slicer. This gives you a sandwich with a shaved beef texture that may remind you of Chicago's Italian beef.

INGREDIENTS

1 large brisket flat (6 to 7 pounds)

½ to ¾ cup Slaughterhouse 2.0 Championship BBQ Rub (recipe follows)

1 cup apple juice or apple cider, in a spray bottle, for spritzing

12 hamburger buns, brushed with 3 tablespoons melted butter and grilled or toasted (see What Else, page 72), for serving

Your favorite sweet-smoky barbecue sauce (I'm partial to my bottled Project Smoke Lemon Brown Sugar or Spicy Apple Barbecue Sauce), or one of the sauces in chapter 10, for serving

Sweet pickle chips, for serving

1. Using a sharp knife, trim the brisket, leaving a layer of fat at least ¼ inch thick (see page 14). Be careful not to over-trim. It's better to err on the side of too much fat than too little.

2. Place the brisket fat side up in the aluminum foil pan.

Sprinkle the rub to coat the brisket on all sides, rubbing it into the meat with your fingertips.

3. Fire up your smoker following the manufacturer's instructions and heat to 250°F. Add the wood as specified by

WHAT ELSE: Most of the briskets in this section are cooked to an internal temperature of around 205°F. This makes them supernaturally moist and cut-with-the-side-of-a-fork tender—the texture we associate with Texas barbecued brisket. Joe's Kansas City Bar-B-Que cooks the meat only to 185°F, which leaves it still sufficiently firm to slice on a meat slicer. Joe's also suggests wrapping the brisket in foil partway through the cook. Imagine that—the "Texas Crutch" (page 60) in Kansas City.

the manufacturer. Place a metal bowl or aluminum foil pan with 1 quart of warm water in the smoker—this creates a humid environment that will help the smoke adhere to the meat and keep your brisket moist.

4. Place the brisket in its pan fat side down in the smoker. Smoke the brisket for 1 hour, then turn it fat side up. Continue cooking the brisket until the outside is darkly browned and the internal temperature registers about 155°F on an instant-read thermometer, 5 to 6 hours, rotating the brisket 180 degrees halfway through so it cooks evenly. Spritz the brisket every hour with apple juice. Refuel your cooker as needed, following the manufacturer's instructions.

Cut Kansas City–style brisket into paper-thin slices on a meat slicer.

5. Wrap the brisket tightly in heavy-duty aluminum foil, crimping the edges to make a tight seal. Insert the probe of a digital thermometer into the meat (it's best to pierce the foil only once). Return the wrapped brisket to the smoker and cook to an internal temperature of 185°F, 2 to 3 hours more.

6. Transfer the wrapped brisket to an insulated cooler and let it rest for 1 to 2 hours. (This allows the meat to relax and its juices to redistribute.)

7. Unwrap the brisket, working over a rimmed sheet pan to collect the juices. Slice the brisket paper-thin on a meat slicer or transfer it to a welled cutting board and slice it with an electric knife.

8. To serve, pile the sliced brisket onto the prepared buns. Spoon on the reserved brisket juices. Add barbecue sauce and sweet pickles.

SLAUGHTERHOUSE 2.0 CHAMPIONSHIP BBQ RUB

YIELD: Makes 1¼ cups

This barbecue rub is classic Kansas City, with sugar to make it sweet and mustard, chili powder, and cayenne to turn up the heat.

INGREDIENTS

¼ cup kosher salt

¼ cup sugar

2 tablespoons chili powder

2 tablespoons dry mustard powder, such as Colman's

2 tablespoons sweet paprika

2 tablespoons granulated garlic

2 tablespoons granulated onion

2 tablespoons dried granulated lemon peel

1 tablespoon freshly ground black pepper

1 tablespoon ground white pepper

1 tablespoon cayenne pepper

Combine the salt, sugar, chili powder, dry mustard, paprika, granulated garlic, onion, lemon peel, and black and white and cayenne peppers in a bowl and stir to mix, breaking up any lumps with your fingers.

Slaughterhouse 2.0 Championship BBQ Rub will keep, in a sealed container at room temperature away from heat and light, for several weeks.

A TALE OF TWO CITIES—AND TWO BRISKETS

These days world-class barbecued brisket can be found across the United States (and across Planet Barbecue), but two American cities are inextricably associated with this epic meat: Austin, Texas, and Kansas City. A recent trip to both revealed some striking differences. (My observations are based on visits to Franklin Barbecue, La Barbecue, and Stiles Switch BBQ in Austin and Q39, Slap's, and Joe's in Kansas City.)

AUSTIN

- **The cut:** Whole packer brisket.

- **The seasonings:** Generally, salt and pepper.

- **The fuel:** Oak is the preferred wood, with mesquite and apple also used.

- **Internal temperature:** Cooked to 205°F (approximately), which makes the brisket tender enough to cut with the side of a fork.

- **Slicing and serving:** Sliced by hand (see page 34). A normal portion includes both point (the fatty part) and flat (the lean part).

- **Condiments:** Sauce is available, but often ignored.

How brisket is done at Franklin Barbecue

KANSAS CITY

- **The cut:** Kansas Citians take a divide-and-conquer approach, cooking the flat and point separately. The former they serve thinly sliced on a meat slicer. The point gets diced, barbecued, and often sauced to sell separately as burnt ends.

- **The seasonings:** You're more likely to find a full-scale barbecue rub than simple salt and pepper.

- **The fuel:** Varies from establishment to establishment, with hickory and oak in preponderance.

- **Internal temperature:** This is one of the biggest differences between KC and Austin barbecue. Pit masters here cook to about 185°F, which leaves the brisket firm enough to cut on a meat slicer. (Texas-style brisket would fall apart.)

- **Slicing and serving:** Another big difference. Again, slicing is done on a meat slicer, with slices just shy of ⅛ inch thick. This makes KC-style brisket a little firmer than its Texas counterpart, but well suited to piling on a sandwich.

- **Condiments:** Kansas City barbecue sauce is thick, sweet, and smoky, and the locals don't hesitate to pour it on.

JASON DADY'S EAST-WEST BRISKET

Where else but in America would a self-described "good old-fashioned corn-fed boy from Nebraska" become a fine dining chef and then a Texas barbecue mogul? Meet Jason Dady, who with his brother, Jake, runs a pair of world-class barbecue joints—Two Bros. BBQ Market and B&D Ice House in San Antonio—not to mention Italian restaurants, a fish shack, and a steakhouse. Jason uses a pungent paprika-fennel-cumin rub at Two Bros. At B&D he slathers the brisket with *gochujang* (Korean chile paste; see What Else) much the way a Kansas City pit master might use ballpark-style mustard or pickle juice. The following recipe borrows the best of both restaurants—the *gochujang* slather from B&D and the Two Bros. spice rub. The result is a brisket with uncommonly savory bark, intense flavor, and wood smoke in abundance.

INGREDIENTS

1 packer brisket
   (12 to 14 pounds)

1 cup *gochujang* (Korean chile
   paste), or as needed

½ to ¾ cup Two Bros. Spice
   Rub (recipe follows)

1. Using a sharp knife, trim the brisket, leaving a layer of fat at least ¼ inch thick (see page 14). Be careful not to over-trim. It's better to err on the side of too much fat than too little.

2. Place the brisket on a rimmed sheet pan. Brush or slather it on all sides with the *gochujang* and refrigerate it, uncovered, to marinate for 30 minutes.

3. Meanwhile, fire up your smoker following the manufacturer's instructions and heat to 250°F. Add the wood as specified by the manufacturer. Place a metal bowl or aluminum foil pan with 1 quart of warm water in the smoker—this creates a humid environment that will help the smoke adhere to the meat and keep your brisket moist.

YIELD: Serves 12 to 14

METHOD: Barbecuing

PREP TIME: 20 minutes

COOKING TIME: 10 to 14 hours, plus 1 to 2 hours for resting

HEAT SOURCE: Smoker or charcoal grill

YOU'LL ALSO NEED: A rimmed sheet pan; wood logs, chunks, or soaked, drained hardwood chips; a metal bowl or aluminum foil pan (for the smoker); heatproof gloves; pink butcher paper (unlined); a digital instant-read thermometer (preferably remote); an insulated cooler; a welled cutting board

WHAT ELSE: Jason cooks his brisket using a unique three-step process: a 12-hour cook, followed by a 12-hour rest, followed by a higher-temperature cook to crisp up the bark. I've streamlined the recipe so you can cook it in a single smoke session. You'll need one ingredient that may be unfamiliar: *gochujang*. This rust-colored chile paste endows your brisket with a spicy, umami-rich base. You can find it in the ethnic food aisle of many supermarkets or online.

4. Sprinkle the spice rub over the meat and rub it in with your fingertips to coat it on all sides. Remove the brisket from the sheet pan and place it, fat side up in the smoker. If using an offset smoker, position the thicker end of the brisket toward the firebox. Cook the brisket until the outside is darkly browned and the internal temperature registers 165°F on an instant-read thermometer, about 8 hours.

5. Remove the brisket from the smoker and tightly wrap it in butcher paper (see page 31). Return it to the cooker.

6. Continue cooking until the internal temperature reaches 205°F and the meat is darkly browned and very tender when

HOW TO RECOGNIZE A PERFECT BRISKET

You know it when you see it, and you know it when you taste it, but what do the pros do when they judge a brisket?

Well, not surprisingly, they use all of their senses.

Sight: A world-class brisket will have a dark, almost black bark (crust). The juices and fat will squirt when you cut into it. In cross section, you should see a well-defined crimson smoke ring extending ⅛ to ⅜ inch inward from the surface into the meat. In a cross section of the point, the seam fat will be translucent and mostly rendered.

Smell: Your brisket will smell smoky and beefy, with the thrilling scents of black pepper and caramelized meat proteins.

Sound: No, brisket doesn't really speak to you out loud (although many pit masters whisper to theirs). But there are a number of pleasing sounds associated with its

preparation: the thunk of the ax as it splits logs; the crackle of the fire; the clang of the heavy metal smoker door; the sizzle of the briskets in the smoke chamber; the crinkle of the butcher paper as you unwrap the meat; the hiss of the knife or clatter of the cleaver on the cutting board as you slice the brisket. And of course, the moans of pleasure as you eat it.

Touch: A properly barbecued brisket will jiggle when you press it. Pick up a slice: It should be tender enough to pull apart with your fingers—but not so soft that it falls apart. Take a bite: The meat should be tender, but should retain a little chew.

Taste: Ah, I've saved the best part for last. Your first impression comes from the bark: smoky, salty, peppery, gritty with spice, and slick with fat. The meat will taste beefy and smoky (though not necessarily in that order)—satisfyingly meaty and luscious with rendered brisket fat.

tested (see page 18), another 2 to 4 hours, or as needed.

7. Place the wrapped brisket in an insulated cooler and let it rest for 1 to 2 hours. (This allows the meat to relax and its juices to redistribute.)

8. To serve, unwrap the brisket and transfer it to a welled cutting board. Pour any juices that accumulated in the butcher paper into a bowl. Slice the brisket across the grain into ¼-inch-thick slices or as desired (see page 34). Arrange the sliced brisket on a platter. Add any juices from the cutting board to the reserved juices in the bowl, spoon them over the sliced brisket, and serve.

TWO BROS. SPICE RUB

YIELD: Makes about 1½ cups

The Two Bros. spice rub offers an orchestral range of flavors—sweet fennel seeds, smoky pimentón, fragrant coriander, and pungent pepper. Roasting the spices adds a subtle smokiness. This recipe makes more rub than you need for one brisket, but you'll be happy you have leftovers.

INGREDIENTS

3 tablespoons black peppercorns

2 tablespoons fennel seeds

2 tablespoons cumin seeds

6 tablespoons sweet paprika

6 tablespoons brown sugar

⅓ cup kosher salt

¼ cup pimentón (Spanish smoked paprika)

2 tablespoons ground coriander

1. Heat a small, dry skillet over medium-high heat. Add the peppercorns, fennel seeds, and cumin seeds and roast until fragrant and toasted, 1 to 2 minutes.

2. Immediately transfer the peppercorns and seeds to a bowl to cool, then grind them to a powder in a spice mill. Pour the powder into a small bowl or jar, and stir in the paprika, brown sugar, salt, pimentón, and ground coriander to combine.

Two Bros. Spice Rub will keep, in a sealed container away from heat and light, for several weeks.

COMPETITION BRISKET VS. RESTAURANT BRISKET—AND HOW THEY DIFFER

You know great brisket when you taste it. What you may not know is that what makes brisket great differs dramatically depending on whether you eat it at a restaurant or at a barbecue competition, like the Jack Daniel's World Championship or the American Royal World Series of Barbecue in Kansas City.

According to Australian-born, Austin, Texas–based (how's that for a pedigree?) barbecue authority Jess Pryles, competition briskets are as primped and fussed over as "contestants in a *Toddlers & Tiaras* beauty pageant." The mission is simple—to combat palate fatigue and stand out among the dozens, sometimes hundreds, of samples a judge must taste in a single sitting.

Teams routinely start with expensive Wagyu or Prime brisket (see page 11), injecting the meat with bouillon or melted butter to make it juicier (see page 252). The preferred cut is a lean brisket flat, which yields neat rectangular slices that are pleasing to look at. Competition briskets tend to be seasoned with complicated rubs and often MSG (to pump up the flavor) and finished with a sweet glaze or barbecue sauce. (American taste buds seem hardwired to respond favorably to sweetness.) Wrapping in foil is common to make the meat hyper-tender. In short, explains Pryles, competition briskets are highly processed and highly manipulated. And this style is self-propagating as new contestants try to emulate brisket that has won in the past.

Restaurant briskets are just the opposite. The good places serve the whole brisket—fatty point and lean flat together—often from cheaper cuts, like

Championship brisket: picture-perfect bark and a pronounced smoke ring

Choice or Choice Plus. (Snow's BBQ in Lexington, Texas, uses Select.) Remember, restaurants exist to make money and every cost savings counts. The seasonings are simple—solely salt and pepper in most places—to keep the emphasis on the meat and the wood smoke. Sauce, when it's available, is almost always served on the side.

Pryles compiled the following chart to show the differences between competition and restaurant briskets.

CHARACTERISTICS	COMPETITION BRISKET	RESTAURANT BRISKET
Approach	Highly manipulated	Done as simply as possible
The meat grade	Often Wagyu or Prime	Often Choice Plus, Choice, or Select
The cut	Usually the lean flat (the slices look better) with fat trimmed to a minimum	Whole brisket with plenty of fat
The wrap	Often in foil to steam the brisket and make it more tender	Often in butcher paper or not at all
The seasonings	Complex rubs, often with MSG	Salt and pepper only
Nitrites	Sometimes applied to the surface of the meat to add a smoke ring	Never
Injector sauces	Bouillon, broth, or melted butter	Rare
Butter or margarine	Brushed on the brisket for extra richness	Rare
Barbecue sauce or finishing sauce	Often brushed on as a glaze	Served on the side or not at all
The philosophy	Cooked to win by standing out in a crowd	Cooked to taste good
The taste	Pot roasty	Smoky

Bottom line: Competition-style briskets may win big, but I know which brisket I'd rather find on my plate.

ASIAN-FLAVOR BRISKET
IN THE STYLE OF KYU

'**ve** eaten a lot of brisket over the years and around the world. But I've never been served Texas-style barbecued brisket with chopsticks. Not until I dined at Kyu restaurant in the Wynwood Arts District in my hometown, Miami. "We're an Asian restaurant with a wood-burning smoker," says chef-owner Michael Lewis. "Why can't we serve American barbecue in the style of Korea, Thailand, or Vietnam?" Why not, indeed? Lewis seasons the meat with sesame oil and a Japanese spice rub. He smokes it for 14 hours in the best Texas tradition. But come time for serving, he pulls a page from the Asian playbook. If you look closely, you'll see that your thick slab of brisket has actually been cut into bite-size slivers you can pick up with chopsticks. Instead of Wonder Bread for making sandwiches, Kyu uses crisp lettuce leaves for wrapping the brisket Asian style. This Pan-Asian dish comes with Vietnamese pickles, Japanese wasabi paste, and a sweet-and-sour Korean barbecue sauce. In a nod to Miami's Caribbean roots, a shot glass of hot sauce next to the brisket derives its firepower from house-fermented Scotch bonnets. In short, you get the smoky awesomeness of Texas barbecued brisket with a kaleidoscope of flavorings from Asia. "I think any food tastes better eaten with chopsticks," says Lewis. "There's better airflow with chopsticks, and the more you're breathing, the more you're tasting." Amen to that.

YIELD: Serves 12 to 14

METHOD: Barbecuing

PREP TIME: 20 minutes

COOKING TIME: 10 to 14 hours, plus 2 hours for resting

HEAT SOURCE: Smoker

YOU'LL ALSO NEED: A Microplane or box grater; a rimmed sheet pan; a perforated, foil-wrapped cardboard smoking platform (optional, see page 30); wood logs, chunks, or soaked, drained hardwood chips; a metal bowl or aluminum foil pan (for the smoker); heatproof gloves; pink butcher paper (unlined); a digital instant-read thermometer (preferably remote); an insulated cooler; a welled cutting board

WHAT ELSE: Kyu chef Michael Lewis seasons his brisket with a Japanese spice blend called *togarashi*. The principal flavorings are peppercorns, dried chiles, citrus zest, sesame seeds, and nori seaweed. Make it from scratch following the recipe here, or source it online or at a Japanese market (for this recipe you'll need ½ to ¾ cup).

To toast sesame seeds (and other seeds and nuts), place them in a dry heavy skillet over medium-high heat and cook, stirring occasionally, until fragrant and lightly browned, a few minutes. Transfer them to a bowl and let cool.

INGREDIENTS

FOR THE TOGARASHI RUB

1 sheet (8 by 8 inches) nori seaweed (optional)

1 heaping tablespoon freshly grated citrus zest (ideally a mix of lemon, lime, orange, and/or grapefruit, grated on a Microplane or the fine holes of a box grater)

3 tablespoons kosher salt

3 tablespoons black sesame seeds (or toasted white sesame seeds)

2 tablespoons freshly cracked black pepper

1½ teaspoons cayenne pepper

FOR THE BRISKET

1 packer brisket (12 to 14 pounds)

2 tablespoons toasted (dark) sesame oil

CONDIMENTS FOR SERVING

3 heads butter lettuce, separated into individual leaves, washed, and spun dry

1 bunch fresh cilantro, washed, shaken dry, and stemmed

3 tablespoons Maldon salt

3 tablespoons freshly cracked black peppercorns

Wasabi paste (see Note)

Vietnamese slaw (page 223)

ANY OR ALL OF THE FOLLOWING SAUCES:

Simple Asian-Flavor Barbecue Sauce (recipe follows)

Korean Barbecue Sauce (page 227)

Your favorite Scotch bonnet–based hot sauce (such as Matouk's from Trinidad)

1. Make the rub: If using nori seaweed, toast the sheet on a hot grill or over a lit burner on your stove (holding it with tongs 2 inches above the flames) until crinkly and crisp, 10 seconds per side. Let it cool for a couple of minutes on a plate, then crumble it into a small mixing bowl. Add the citrus zest, salt, sesame seeds, and black and cayenne peppers, and mix together with your fingers. Set aside.

2. Using a sharp knife, trim the brisket, leaving a layer of fat at least ¼ inch thick (see page 14). Be careful not to over-trim. It's better to err on the side of too much fat than too little.

3. Place the brisket on a rimmed sheet pan. Brush the brisket on all sides with the sesame oil, then season it all over with the *togarashi* mixture, rubbing the spices into the meat with your fingertips. If using a cardboard platform (see You'll Also Need), arrange the brisket fat side up on top of it. This is optional, but it keeps the bottom of the brisket from drying out and burning.

4. Meanwhile, fire up your smoker following the manufacturer's instructions and heat to 250°F. Add the wood as specified by the manufacturer. Place a metal bowl or aluminum foil pan with 1 quart of warm water in the smoker—this creates a humid environment that will help the smoke adhere to the meat and keep your brisket moist.

5. Place the brisket (on its cardboard platform, if using) fat side up in the smoker. If using an offset smoker, position the thicker end of the brisket toward the firebox. Cook the brisket until the outside is darkly browned and the internal temperature registers 200° to 205°F on an instant-read thermometer, 10 to 12 hours, or as needed. Refuel your cooker as needed, following the manufacturer's instructions.

6. Remove the brisket from the smoker and tightly wrap it in butcher paper (see page 31). Place the wrapped brisket in an insulated cooler. Let it rest for 2 hours. (Note: Lewis does his wrapping at the end, not two-thirds of the way through

the cook in the style of Aaron Franklin; see page 31.)

7. Unwrap the brisket and transfer it to a welled cutting board. Pour any juices that accumulated in the butcher paper into a bowl. Slice the brisket across the grain into ¼-inch-thick slices. Stack the slices three at a time and cut the stacks widthwise into ½-inch-wide slivers. Transfer the brisket slivers to a platter. Pour the reserved juices over the meat.

8. Assemble the condiments: Arrange the lettuce leaves and cilantro in bowls or on a plate. Place the salt, pepper, wasabi paste, and Vietnamese slaw in individual small bowls. Set out the barbecue sauces and hot sauce in bowls or shot glasses.

9. To eat, place a few pieces of brisket on a lettuce leaf. Add your condiments and sauces of choice and pop the bundle into your mouth. The proper eating implement? Chopsticks, of course.

NOTE: To make wasabi paste, combine 2 tablespoons wasabi powder with 2 tablespoons warm water in a small bowl, and stir to form a paste. Let stand to thicken, 5 minutes, before using.

SIMPLE ASIAN-FLAVOR BARBECUE SAUCE

YIELD: Makes 2 cups

This lightning-quick condiment is what I call a "doctor sauce"—you start with commercial barbecue sauce and doctor it with Asian flavorings such as sesame oil and soy sauce. The sesame seeds provide a pleasing nuttiness and crunch.

INGREDIENTS

1½ cups of your favorite sweet American barbecue sauce (such as Project Smoke Lemon Brown Sugar Barbecue Sauce or KC Masterpiece) or any of the sauces in this book

2 tablespoons soy sauce

2 tablespoons toasted (dark) sesame oil

2 tablespoons rice vinegar or cider vinegar

2 tablespoons toasted white sesame seeds or black sesame seeds (see What Else, page 68)

Combine the ingredients in a bowl and whisk to mix.

Simple Asian-Flavor Barbecue Sauce will keep, in a sealed container in the refrigerator, for several weeks.

JAMAICAN JERK BRISKET

Let's start with the obvious. Jerk brisket isn't really Jamaican. The local meat of choice there is whole hog—ingeniously boned and butterflied so no section is more than 3 to 4 inches thick. That's because the traditional way to cook jerk in Jamaica is not in a stick burner or closed smoker but by direct grilling on a pimento (allspice) wood grate over smoky pimento wood embers. (The heat is low and the process takes the better part of a day, so you're still cooking low and slow.) But jerk seasoning—that ferociously fiery blend of Scotch bonnet chiles, allspice, nutmeg, soy sauce, salt, garlic, rum, and other seasonings—works wonders with the beefy richness of brisket. And Jamaicans prize the flavor of wood smoke as much as any Texan. I give you an electrifying jerk brisket that will definitely make you sit up and take notice. In Jamaica, jerk is served with cornmeal fritters called festivals (you'll find a great recipe for these in my book *The Barbecue! Bible*). The closest equivalent in the United States would be hush puppies. Alternatively, you can pile the brisket slices on buttered, grilled brioche rolls or hamburger buns.

YIELD: Serves 12 to 14

METHOD: Barbecuing

PREP TIME: 30 minutes, plus marinating for 6 hours to overnight

COOKING TIME: 10 to 14 hours, plus 1 to 2 hours for resting

HEAT SOURCE: Smoker or charcoal grill

YOU'LL ALSO NEED: Pimento wood chunks or chips (or your favorite hardwood), the latter soaked for 30 minutes, then drained; a metal bowl or aluminum foil pan (for the smoker); pink butcher paper (unlined); heatproof gloves; a digital instant-read thermometer (preferably remote); an insulated cooler; a welled cutting board

INGREDIENTS

1 packer brisket (12 to 14 pounds)

3 cups jerk seasoning, homemade (recipe follows) or your favorite commercial brand

5 pimento leaves or bay leaves

2 tablespoons allspice berries (preferably Jamaican)

Buttered toasted brioche rolls or hamburger buns (see What Else, optional), for serving

1. Using a sharp knife, trim the brisket, leaving a layer of fat at least ¼ inch thick (see page 14). Be careful not to over-trim. It's better to err on the side of too much fat than too little. Make a series of ½-inch-deep cuts on all sides of the meat using the tip of a paring knife, twisting the blade to widen the holes. (This helps with the absorption of the jerk seasoning.)

2. Using a rubber spatula, slather the brisket with jerk seasoning on all sides. Force it into the holes you made with the paring knife. Marinate, covered, in the refrigerator for at least 6 hours or overnight—the longer it marinates, the richer the flavor.

3. Fire up your smoker, cooker, or grill following the manufacturer's instructions and heat to 250°F. Add the wood as specified by the manufacturer. If using a water smoker, add the pimento leaves and allspice berries to the water pan. Otherwise, place these flavorings in a metal bowl or aluminum foil pan with 1 quart warm water and place the bowl in the smoker.

4. Scrape the excess jerk marinade off the brisket with a spatula. Place the brisket fat side up in the smoker. If using an offset smoker, position the thicker end toward the firebox. Cook the brisket until the outside is darkly browned and the internal temperature registers about 165°F on an instant-read thermometer, about 8 hours. Refuel your cooker as needed, following the manufacturer's instructions.

5. Remove the brisket from the smoker and tightly wrap it in butcher paper (see page 31). Return it to the cooker.

6. Continue cooking until the internal temperature is around 205°F and the meat is very tender when tested (see page 18), another 2 to 4 hours, or as needed.

7. Place the wrapped jerk brisket in an insulated cooler and let it rest for 1 to 2 hours. (This allows the meat to relax and its juices to redistribute.)

8. Unwrap the brisket and transfer it to a welled cutting board. Pour any juices that accumulated in the butcher paper into a bowl. Slice the brisket across the grain into ¼-inch-thick slices. Layer the slices onto the toasted rolls, if desired. Add any juices from the cutting board to the juices in the bowl, spoon them over the meat, and serve.

JERK SEASONING

YIELD: Makes 3 cups

Jamaican jerk seasoning is an incendiary amalgam of Scotch bonnet chiles (or you can use their more readily available cousins, habaneros), alliums, allspice, and rum, with an overall flavor profile that's sweet, salty, spicy, and pugnacious with chile hellfire. For milder jerk seasoning, I seed the chiles.

INGREDIENTS

3 tablespoons allspice berries (preferably Jamaican)

3 tablespoons whole black peppercorns

1 cinnamon stick, broken into pieces, or 2 teaspoons ground cinnamon

1 teaspoon ground nutmeg

2 dried pimento leaves or bay leaves, crumbled

4 to 6 Scotch bonnet or habanero chiles (or to taste), stemmed and seeded (for authentic and *really* fiery jerk seasoning, leave the seeds in)

4 cloves garlic, peeled and roughly chopped

2 bunches scallions, trimmed, white and green parts roughly chopped

A 2-inch piece of fresh ginger, peeled and roughly chopped

2 tablespoons fresh thyme leaves (strip them off the branches) or 2 teaspoons dried thyme

2 tablespoons sea salt, plus extra as needed

2 tablespoons dark brown sugar

½ cup soy sauce

½ cup vegetable oil

½ cup distilled white vinegar

½ cup dark rum

⅓ cup freshly squeezed lime juice

1. Place the allspice berries, peppercorns, cinnamon, nutmeg, and pimento leaves in a spice mill and grind to a fine powder. You may need to work in several batches.

2. Transfer the ground spices to a food processor fitted with a chopping blade. Add the Scotch bonnets, garlic, scallions, ginger, thyme, salt, and sugar and

finely chop. Gradually work in the soy sauce, oil, vinegar, rum, and lime juice. Process to a loose paste. Add salt to taste; the jerk seasoning should be quite salty.

Jerk Seasoning will keep, in a sealed jar in the refrigerator, for several weeks. (Place a sheet of plastic wrap between the mouth of the jar and the lid to prevent the latter from corroding.)

TUFFY STONE'S BURNT ENDS

YIELD: Serves 6 to 8 as a starter, or 4 as a main course (makes about 48 burnt ends)

METHOD: Barbecuing

PREP TIME: 20 minutes

COOKING TIME: 6 to 7 hours for the brisket, plus 1 hour for resting, and 30 minutes for the burnt ends

HEAT SOURCE: Smoker or charcoal grill

YOU'LL ALSO NEED: Three 13-by-9-inch aluminum foil pans; wood logs, chunks, or soaked, drained hardwood chips; heavy-duty aluminum foil; an insulated cooler

WHAT ELSE: The recipe is a little involved, but you can make the rub and sauce ahead of time.

In recent years, burnt ends have morphed from simple brisket trimmings into a freestanding starter or even main course in their own right, consisting of bite-size cubes of barbecued brisket point or flat re-smoked with sweet barbecue sauce. And no one makes them better than French-trained chef turned *BBQ Pitmasters* reality TV star Tuffy Stone. Founder of the Cool Smoke barbecue team, Tuffy is one of the winningest competition barbecuers on the planet, with more than forty grand championships and five world championships to his credit. Tuffy's burnt ends are a triumph of the new-style burnt end, fusing the perfect ratio of smoke to spice and meat to sweet into a morsel you can eat in a single bite. Think of them as brisket candy, and don't think of firing up your smoker without trying them.

INGREDIENTS

FOR THE RUB

½ cup turbinado sugar (such as Sugar in the Raw)

⅓ cup kosher salt

¼ cup chili powder

2 tablespoons ground cumin

4 teaspoons cracked black peppercorns

4 teaspoons granulated onion

4 teaspoons granulated garlic

1 teaspoon cayenne pepper

FOR THE BRISKET

1 brisket point (4 to 5 pounds)

1 tablespoon extra virgin olive oil, or more as needed

1 cup apple juice, in a spray bottle for spritzing

1 tablespoon granulated onion

Cool Smoke Barbecue Sauce (recipe follows), for coating and serving

1. Make the rub: Combine the ingredients in a mixing bowl and stir, breaking up any lumps in the sugar with your fingers. (Note: This makes more rub than you'll need for the burnt ends. Store any excess in a sealed jar away from heat and light—it will keep for several weeks.)

2. Using a sharp knife, trim the brisket, leaving a layer of fat at least ¼ inch thick (see page 14). Be careful not to over-trim. It's better to err on the side of too much fat than too little.

3. Brush the brisket on all sides with olive oil to coat it evenly. Place the brisket in an aluminum foil drip pan and season it on all sides with the rub—you'll need ½ to ¾ cup.

4. Fire up your smoker, cooker, or grill following the manufacturer's instructions and heat to 275° to 300°F. Add the wood as specified by the manufacturer.

5. Place the brisket point in its pan, fat side up, in the smoker. Cook for 1 hour, then spray the brisket with apple juice to moisten it. Continue smoking until darkly browned, 3 hours, spraying the brisket with apple juice every 30 minutes.

6. Lay 2 overlapping sheets of heavy-duty aluminum foil on your work surface. Crimp them together to form a seal—the resulting sheet should be about 2 feet wide. Place the brisket point on top, sprinkle it with the granulated onion, and spray it generously with apple juice. Tightly wrap the brisket in the foil, pleating the seams to make a tight seal. Return the wrapped brisket point, fat side up, to the cooker.

7. Continue cooking until the brisket is very tender and the internal temperature registers 205°F on an instant-read thermometer, 2 to 3 hours more.

8. Place the wrapped brisket point in an insulated cooler and let it rest for 1 hour. (This allows the meat to relax and its juices to redistribute.)

9. Unwrap the brisket point and transfer it to a welled cutting board. Using a sharp knife, cut the meat into 1-inch cubes. Transfer the pieces in a single layer to a couple of aluminum foil drip pans. Pour 1 cup of the sauce (or as needed) over the brisket, gently tossing to coat the cubes.

10. Place the pans in the smoker and cook until the brisket cubes are sizzling and caramelized, 30 minutes or so. Serve the burnt ends hot off the smoker, with the remaining sauce on the side.

COOL SMOKE BARBECUE SAUCE

YIELD: Makes about 2 cups

Sweet, spicy, and smoky, this sauce by Tuffy's Cool Smoke barbecue team is everything you want a barbecue sauce for brisket to be.

INGREDIENTS

1½ cups ketchup

½ cup dark brown sugar

⅓ cup distilled white vinegar

2 tablespoons molasses

2 tablespoons apple cider vinegar

1½ tablespoons Worcestershire sauce

1 tablespoon pimentón (Spanish smoked paprika)

2 teaspoons chili powder

1 teaspoon ground cumin

1 teaspoon granulated onion

1 teaspoon granulated garlic

Kosher salt and freshly ground black pepper

Combine the ketchup, brown sugar, white vinegar, molasses, apple cider vinegar, Worcestershire sauce, pimentón, chili powder, cumin, granulated onion, and granulated garlic in a medium-size saucepan with ⅓ cup water and whisk to mix. Bring the mixture to a boil over medium-high heat, then reduce the heat and gently simmer, whisking often, until the sauce is thick and richly flavored,

10 to 15 minutes. If the sauce thickens too much, add a few tablespoons of water. Correct the seasoning, adding salt and pepper to taste: The sauce should be highly seasoned.

Cool Smoke Barbecue Sauce can be prepared ahead of time. It will keep, in a sealed container in the refrigerator, for several weeks.

WILL THE REAL BURNT ENDS PLEASE STAND UP?

In the beginning, burnt ends were burnt edges: charred, crusty, smoked brisket trimmings deemed too calcified or misshapen to serve customers paying good money for a plate of barbecue. They were brisket scraps, really—smoky and salty, with nary a drop of barbecue sauce, sweet or otherwise. And you still find them at a few Texas barbecue joints, like Louie Mueller Barbecue in Taylor, Texas.

But in the last ten years, burnt ends have morphed into a sort of meat candy comprised of cubes of cooked brisket slathered with sweet barbecue sauce. All too often, there's nothing "burnt" or edgy about them. Some places now serve "burnt ends" made from sausage or spareribs. Really.

History credits the landmark Kansas City barbecue joint, Arthur Bryant's, with the invention of burnt ends—a way to reward customers who waited long enough to be at the head of the line when the restaurant opened. (Ever notice how you always wait in a line at a good barbecue joint?)

As far as I'm concerned, "real" burnt ends are smoky, salty scraps cut from the burned edges of a well-barbecued brisket—sauce need not apply.

Here's how Calvin Trillin reminisced about them in his mythical celebration of Kansas City cuisine, *Alice, Let's Eat*:

I dream of those burned edges. Sometimes, when I'm in some awful overpriced restaurant in some strange town—all of my restaurant-finding techniques having failed, so that I'm left to choke down something that costs $7 and tastes like a medium-rare sponge—a blank look comes over my face: I have just realized that at that very moment someone in Kansas City is being given those burned edges free.

The problem with burnt ends is that there just aren't enough of them. For once you trim a smoked brisket, there's a lot more meat to go around than scraps.

To meet the demand for a delicacy that was once a by-product, Kansas City restaurants started dicing cooked brisket points and dousing them with barbecue sauce. The good places returned them to the pit to cook the sauce into the meat and caramelize it. The not-so-good places poured sweet barbecue sauce over the brisket and served it like French fries smothered with ketchup.

Personally, I'm not a big fan of sauce-slathered burnt ends. I believe a proper brisket and its ends deserve to be eaten on its own without sauce. But many people do like sweet-sauced burnt ends. On page 74, you'll find one of the best—spice-stung, sauce-slathered burnt ends from one of the winningest competition barbecuers and host of the *BBQ Pitmasters* TV show, Tuffy Stone.

BRISKET "STEAKS"
WITH SHALLOT SAGE BUTTER

The brisket "steak" takes me back to my Barbecue University days at the Greenbrier resort in White Sulphur Springs, West Virginia. A chef there had the genius idea to cook thick slabs of barbecued brisket on a screaming hot grill, just as you would a New York strip. This gave the brisket a sizzling, crusty exterior that lay midway between traditional barbecued brisket and steak, with a handsome smoky crosshatch of grill marks. (It's also a great way to repurpose leftover barbecued brisket.) To this, add a shallot sage butter and a dusting of fiery fresh horseradish and you may just barbecue your next brisket solely to turn it into steak. Note: If you like your steaks lean, cut them from the flat. If you like them richer and fattier, cut them from the point. You've probably guessed by now that I like the latter.

YIELD: Serves 4

METHOD: Direct grilling

PREP TIME: 5 minutes

COOKING TIME: 4 to 8 minutes

HEAT SOURCE: Grill

YOU'LL ALSO NEED: A Microplane or other fine-hole grater

WHAT ELSE: I take a savory approach to these steaks, basting them with Shallot Sage Butter and grating fresh horseradish root on top. (It's amazing how fiery fresh horseradish invigorates the smoky meat.) Alternatively, you could take the sweet route, seasoning the steaks with barbecue rub instead of salt and pepper, and slathering them with your favorite sweet barbecue sauce in place of the butter.

INGREDIENTS

Vegetable oil, for oiling the grill grate

2 pounds barbecued brisket (about 4 pounds uncooked; see pages 25 to 35), cut across the grain into 1¼-inch-thick slices

Coarse sea salt and freshly ground black pepper

Shallot Sage Butter (recipe follows)

A 2-inch chunk of fresh horseradish root, peeled

1. Set up your grill for direct grilling (see page 81) and heat to high. Brush or scrape the grill grate clean and oil it well.

2. Season the brisket slices on both sides with salt and pepper. Brush the slices on both sides with half the Shallot Sage Butter; set the remaining butter aside.

3. Arrange the brisket slices on the grill running diagonal to the bars of the grate. Grill until browned on the bottom,

2 to 4 minutes, giving each slice a quarter turn halfway through to lay on a crosshatch of grill marks.

4. Gently flip the brisket slices and grill the other side the same way, 2 to 4 minutes more.

5. Serve the brisket steaks hot off the grill, with the remaining Shallot Sage Butter spooned over them and the fresh horseradish grated on top with a Microplane or other fine-hole grater.

SHALLOT SAGE BUTTER

YIELD: Makes ½ cup

Shallot Sage Butter brings a Mediterranean note to a smoked meat with deep American roots. Allium lovers can substitute garlic for the shallots.

WHAT ELSE: For an extra hit of flavor and an irresistible crackly crunch, I like to add a handful of fried whole sage leaves to the steaks along with this butter. To make them, fry the fresh leaves in olive oil over medium-high heat for a few seconds until crisp. Drain on paper towels until ready to use.

INGREDIENTS

8 tablespoons (1 stick) unsalted butter

2 to 3 large shallots, peeled and minced (½ cup)

2 tablespoons chopped fresh sage leaves (plus an optional handful of whole leaves; see What Else)

Melt the butter in a saucepan over medium heat. Add the shallots and sage and cook until just beginning to brown, 3 minutes. Remove from the heat and keep at room temperature until ready to use. Reheat the butter gently if it solidifies.

DIRECT GRILLING

To direct grill on a charcoal grill, mound the lit coals towards the back, raking them into a single layer of embers in the center of the grill, leaving the front third of the grill coal-free. This gives you a hot zone for searing (in the back), a medium zone for cooking (in the center), and a coal-free safety zone in the front for keeping food warm or for dodging flareups. On a gas grill, set the rear burner (or burner on one side) on high, the center burner on medium, and leave the front burner (or burner on the other side) off. In either case, control the heat by moving the food closer to or farther away from the hot zone.

BRISKET IN A HURRY

When it comes to cooking brisket, three words have been the credo of the barbecue community for decades: "low and slow."

In other words, cook it at a *low* temperature and *slowly*—for a long time—to render the brisket fat and convert the tough collagen to tender gelatin.

So when *Texas Monthly*'s barbecue editor, Daniel Vaughn, broke the news of the "hot and fast" method proposed by Roland Lindsey, pit master–owner of Bodacious Bar-B-Q in Longview, Texas (incidentally, the first place I experienced Texas barbecue), the blogosphere erupted with understandable emotion.

If you could really cook a respectable brisket in 3 to 4 hours, why have so many of us endured predawn wake-up calls or overnight smoke sessions?

Well, the controversy reached Barbecue University recently ("BBQ U" is the three-day class I teach each year at the Broadmoor resort in Colorado Springs, Colorado), so we decided to put it to the test. Steve Nestor, a student from the Boston area, posed the question; naturally, we drafted him to try it.

In a nutshell, the hot-and-fast method calls for cooking a full packer brisket at 400°F instead of the traditional 250°F. The supposed secret is to rest the wrapped brisket in an insulated cooler for at least 2 hours to allow the meat to relax.

We used a Weber kettle grill set up for indirect grilling. (Most smokers don't get that hot.) We fueled it with natural lump charcoal and added cherry chunks to generate wood smoke. We wrapped the brisket in unlined butcher paper at 165°F and continued cooking it to an internal temperature of 205°F. The total cooking time was just north of 4 hours.

I confess: I was dubious. The internal temperature may have been right, but the brisket sure didn't feel right. It flunked the "bend" test and lacked the "jiggle" I associate with a properly cooked brisket (see page 32).

We rested it in an insulated cooler for the prescribed 2 hours. Much to my surprise, the meat softened considerably during that time, and when we cut into it, we tasted not a top-tier brisket, but a respectable second flight.

The flat was a bit tougher than a low-and-slow brisket, but it would be okay thinly sliced on a sandwich.

The point was moist and succulent. You could see the white intramuscular fat (which in a low-and-slow cook would melt out), but the mouthfeel was luscious, the way a brisket point should be.

Both parts had a well-defined smoke ring and pronounced smoke flavor.

Bottom line: You wouldn't mistake a hot-and-fast brisket for meat smoked low and slow the traditional way. But if you're crunched for time, the hurried-up version is certainly better than nothing.

KOREAN GRILLED BRISKET

Brisket is enjoyed the world over, and exploring how it varies from food culture to food culture has been one of the great thrills of writing this book. But there's one virtually universal article of faith: Brisket requires long, slow cooking with moist, gentle heat to make it tender and palatable. Consequently, you cook brisket in a smoker or at a low heat in the oven, in a steamer, slow cooker, stew pot, or soup pot. The one place you'd never cook it is directly over high heat on a grill. Or so I believed until I visited Kang Ho Dong Baekjeong restaurant in the heart of New York's Koreatown. Here, chef Mike Sim slices frozen brisket points across the grain on a meat slicer. The slices come so paper-thin that the meat cooks in a matter of seconds. It simply doesn't have the time or heft to get tough. You could think of this direct grilled brisket as steak on steroids, with a rich, meaty, beefy flavor every bit as intense as slow-cooked brisket, but as easy to chew as New York strip. The brisket itself comes unseasoned. The fireworks come from an eye-popping selection of sauces and condiments collectively known as *banchan* (see page 89). Like so much Korean grilled meat, you eat grilled brisket wrapped in lettuce leaves, taco-style. Think of it as barbecue health food.

YIELD: Serves 6 to 8

METHOD: Direct grilling

PREP TIME: 15 minutes, plus several hours or overnight to freeze the brisket

COOKING TIME: Minutes rather than hours!

HEAT SOURCE: Ideally, a hibachi, or a charcoal or gas grill

YOU'LL ALSO NEED: An electric meat slicer or food processor fitted with a slicing disk (this works best on a processor with a fixed-blade slicing disk); small tongs (full-size tongs would be cumbersome to handle such small, thin slices of meat); chopsticks

INGREDIENTS

2 pounds brisket point or cross section of point and flat together

1 head green leaf lettuce, such as butter lettuce or romaine, separated into leaves, washed, and spun dry

CONDIMENTS (ANY OR ALL OF THE FOLLOWING)

Coarse sea salt

Toasted (dark) sesame oil

Wasabi Soy Dipping Sauce (recipe follows)

Chile Jam (*Ssamjang*—page 88) or *gochujang* (Korean chile paste—see What Else, page 61)

Korean Cucumber Salad (page 237)

WHAT ELSE: The easiest way to slice the meat for this extraordinary brisket is on an electric meat slicer. Serious carnivores may own one already. I've come up with a work-around using a food processor with a sturdy slicing blade. In a pinch, you could try hand slicing with a very sharp chef's knife or santoku, in which case, freeze the brisket until it is partially frozen, not hard as a rock. Note: Many Asian markets sell pre-sliced brisket in the frozen foods section—especially if you live in an area with a large Korean community.

Make the Chile Jam, Wasabi Soy Dipping Sauce, and Korean Cucumber Salad a few hours before you intend to cook and serve the brisket.

1. Using a sharp knife, trim the brisket, leaving a layer of fat at least ½ inch thick (see page 14); you'll need more fat than usual here because you'll be direct grilling the brisket (see page 81) and you want to keep it moist. Save a few pieces of that fat in the refrigerator for greasing the grill grate.

2. If you have an electric meat slicer, wrap the whole brisket point in plastic wrap and place it in the freezer. If you plan to use a food processor, cut the brisket point along the grain into chunks just narrow enough to fit in the processor feed tube. (Take note of which way the grain of the meat—the meat fibers—runs: When it comes time for slicing, it's

very important to cut it across the grain.) Wrap the chunks in plastic wrap and freeze until solid, several hours or overnight.

3. If you have an electric meat slicer, unwrap the brisket and use the slicer to cut the frozen brisket across the grain into paper-thin slices. As they come off the slicer, they'll naturally curl. Arrange the slices on a platter. If using a food processor, install the thin slicing blade. Place the unwrapped, frozen brisket chunks in the feed tube (the grain of the meat should run vertical and parallel to the feed tube). Turn on the processor and slice the meat. (The slices won't be quite as pretty as those made on a

Thinly slice the frozen brisket in a food processor fitted with a slicing blade.

Direct grill the paper-thin brisket slices on a hibachi.

meat slicer, but you will get the requisite thinness.) Arrange the slices on a platter.

4. Transfer the sliced brisket on its platter to the freezer and keep it there until ready to grill. (The brisket can be sliced and frozen several hours ahead.)

5. Just prior to grilling, heat your grill to high. Brush or scrape the grill grate clean. Grease the grate with reserved chunks of brisket fat. Place the sea salt in a small bowl and the sesame oil in another. (Or if you like sesame sea salt, place the salt in a small bowl and gently pour the sesame oil over it so the salt remains in a pile in the center.) Set out the remaining condiments in bowls.

6. When the grill is hot, arrange the brisket slices on the grate and grill until browned on both sides, 30 seconds per side, or until cooked to taste. For even more fun, place the hibachi in the center of the table (outdoors only) and have each guest grill his or her own meat.

7. Enjoy immediately, using chopsticks to dip a grilled brisket slice in salt, sesame oil, or Wasabi Soy Dipping Sauce, then place it on a lettuce leaf (spread with Chile Jam for even more flavor, if you like). Add some cucumber salad. From there, just roll it up and pop it into your mouth. It's simply one of the most amazing brisket dishes on Planet Barbecue.

WASABI SOY DIPPING SAUCE

YIELD: Makes about 3 cups

A variation on this sauce turns up wherever Koreans grill meat. Soy sauce makes it salty; sugar makes it sweet; rice vinegar gives it sharpness; sliced serranos crank up the heat. Some versions include diced Asian pear; others, scallions or onions. The wasabi lends a Japanese note—an innovation I've seen only at Baekjeong. As you dip the pieces of brisket in the sauce, the meat juices make it all the more flavorful.

INGREDIENTS

2 tablespoons wasabi powder

½ cup plus 2 tablespoons warm water

½ cup sugar

1 cup soy sauce

½ cup rice vinegar

2 serrano chiles, stemmed and sliced crosswise paper-thin

½ medium onion, cut into ¼-inch dice

¼ cup coarsely chopped fresh cilantro or mint

1. Combine the wasabi powder and 2 tablespoons warm water in a small bowl and stir with chopsticks to form a paste. Let stand to thicken, 5 minutes.

2. Place the sugar and remaining ½ cup warm water in a mixing bowl and whisk until the sugar is dissolved. Whisk in the soy sauce and rice vinegar and let the mixture cool to room temperature. Stir in the chiles, onion, and cilantro or mint.

3. To serve, ladle the dipping sauce into as many small bowls as you have eaters. Spread a dab of wasabi paste onto the edge of each bowl, so that each person can add as much wasabi as he or she desires.

Wasabi Soy Dipping Sauce can be made a few hours ahead of time (store it in a sealed container in the refrigerator), but it tastes best served the same day.

CHILE JAM (SSAMJANG)

YIELD: Makes 1 cup

*S*samjang is another indispensable Korean barbecue condiment. The name literally means "wrap paste," and the idea is that you spread some of this spicy, salty, garlicky, mildly fiery paste on the lettuce leaves used to wrap and eat the grilled brisket. This recipe probably makes more than you'll need at a single grill session—it will keep for several weeks in the refrigerator and it's infectiously delicious.

INGREDIENTS

½ cup miso (preferably Korean; see Note)

½ cup *gochujang* (Korean chile paste—see What Else, page 61)

1 tablespoon toasted (dark) sesame oil

1 clove garlic, minced

Combine the miso, *gochujang*, sesame oil, and garlic in a mixing bowl and stir or whisk to mix. If the mixture seems too thick, add a tablespoon or two of cold water to thin it.

Chile Jam will keep, in a sealed container in the refrigerator, for several weeks.

NOTE: I like to use Korean *doenjang*, a miso-like fermented soybean paste that's typically available at Korean food markets. If you can't find it, red or white Japanese-style miso will work just fine.

KOREAN BRISKET

"Brisket is one of the most esteemed beef cuts in Korea," says Mike Sim, executive chef of the popular Baekjeong restaurant in New York's Koreatown. "We cook it on the grill." (Notice he said "grill"—more on that in a minute.) "We simmer it in stews and braise it with *gochujang*. We boil it to make broth, which we ladle over cold sliced brisket and glass noodles to make the most refreshing dish you can imagine for summer."

But Korean brisket achieves its apotheosis in the one place you'd never expect to find this tough cut of steer: on a grill. The secret involves a freezer, a meat slicer, and a fine white powder called meat glue.

Baekjeong is the sort of restaurant where Korean expats come to feel at home and where Americans come to feel Korean. The brainchild of Korean television wrestling star Kang Ho Dong, this popular chain has outlets in New York, Los Angeles, and, of course, across East Asia.

I've come here on an icy afternoon to get a crash course on Korean brisket surgery. Chef Sim produces a huge slab of beef that Texas barbecue buffs would recognize as a packer brisket. He trims off some of the fat—just a little—then cuts the brisket into four quadrants. He sprinkles them with transglutaminase (meat glue) and piles a lean quadrant atop a fatty quadrant. He swaddles the resulting hunk in a large sheet of plastic wrap, twisting the edges to create a roll that looks vaguely like a brisket bologna. The roll goes in the freezer until it's as hard as a log—indispensable for slicing it thin enough to grill.

The second prerequisite is a meat slicer, which Mike switches on the moment brisket is ordered. Off come paper-thin round slices of gorgeously marbled, shockingly red meat veined with fat and with a thick patch of fat in the center. As the brisket thaws, it curls into handsome rolls that make me think of beef cannelloni shells.

Meanwhile, one of Baekjeong's servers has lit the circular gas grill in the center of my stainless steel–topped table. Holding a piece of brisket fat with tongs, he greases the grate—an inverted metal plate honeycombed with slits to let the fire through—then lays the thin shavings of beef on top. In 30 seconds they're cooked (a little longer if you like them browned crisp).

If this were Texas, you'd eat the brisket slapped on a slice of white bread. This being Korea (or at least Koreatown), you eat the meat taco-style, with lettuce leaves standing in for the tortillas. There are four possible condiments: sea salt for the purist; sea salt with a slick of sesame oil, which adds a nice nutty counterpoint to the meat; a sweet-tart-salty dipping sauce spiked with onion and chile slices; and a salty, garlicky paste made with Korean miso and *gochujang*.

You might think you're done, but you've just scratched the surface, because you can also load your brisket lettuce bundle with *banchan*—a plentiful array of pickles, salads, and condiments. In short, it's brisket as a gustatory musical and you get to customize the chorus line.

But what's most amazing of all is the cooking method: This is one of the only brisket dishes in the world that you grill like steak.

Chapter 3

BRISKET CURED

Long before there was refrigeration, there was salt. Salt for brining. Salt for curing. These ancient preserving methods kept meat safe for most of human history. And in the process, they gave us three of the world's great incarnations of brisket: corned beef, pastrami, and Montreal smoked meat. In this chapter, you'll learn how to make all three. You'll also experience a lesser-known, but no less worthy Irish specialty: spiced beef. And once you've mastered curing, I'll show you how to prepare superlative Irish corned beef and cabbage (the secret is buttering the broth) and a *kung pao* pastrami that will light up your taste buds like fireworks on Lunar New Year.

OLD SCHOOL PASTRAMI

Picture the perfect pastrami. The exterior black as bitumen. The interior a bright shade of pink, like a drag queen's hairdo. The stunning striations of meat and fat rendered iridescent by curing salt. The bite of black pepper and coriander seed overlaid with the subtle scent of wood smoke. And that's *before* the taste—beefy, salty, garlicky—with spice, meat, and fat in luscious equipoise. It's the sort of pastrami you get at Katz's Deli or Pastrami Queen in New York City. And you're about to make it at home. It won't be difficult, but it *will* require a virtue in short supply in our age of reduced attention spans and instant gratification: patience. It takes a full 12 days to pickle the meat in a brine scented with garlic and onion. You'll need to roast the spices in a skillet (to intensify their flavor) and grind them from scratch to make the rub. You'll need 8 to 10 hours of smoking to give the meat the requisite smoke flavor and 2 to 3 hours of steaming or resting to make it tender. And you'll need to use one ingredient that you might be unfamiliar with, a curing salt called Prague Powder #1. (Consumed in excess, it can kill you.) But persevere, dear reader, because pastrami is one of the most awesome manifestations of brisket on Planet Barbecue. The first time you cut into a home-cured, house-smoked pastrami, you'll feel immense pride, deep satisfaction, and peak gustatory pleasure.

YIELD: Serves 8 to 10

METHOD: Smoking, steaming

PREP TIME: 20 minutes for the brine and spice rub, plus 12 days for brining the brisket

COOKING TIME: 7 to 8 hours for smoking the brisket, plus 2 to 3 hours for steaming (or another 2 to 3 hours for smoking, and 1 to 2 hours for resting)

HEAT SOURCE: Smoker or charcoal grill (like a Weber kettle), then a stove or oven (sorry, folks—you won't get the right smoke flavor on a gas grill)

2 jumbo (2.5-gallon) resealable heavy-duty plastic bags; a large baking dish or a plastic bucket; spice mill; rimmed sheet pan; metal bowl or aluminum foil pan (for the smoker); hickory or other hardwood chunks or chips (the latter soaked in water for 30 minutes, then drained); heatproof gloves; pink butcher paper (unlined); large aluminum foil pan; a steamer (see page 96) or a large insulated cooler

INGREDIENTS

FOR THE BRISKET

1 section (about 8 pounds) brisket (preferably with both point and flat)

FOR THE BRINE

1 gallon (4 quarts) cold water

1 cup kosher salt

1 tablespoon Prague Powder #1 (see box, page 106)

6 juniper berries, lightly crushed with the side of a knife (or 2 tablespoons gin)

2 teaspoons yellow mustard seeds

1 teaspoon celery seeds

8 cloves garlic, peeled and cut in half widthwise

1 small onion, peeled and quartered

FOR THE RUB

½ cup whole coriander seeds

½ cup whole black peppercorns

1. Using a sharp knife, trim the brisket, leaving a layer of fat at least ¼ inch thick (see page 14). Be careful not to over-trim. It's better to err on the side of too much fat than too little. Place it in a jumbo resealable heavy-duty plastic bag set inside a large baking dish (or plastic bucket).

2. Make the brine: Combine 2 quarts of the cold water with the kosher salt, Prague Powder #1, juniper berries, mustard seeds, and celery seeds in a large stockpot, and bring to a boil over high heat, whisking until the salts are dissolved. Remove the pot from the heat and stir in the remaining 2 quarts of cold water. Let the brine cool to room temperature.

3. Add the brine to the brisket in the bag, along with the garlic and onion, and seal it shut. Place this in a second jumbo resealable heavy-duty plastic bag (to contain any leaks), seal it, and place the bagged brisket in the baking dish in the refrigerator. Brine the brisket for 12 days, turning the bag over each day so the brisket brines evenly.

4. On the 12th day, make the rub: Toast the coriander seeds and peppercorns in a large dry skillet over medium-high heat, stirring so they toast evenly, until fragrant, 1 minute. Working in batches, coarsely grind the toasted spices in a spice mill. Place in a small bowl and stir to mix.

5. Drain the brisket, discarding the brine. Rinse the brisket thoroughly in cold water, then blot it dry with paper towels. Place the brisket on a rimmed sheet pan. Season it generously on all sides with the rub, using your fingertips to rub the spices into the meat in a thick layer.

6. Fire up your smoker, cooker, or grill following the manufacturer's instructions and heat to 250°F. Add the wood as specified by the manufacturer. Place a metal bowl or aluminum foil pan with 1 quart of warm water in the smoker—this creates a humid environment that will help the smoke adhere to the meat and keep your brisket moist.

7. Transfer the brisket from the pan and place it fat side up in the smoker. Cook until the outside is darkly browned and the internal temperature registers about 175°F on an instant-read thermometer, 7 to 8 hours. Refuel your cooker as needed, following the manufacturer's instructions.

8. Set up a steamer following the instructions on page 96. Place the pastrami fat side up on the rack. Steam it until very tender, 2 to 3 hours.

When serving pastrami cold, thinly slice it on a meat slicer for deli-worthy sandwiches.

9. Transfer the pastrami to a welled cutting board. At this point, you can serve it warm or cold. For hot pastrami, use a long sharp knife to slice the meat across the grain as thickly or thinly as you desire. For cold pastrami, let it cool to room temperature, then refrigerate it until cold and firm. Cut it into paper-thin slices on a meat slicer or by hand.

VARIATION

Smoked Pastrami (Hold the Steam): Once the domain of the delicatessen, pastrami has been embraced by a new generation of barbecue restaurants. Here, the entire cook is done in the smoker without the traditional step of steaming. This produces an equally fabulous pastrami—

WHAT ELSE: Traditionally, pastrami was made not with brisket but with another tough, fatty cut from the steer's undercarriage: beef navel. (Think the bovine equivalent of pork belly.) In recent years, a new generation of pit masters—guys like Tim Rattray at the Granary in San Antonio and Joe Carroll at Fette Sau in Brooklyn and Philadelphia—has added house-smoked pastrami to the traditional barbecue repertoire, and in the process, brisket has become the preferred beef for curing and smoking. I call for an 8-pound chunk of brisket—a flat if you like your pastrami lean; a section with both flat and point if you like it fatty.

perhaps a bit smokier and drier than the deli version. To do this, cook the pastrami through step 7. Wrap the pastrami in unlined butcher paper, following the instructions on page 31. Return the pastrami to the smoker and continue cooking until the internal temperature reaches around 205°F, another 2 to 3 hours, or as needed. Place the wrapped pastrami in an insulated cooler and let it rest for 1 to 2 hours. Serve as described above.

NOTE: Pink curing salt, also known as Prague Powder #1 or InstaCure #1, can be found at some butcher shops or online. Do not confuse it with Himalayan pink salt.

HOW TO SET UP A STEAMER

Steaming is an essential step in preparing pastrami and Montreal smoked meat. Restaurants use professional steamers, but it's easy to rig one up at home. Here are four simple configurations. Whichever one your choose, you'll want to replenish the water as needed to keep the level at a couple of inches.

- **In a Chinese bamboo steamer:** If you own a wok or you know your way around Chinatown, use a Chinese bamboo steamer. Fill the bottom of a large wok with water to a depth of about 2 inches. Place the appropriately sized bamboo steamer on top. (You may need to seal any steam leaks around the outside with rolled wet paper towels.) Add the cured brisket, cover, and steam as directed.

- **In a round pot or Dutch oven:** Place three open empty mason jars or cans in the bottom of a large round pot or Dutch oven. Fill them with water and add water to the pot to reach a depth of about 2 inches. Set a round wire cake rack atop the jars and place the cured brisket on top. Bring the water to a boil and tightly cover. Steam as directed.

- **With a steaming basket:** This is better for smaller cuts of cured brisket. Place the largest folding steaming basket you can find in the bottom of a large pot or Dutch oven. Place the cured brisket on top. Add water to a depth of about 2 inches (it should be below the bottom of the basket). Cover the pot and steam as directed.

- **In the oven:** Place a wire rack in a roasting pan or large Dutch oven. (If the rack sits too low to add water, raise it on open water-filled mason jars or cans.) Add boiling water to a depth of about 2 inches. Place the cured brisket on the rack. Tightly cover the roasting pan with aluminum foil or the Dutch oven with the lid. Place in a 350°F oven and steam as directed.

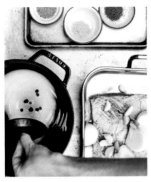

1. Make the brine.

4. Rinse the brined brisket with cold water.

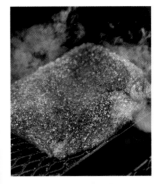

7. Smoke the brisket in your favorite cooker.

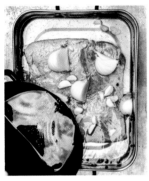

2. Pour the brine over the brisket.

5. Roast the spices before grinding.

8. Steam the brisket (here in a bamboo steamer).

3. Brine the brisket.

6. Crust the brined brisket with the pastrami rub.

9. The steamed brisket is ready for slicing.

PASTRAMI: A DELI ICON

Quick—think of your favorite meat at your neighborhood delicatessen. You're not alone if you named pastrami.

This pepper- and coriander-crusted meat—black on the outside, shocking pink inside, salty, mildly smoky, intensely garlicky—is one of the world's great brisket success stories. And how it arrived at the American delicatessen is a journey as remarkable as the four-step process required to cook it.

You may be surprised to learn that, in the beginning, pastrami wasn't Jewish. It wasn't smoked. It wasn't even beef.

Pastrami originated in Turkey, where it was made with lamb, goat, water buffalo, or even camel. It went by the name *basturma*—derived from the Turkish verb *bastir*—"to cure" or "to press." Imagine arm-long strips of meat, salted first, then pressed, then rubbed with cumin, fenugreek, hot paprika, and other aromatic spices. The final step was air-drying, producing a cured meat similar to Italian *bresaola*. You still find *basturma* throughout Turkey and the Middle East today, where it's thinly shaved over scrambled eggs or sliced paper-thin to munch with *raki* (anise liqueur) as an aperitif.

According to Robert Moss, author of a fascinating essay "How Pastrami Really Arrived in New York City" on SeriousEats .com, by the time the preparation reached what today is Romania (a Turkish province during the Ottoman Empire), it had morphed into *pastroma*. A commercial dictionary of the period described it as "ox, sheep, or goat's flesh, salted, with garlic and spices, and dried in the sun for winter food." Garlic had become a primary flavoring (after all, this was Romania). Later reports cite another inexpensive and widely available meat of the time: goose. In the 1850s, the Romanian port city of Braila on the Danube was a major *pastroma* exporter.

Between 1881 and 1914, more than 75,000 Romanian Jews immigrated to New York City—many of them to the Lower East Side. They brought their love of *pastroma*, dispensing it at grocery stores and kosher butcher shops that sprang up on Rivington, Allen, and Delancey Streets. One thing they couldn't agree on was spelling. Newspaper ads of the period refer to "pastrame," "pastromie," "pestrame," "pastromi," "pasturma," "pastromer," and "pastroma."

So, who first served a pastrami sandwich in the United States? Here, too, debate rages, with Sussman Volk (founder of Volk Provisions) and Willy Katz (founder of Katz's Deli) being the top contenders. *Eater* food critic Robert Sietsema explores the chronology and much else about pastrami's history in his mouthwatering book *New York in a Dozen Dishes*.

Contender #1, Sussman Volk, emigrated from Lithuania and opened a butcher shop somewhere between 1888 and 1903. (Family accounts differ from commercial records of the period.) A much-repeated story holds that Volk agreed to store a steamer trunk for a Romanian friend, who, by way of thanks, shared his recipe for pastrami. Volk began selling it at his butcher shop. So popular was the new meat that Volk rented a storefront at 88 Delancey Street, installed tables and chairs, and began selling pastrami sandwiches to what were soon standing-room-only crowds. The delicatessen was born.

The Katz family (owners of the landmark Katz's Deli), on the other hand, credits Willy Katz with serving New York's first pastrami sandwich. The family sets the date at 1888, when Morris and Hyman Iceland opened a delicatessen called Iceland Brothers. Katz bought it in 1903, changing the name to Iceland & Katz, then simply Katz's Delicatessen in 1910. (Immigration and municipal records set the dates somewhat later.) What's important either way is that, by the early twentieth century, pastrami had become a delicatessen icon.

Almost as iconic is the famous scene in the movie *When Harry Met Sally . . .* , in which Meg Ryan loudly fakes an orgasm while eating a pastrami sandwich at Katz's Deli. (A woman at the next table utters the immortal line "I'll have what she's having.") The late writer-director Nora Ephron conceived the scene during one of her weekly lunches with Rob Reiner at Katz's. You can still sit at that table today and people line up to do so. According to Katz's current owner, Jake Dell, customers like to re-enact the scene—some with brio equal to that of Ms. Ryan.

For most of the twentieth century, pastrami was made the traditional way—first brined, then rubbed, then smoked, and finally steamed. Over the years, the original beef cut—navel (the bovine analogue to the pork belly)—gave way to leaner brisket, although a few holdouts, like Katz's, still make pastrami with beef navel.

And the latest chapter in pastrami's colorful history? In 2007, Joe Carroll began serving barbecued brisket pastrami at Brooklyn's Fette Sau (more on this remarkable barbecue joint on page 51). Tim Rattray made it a weekly special at the Granary in San Antonio. Billy Durney serves an amazing barbecued pastrami at Hometown Bar-B-Que in Red Hook, Brooklyn. These new school briskets are smokier than their delicatessen counterparts. Some pit masters even skip the step of steaming.

On page 93, you'll find an Old School Pastrami in the style of Katz's Deli. On page 100, there's a New School Pastrami—flavored with fish sauce and makrut (kaffir) lime leaves—from Harry & Ida's Meat & Supply Co., also in Manhattan. On page 109, you'll find a fiery Kung Pao Pastrami in the style of chef Danny Bowien of Mission Chinese in San Francisco and Manhattan.

Which is to say, this ancient cured meat from Turkey continues to evolve.

Katz's: landmark pastrami since 1888

NEW SCHOOL PASTRAMI

YIELD: Serves 8 to 10

METHOD: Smoking, steaming

PREP TIME: 30 minutes to make the brine and rub, plus 7 days to brine the pastrami

COOKING TIME: 6 to 7 hours for smoking, plus 2 to 3 hours for steaming

HEAT SOURCE: Smoker or charcoal grill (like a Weber kettle), then a stove or oven (sorry, folks—you won't get the right smoke flavor on a gas grill)

YOU'LL ALSO NEED: 2 jumbo (2.5-gallon) resealable heavy-duty plastic bags; a large baking dish or a plastic bucket; a rimmed sheet pan; a metal bowl or aluminum foil pan (for the smoker); oak and hickory or other hardwood chunks or chips (the latter, soaked in water for 30 minutes, then drained); a steamer (see page 96)

Harry & Ida's Meat & Supply Co. burst onto New York's deli scene in 2015, with a decidedly new take on pastrami. Here was a delicatessen that cured its own meats, using exotic flavorings such as Asian fish sauce, makrut (kaffir) lime leaves, and maple sugar. Unlike traditional spots, Harry & Ida's proprietor, Will Horowitz, starts with brisket points (not whole briskets or beef navels). He smokes them with oak and hickory, and thanks to a 3-hour steaming process, the meat comes out tender enough to slice with the side of a fork. ("Water is an essential part of making pastrami," Horowitz says.) This enables him to serve it in 1-inch-thick steaks, not thinly sliced, as at most delicatessens. He piles these steaks not on the traditional rye bread but on soft puffy hoagie rolls. You can't eat pastrami without mustard, and Will's contains anchovies. (You've probably gathered by now that Will is obsessed with umami flavors.) The traditional pickles give way to a crispy-creamy Cucumber, Buttermilk, and Rye Berry Salad (page 239). And each pastrami sandwich is lavished with fresh dill—"a ton of fresh dill," insists Will—which provides an unexpected counterpoint to the salty richness of the pastrami. It is, in short, the ultimate pastrami sandwich—and if it took flavorings from Scandinavia and Southeast Asia to get there, well, I'm sure Will's great-grandparents, Harry and Ida, would have approved.

INGREDIENTS

FOR THE BRISKET

2 brisket points (3 to 4 pounds each, 6 to 8 pounds total)

FOR THE BRINE

1 gallon (4 quarts) cold water

⅓ cup Asian fish sauce

1½ cups kosher salt

¾ cup maple sugar or light or dark brown sugar

1 tablespoon Prague Powder #1 (also known as pink curing salt; see box, page 106)

2 bay leaves

2 makrut (kaffir) lime leaves, or 2 strips fresh lime zest, each ½ inch wide and 1½ inches long

1 tablespoon whole black peppercorns

1 tablespoon juniper berries, lightly crushed with the side of a knife (or 3 tablespoons your favorite gin)

1 tablespoon allspice berries, lightly crushed with the side of a knife

1 tablespoon coriander seeds

1 tablespoon mustard seeds

1 tablespoon chopped fresh garlic

1 cassia or cinnamon stick (cassia comes in smooth sticks, and cinnamon in shaggy sticks—both have a cinnamon flavor)

FOR THE RUB

¼ cup coarsely ground black pepper

¼ cup maple sugar or light or dark brown sugar

2 tablespoons ground coriander

4 teaspoons garlic powder

4 teaspoons chili powder

4 teaspoons sweet paprika

1 teaspoon cayenne pepper

FOR SERVING (OPTIONAL)

Hoagie rolls (you'll need 4 to 6 per brisket point), cut almost in half lengthwise and opened like a book

Anchovy Mustard (recipe follows)

1 bunch fresh dill, stemmed and torn into sprigs

Cucumber, Buttermilk, and Rye Berry Salad (page 239)

1. Using a sharp knife, trim the brisket points, leaving a layer of fat at least ¼ inch thick (see page 14). Be careful not to over-trim. It's better to err on the side of too much fat than too little. Place them in a jumbo heavy-duty resealable plastic bag set in a large baking dish (or plastic bucket).

2. Make the brine: Place 2 quarts of the cold water, the fish sauce, salt, sugar, Prague Powder #1, bay leaves, makrut (kaffir) lime leaves, peppercorns, juniper berries, allspice berries, coriander seeds, mustard seeds, garlic, and cassia in a large stockpot and bring to a boil over high heat, whisking until the sugar and salts are dissolved. Remove the pot from the heat and stir in the remaining 2 quarts of cold water. Let the brine cool to room temperature.

3. Add the brine to the brisket points in the bag and seal it shut. Place this bag in a second jumbo resealable heavy-duty plastic bag (to contain any leaks) and place the bagged brisket in the baking dish in the refrigerator. Brine the points for 7 days, turning the bag over each day so the meat brines evenly.

4. On the 7th day, make the rub: Place the pepper, sugar, coriander, garlic powder, chili powder, paprika, and cayenne in a bowl and mix together, using your fingers to break up any lumps.

5. Drain the briskets, discarding the brine. Rinse the briskets thoroughly with cold water and blot dry with paper towels. Place the briskets on a rimmed sheet pan. Season them generously on all sides with the rub, using your fingertips to rub the spices into the meat in a thick layer.

6. Fire up your smoker, cooker, or grill following the manufacturer's instructions and heat to 250°F. Add the wood as specified by the manufacturer. Place a metal bowl or aluminum foil pan with 1 quart of warm water in the smoker—this creates a humid environment that will help the smoke adhere to the meat and keep your brisket moist.

7. Transfer the brisket points from the pan and place them fat side up in the smoker. Cook until the outside is darkly browned and the internal temperature registers about 175°F on an instant-read thermometer, 6 to 7 hours. Refuel your cooker as needed, following the manufacturer's instructions.

8. Set up a steamer following the instructions on page 96. Place the pastrami fat side up on the rack. Steam it until very tender, 2 to 3 hours. Keep the pastrami warm until serving.

9. To serve, transfer the pastrami to a welled cutting board and use a long, sharp knife to slice the pastrami as thickly or thinly as you desire. Pile it on hoagie rolls slathered with Anchovy Mustard and heaped with fresh dill, with the cucumber salad on the side.

ANCHOVY MUSTARD

YIELD: Makes 1 cup

Anchovy gives this mustard a briny umami flavor, while the preserved lemon (available at Whole Foods, gourmet shops, and online) adds a salty, tangy, lemony tartness. If preserved lemon is unavailable, add ½ teaspoon finely grated lemon zest and 1 tablespoon fresh lemon juice.

INGREDIENTS

1 anchovy fillet, minced

1 tablespoon minced preserved lemon

1 cup coarsely ground deli-style mustard

Combine the anchovy, preserved lemon, and mustard in a mixing bowl and whisk to mix.

Anchovy Mustard will keep, in a sealed jar in the refrigerator, for several weeks.

BRISKET WHISPERER—WILL HOROWITZ

If Will Horowitz wants to tinker with his century-old family pastrami recipe, he's certainly earned the right. His great-grandparents, Harry and Ida—namesakes of his pastrami emporium in Manhattan—ran a delicatessen in Harlem. (They cured their pastrami and sauerkraut in buckets on the fire escape.) Will earned dual degrees in writing and Tibetan Buddhism and became a survivalist, then a chef. His fascination with fermenting and curing dates from his survivalist days, and his food prep area looks as much like a biology lab as it does a kitchen.

What? You haven't heard of Will or the Ducks Eatery and Harry & Ida's restaurants he runs with his sister, Julie? I bet you've heard of their latest creation—a smoked watermelon "ham" that recently rocked the blogosphere. (There's currently a one-month waiting list for this curiosity, which retails for $75.) Will cures and smokes all sorts of foods you wouldn't expect, from seaweed and mushrooms to radishes, and his watermelon ham is just the most recent, er, fruit of an omnivorously curious mind and a chef's willingness to try anything.

That includes deconstructing traditional deli pastrami, enriching the brine with Asian fish sauce, maple sugar, and makrut (kaffir) lime leaves. (You'll find the recipe on page 100.) As for the barbecued brisket served at Ducks Eatery, "it took me a solid year of experimenting to get the meat we serve today," Will says. One secret is to vary the cooking temperature during the 15-hour cook, starting low (230°F) for the first three hours to set the smoke flavor, then boosting the heat as high as 325°F to build the bark. Will finishes the brisket at 250°F to gelatinize the collagen and render the fat. But don't ask to see his instant-read thermometer. "I haven't taken a temperature in eight years," he says. "We check all our briskets by feel."

So what is it about brisket that has inspired Will to make it the focal point of two restaurants? "I love the heritage and family tradition. I love how it can be simultaneously so fatty and luscious and so lean. Ultimately, I love the challenge of cooking a cut of meat comprised of two different muscles that behave completely differently in the smoker. There are a lot of paths to the top of the mountain. Take your time and you'll get there."

As the owner of both a deli and a restaurant that has been described as a New Wave barbecue joint, Horowitz thinks a lot about the connection between pastrami and Texas brisket.

"Both originated with Eastern Europeans (Romanian Jews in the case of the former; Austrian and Czech butchers in the case of the latter)." Both used spice and smoke to preserve meat before the advent of refrigeration. "And what is the classic pastrami seasoning but a Texas salt and pepper rub fortified with garlic and coriander?" Will asks with a smile.

Like many of the new generation of brisket masters, Will is deeply concerned about sustainability, including the lessons we can learn from a plant-based diet. His pastrami sandwich comes with a veritable farmers' market of rye berries, cucumbers, and fresh dill. "Sure, we could buy cheaper brisket and boost our output," he says. "We prefer to work with meat from local farmers."

"Cook with compassion," Will says. "Remember, your brisket comes from what was once a living, breathing creature. Your job as a cook is to be a storyteller. Tell the story of this beautiful cut of meat as simply and as perfectly as you can."

CURING SALTS

Corned beef, pastrami, and Montreal smoked meat are some of the world's most delectable manifestations of brisket. One is boiled; two are smoked; and two may or may not be steamed. But they all have one thing in common: All owe their vivid pink color, iridescent sheen, and soulful umami flavor to a curing salt called sodium nitrite.

Wait: Aren't sodium *nitrite* and its sibling, sodium *nitrate*, artificial ingredients added by evil food manufacturers and indisputably shown to cause cancer?

So they were accused in the 1980s, and while nitrites have long since been exonerated, a certain prejudice toward them persists to this day.

Nitrites occur naturally in both mineral deposits and plants. (Sodium nitrite—$NaNO_2$—has two oxygen atoms for every nitrogen atom; sodium nitrate—$NaNO_3$—has three.) Both give cured meats their shimmering rosy hue. They do so by binding with the myoglobin in beef and other red meats, converting it to nitrosomyoglobin, which turns cooked meat pink.

More importantly, nitrites and nitrates greatly reduce the risk of a potentially fatal foodborne illness called botulism. And when combined with salt, they greatly extend cured meat's shelf life. They also create a unique cluster of flavors—salty, hammy, cheesy. You can make corned beef and pastrami without nitrites, but they won't look or taste quite right.

So how did sodium nitrite get such a bad rap? Well, for starters, when consumed in large quantities, it can be toxic. (That's why manufacturers dilute it with table salt and dye it pink as a warning.) It was also linked to higher cancer rates in a handful of questionably accurate experiments in the 1970s.

There's just one catch: Sodium nitrite occurs naturally in many vegetables, including celery, spinach, carrots, and beets. In fact, according to the American Meat Institute (an organization admittedly pro-curing salt), more than 90 percent of our daily nitrite intake comes from vegetables. The USDA allows up to 156 parts per million (PPM) of sodium nitrite in corned beef, pastrami, and other cured meats. A daily serving of vegetables can contain up to 1,900 PPM! Case closed.

The curing salt you'll use in this book is sodium nitrite. (Sodium nitrate is used in slow cures—for salami, for example—that take place over several months.) Nitrites are sold under several names, including:

- Pink curing salt (*sel rose* in French)

- Prague Powder #1

- InstaCure #1 or Quick Cure

- Morton Tender Quick

Regardless of what you call it, curing salt contains roughly 6 percent pure sodium nitrite mixed with 92 percent table salt, with small traces of an anti-caking agent and red food dye to color the mixture pink. (Don't confuse the latter with Himalayan salt, which is naturally pink.)

When working with curing salt, a little goes a long way: 4 ounces will cure 100 pounds of meat.

Sodium nitrite is safe, effective, and indispensable for making pastrami, corned beef, and other cured meats, but never forget that, consumed in excess, it can be toxic. Follow the manufacturer's instructions—and the recipes in this book—and you'll be fine.

One cut of meat cured four ways. Clockwise from top right: pastrami, corned beef, smoked corned beef, and Montreal smoked meat

BRISKET HACKS:

- When curing brisket, label the package accurately with the date you began and your target date. Cure the meat in the refrigerator. Turn it daily so it cures evenly. Drain it well, then rinse the meat thoroughly with cold water and pat it dry. When making pastrami or smoked meat, drain and rinse off the brine or rinse off the cure, then pat it dry with paper towels before smoking.

- When brining, make sure the brisket is completely submerged in brine by weighting it with a dinner plate or tightly sealed bags of ice. (Replace as needed.)

- When dry curing, thoroughly mix the curing salt with the other dry flavorings *before* applying them to the brisket.

KUNG PAO PASTRAMI

There are two ways to approach restaurants, just as there are two philosophies for living your life. The first is to find places you like and return to them often for your tried-and-true favorite dishes. This guarantees meals you will like in surroundings that make you comfortable. The other approach is to constantly seek new experiences, forsaking the comfort of the familiar for a shot at the unplanned and extraordinary. My wife adheres to the first school, so when she picks the restaurant, I know I'm in for a good meal. I'm all about the thrill of the new, which means that often I'm disappointed, but occasionally I'm blown away. So for me to return to the *same* restaurant and order the *same* dish in the space of two weeks—and this in one of the most sophisticated restaurant cities in North America that I've flown 3,000 miles to visit—well, that suggests a pretty astonishing meal. But that's exactly what I did at Mission Chinese in San Francisco. You won't find the dish that so captivated me—stir-fried *kung pao* pastrami—at your average Chinese restaurant in North America or China. Then again, Mission Chinese chef-owner Danny Bowien was born in Korea and raised in Oklahoma, and his first claim to culinary fame involved not Asian food, but winning a Pesto World Championship. Bowien's take on traditional *kung pao* features two decidedly non-Chinese ingredients: pastrami and potatoes. The sauce roars in like a SWAT team, assaulting you with salt, garlic, chile hellfire, and tongue-numbing Sichuan peppercorns. Eating it will hurt your taste buds, and the only way to get relief is to take another bite. What follows is a streamlined version of Danny Bowien's masterpiece.

YIELD: Serves 4 as a starter, or 2 as a main course

METHOD: Stir-frying

PREP TIME: 20 minutes

COOKING TIME: 10 minutes

HEAT SOURCE: Stove or grill side burner

YOU'LL ALSO NEED: A metal strainer; a wok; a wok spatula

WHAT ELSE: You may need to take a trip to an Asian market to make this one. For chile paste, you want a hot, salty Chinese version (*la jiao jiang*) or *sambal oelek* from Indonesia. Chinese hot bean paste (*dou ban jiang*—another condiment made with chiles and soybeans) piles on more salty-garlicky flavors. (I've made it optional.) Tianjin peppers (rust-colored dried chiles) pump up the heat even further. (In a pinch, substitute 2 to 3 teaspoons hot red pepper flakes.) Sichuan peppercorns don't belong to the pepper family at all, but they are tiny reddish dried berries that possess the odd property of simultaneously numbing and cooling your mouth. There's no substitute, but if unavailable, your stir-fry will still taste pretty remarkable without them.

INGREDIENTS

1 pound thick-sliced pastrami (make your own following the recipe on page 93, or ask the deli guy to slice it ¼ inch thick)

2 tablespoons Chinese chile paste or *sambal oelek*

2 tablespoons soy sauce

2 tablespoons Chinese rice wine (Shaoxing), sake, or Scotch whisky

1 tablespoon Chinese hot bean paste (optional)

2 teaspoons sugar

½ cup peanut oil

12 ounces Yukon gold potatoes, peeled and cut into ½-inch dice (enough to make 1 cup)

1 tablespoon Sichuan peppercorns

3 to 6 dried Chinese chile peppers (Tianjin peppers), or to taste

A 1-inch piece of fresh ginger, peeled and cut into matchstick slivers

2 cloves garlic, peeled and minced

4 scallions, trimmed and thinly sliced crosswise (set aside 1 tablespoon of the green parts for garnish)

4 ribs celery, cut on the diagonal into ¼-inch slices

2 serrano or jalapeño chiles (or to taste), stemmed and thinly sliced crosswise

1 cup unsalted dry-roasted peanuts

1. Cut the pastrami slices crosswise into 1-inch pieces and set aside.

2. Make the sauce: Combine the chile paste, soy sauce, rice wine, bean paste (if using), and sugar in a small bowl and whisk to incorporate.

3. Place a metal strainer over a heatproof bowl and line a plate with paper towels. Heat the peanut oil in a wok over high heat or on a hot grill set up for direct grilling (see page 81). Add the potatoes and fry, stirring with a wok spatula,

until golden, 6 to 8 minutes. Pour the fried potatoes and oil into the strainer and drain for 2 minutes. Reserve the oil that has collected in the bowl and transfer the potatoes from the strainer to the prepared plate; blot any excess oil off the potatoes with a paper towel.

4. Return 3 tablespoons of the strained oil to the wok. Add the Sichuan peppercorns and dried chiles and stir-fry over high heat (or on the hot grill) until fragrant, 10 seconds. Add the ginger, garlic, scallions, celery, and fresh chiles and stir-fry until aromatic and beginning to brown, 30 seconds. Add the pastrami, ¾ cup peanuts, and the potatoes to the wok and stir-fry until fragrant, 2 minutes.

5. Stir the sauce to reincorporate the ingredients and add it to the wok. Stir-fry until the sauce boils, thickens, and coats the other ingredients, 1 minute.

6. Sprinkle the remaining ¼ cup peanuts and 1 tablespoon scallion greens on top and serve at once directly from the wok.

CLASSIC CORNED BEEF

You can't get more Jewish than a corned beef sandwich on rye bread, right? Or can you? According to Irish cooking authority Darina Allen, the Irish have been "corning" (pickling) beef since the eleventh century. Between the 1680s and 1825, beef corning was the biggest industry in County Cork. Corned beef from Cork was exported across the British Empire, from Newfoundland to the West Indies. It was the Irish immigrants in New York at the turn of the last century who made corned beef the St. Patrick's Day icon it is today. So where does the Jewish connection come in? The Irish corned beef, but not necessarily brisket. They adopted the latter from their Jewish neighbors on Manhattan's Lower East Side. Curiously, the term *corned* comes not from the grain we eat on the cob (or use to brew whiskey) but from the medieval word for a large kernel of salt. You could think of corning as brining—with the addition of pickling spices, such as bay leaves, peppercorns, mustard seeds, allspice, and ginger. Here's a traditional corned beef that's surprisingly easy to make. It tastes equally great cold in sandwiches or hot with boiled potatoes and cabbage, and can be used deliciously to make the Double-Down Reuben sandwich on page 213 or Corned Beef Hash on page 184. And on page 116 you'll find a Raichlen twist: a corned beef you cook in a smoker. Just don't wait until St. Patrick's Day to try them.

YIELD: Serves 6 to 8

METHOD: Boiling or braising

PREP TIME: 15 minutes, plus 8 days to cure the brisket, plus another 1 hour for soaking

COOKING TIME: 2½ to 3½ hours

HEAT SOURCE: Stove, oven

YOU'LL ALSO NEED: A large, nonreactive stockpot; 2 jumbo (2.5-gallon) resealable heavy-duty plastic bags; a baking dish or a plastic bucket; a colander; a Dutch oven with a tight-fitting lid; a welled cutting board

"Corn" the brisket in a brine flavored with pickling spice.

INGREDIENTS

FOR CORNING (CURING) THE BEEF

2 cups hot water

1 cup coarse sea salt or kosher salt

½ cup light or dark brown sugar

¼ cup Pickling Spice (recipe follows, or use your favorite commercial brand)

2 teaspoons Prague Powder #1 (pink curing salt; see box, page 106)

2 cups ice water

¼ cup Irish whiskey

1 beef brisket flat (3 to 4 pounds)

FOR COOKING THE CORNED BEEF

1 whole clove

1 bay leaf

1 medium onion, peeled and quartered

3 carrots, peeled and trimmed

3 ribs celery

FOR SERVING

Sliced rye bread and mustard (optional)

Boiled potatoes and/or cabbage (optional)

1. Make the brine: Combine the hot water, coarse salt, brown sugar, pickling spice, and Prague Powder #1 in a nonreactive stockpot. Bring to a boil on the stovetop over high heat. Let cool to room temperature, then stir in the ice water and whiskey.

2. Meanwhile, using a sharp knife, trim the brisket, leaving a layer of fat at least ¼ inch thick (see page 14). Be careful not to over-trim. It's better to err on the side of too much fat than too little.

3. Place the brisket in one of the jumbo resealable heavy-duty plastic bags. Add the brine and seal the bag. Place it in

another resealable plastic bag (to catch any leaks), seal it, and place the bagged brisket in a baking dish or plastic bucket.

4. Brine the corned beef in the refrigerator for 8 days, turning the bag daily.

5. Drain the brisket in a colander, discarding the brine. Fill a stockpot with fresh cold water, add the brisket, and let soak for 1 hour, then drain again.

6. Preheat the oven to 300°F.

7. Place the corned beef in a Dutch oven and add water to cover by a depth of 1 inch. Bring to a boil over medium-high heat. Reduce the heat to a simmer and skim off any foam that rises to the surface, using a ladle or slotted spoon.

8. Use the clove to pin the bay leaf to one of the onion quarters. Add the onion to the brisket pot along with the carrots and celery. (Note: If you like your carrots and celery with a little chew to them, add them after 2 hours of braising.)

9. Cover the Dutch oven with the lid or aluminum foil, crimped to fit tightly, and place it in the oven. Braise the corned beef until very tender (test it by inserting a fork—it should

pierce the meat easily), 3 to 3½ hours, or as needed.

10. Transfer the corned beef to a welled cutting board. At this point, you can serve it hot or cold. For hot corned beef, use a long, sharp knife to slice the meat across the grain into ¼-inch-thick slices. (Reserve some of the broth for spooning on top.) Serve on rye bread with mustard or with boiled potatoes and/or cabbage. For cold corned beef, let it cool to room temperature, then refrigerate it until cold and firm. Cut it into paper-thin slices on a meat slicer or by hand and serve it on rye bread with mustard.

PICKLING SPICE
YIELD: Makes ¼ cup

I prefer this pickling spice to commercial blends because you can customize the flavorings and make sure the spices are fresh.

INGREDIENTS

10 juniper berries

6 allspice berries

6 whole cloves

2 dried bay leaves, crumbled

1 cinnamon stick (3 inches), broken into 3 or 4 pieces

1 tablespoon whole black peppercorns

1 tablespoon coriander seeds

2 teaspoons mustard seeds

½ teaspoon ground ginger

Combine the ingredients in a mixing bowl and stir to mix. Pickling Spice will keep, in a sealed jar at room temperature away from heat and light, for at least 2 months.

CORNED BEEF THROUGH THE AGES

Attman's Deli on Lombard Street in Baltimore, where I grew up, may not serve the best corned beef in America. But if someone else does it better, I've yet to find it. Attman's simmers its cured beef briskets in waist-high cauldrons, much as it did when the restaurant opened in 1915. They slice it so thin that you can almost read through it, and they pile it so high on rye bread that your jaws will ache from opening wide enough to take a bite.

Lombard Street was Baltimore's answer to Delancey Street in New York, and in my grandfather's day, you could get world-class corned beef from a half-dozen delis and meat markets there. Today, most deli corned beef comes from giant factories, and while it's reasonably tasty, you'd never mistake it for Attman's. Or for Katz's Deli in Manhattan, or Manny's in Chicago, or Langer's in LA.

Corned beef? Delicatessen? Wait: Didn't corned beef come from Ireland? Isn't corned beef what you eat on St. Patrick's Day—whether you're Irish American or not? So how did it get from the Emerald Isle to the New York–style delicatessen?

In the beginning, the Irish raised cattle mostly as draft and dairy animals. What little meat people ate came primarily from pigs and sheep. That changed when the English conquered Ireland in the twelfth century. To sate England's appetite for beef, English landlords established huge cattle farms in Ireland (displacing Irish farmers in the process). By the 1800s, Ireland was exporting tens of thousands of cattle to England each year.

That all changed with the Cattle Acts of 1663 and 1667, explains Shaylyn Esposito in a fascinating Smithsonian.com article titled "Is Corned Beef Really Irish?" Promulgated to protect the English beef industry, these acts forbade the export of live Irish cattle to England. Irish beef prices plummeted, forcing the nation's meat merchants to salt their surplus inventory to keep it from spoiling.

The first reference to corned beef appears in a twelfth-century comic poem called *Aislinge Meic Con Glinne* (*The Vision of Mac Conglinne*). Back then, beef was cured with sea ash (burned seaweed) instead of salt. In the age before refrigeration (make that most of human history), "corning" (salt curing) was the most effective way to preserve meat. Butchers used coarse rock salt, whose large grains were the size and shape of barley corns. These "corns of salt" gave rise to the name *corned beef*.

Thanks to Eire's abundant beef and low salt tax (10 percent of England's at the time), Irish corned beef became big business. It fed the sailors in the Royal Navy, foot soldiers in Wellington's army, and armies of slaves on Caribbean plantations. It was exported to Colonial America and to British outposts throughout India, Africa, and Asia. It even went to England's archenemy, France. Dublin, Cork, and Belfast grew rich on a corned beef industry that literally fed the world.

Sadly, the only people who weren't eating much corned beef themselves were the Irish. Corned beef was too expensive for the average farmer or factory worker.

The Irish wouldn't start eating corned beef in substantial quantities until the mid-1800s when a million or so immigrants—refugees from the potato famine—settled in New York City. Wages were higher in America and beef was plentiful, which meant that Irish immigrants could now afford a meat that had been financially off-limits for centuries. And where did they buy it? From other immigrants—Eastern European Jews—who turned a cheap tough cut from the steer's undercarriage into a newly coined delicacy: kosher-style corned beef brisket.

Today's corned beef differs dramatically from its eighteenth-century Irish namesake. Back then, butchers corned any tough cut of beef—neck, shank, belly. Today, we use only brisket. In the old days, the meat was heavily salted with rock salt, with saltpeter (potassium nitrate) added as a preservative. (Yes, the same saltpeter used to make gunpowder.) Today, corned beef is brined with pickling spices, such as allspice, cloves, mustard seed, and bay leaves. It owes its iridescent pink sheen and umami tang to a more modern curing salt, sodium nitrite. To be sure, it's salty, but not nearly as salty as the tinned corned beef of the Industrial Revolution.

One thing is certain: Corned beef's popularity hasn't waned over the centuries. Abraham Lincoln served corned beef at his first inaugural dinner in 1861. More recently, NASA astronaut John Young snuck a corned beef sandwich in his spacesuit pocket prior to boarding his flight on Gemini 3. As for the modern-day Irish? On St. Patrick's Day, most still prefer lamb or bacon to corned beef. And they never drink green beer.

Resistance is futile: A great corned beef Reuben can tempt even the most die-hard dieter.

SMOKED CORNED BEEF

YIELD: Serves 6 to 8

METHOD: Smoking

PREP TIME: 15 minutes, plus 8 days to cure the corned beef

COOKING TIME: 6 to 8 hours, or as needed, plus 1 to 2 hours for resting

HEAT SOURCE: Smoker or grill

YOU'LL ALSO NEED: Hickory or other hardwood chunks or chips (if using the latter, soak in water to cover for 30 minutes, then drain); a metal bowl or aluminum foil pan; heatproof gloves; heavy-duty aluminum foil; a Dutch oven; an insulated cooler; a welled cutting board

WHAT ELSE: Made from the brisket flat, corned beef is leaner than pastrami. So I like to wrap it in foil two-thirds of the way through smoking—the built-up steam breaks down tough muscle fibers, tenderizing the meat.

L ike most brisket dishes, traditional corned beef requires a slow, low-temperature cook in a moist environment to render it tender. Did someone say low and slow? Sounds like barbecue, and the only thing missing is wood smoke. Some years ago, I had the idea to smoke corned beef instead of braising it. Think of it as pastrami, but without the peppery crust. (It's the perfect cured meat for people who find pastrami too garlicky.) The smoke lends a complexity and depth of flavor you just don't find in traditional corned beef.

INGREDIENTS

1 recipe Classic Corned Beef (page 111), prepared through step 5

Rye bread, mustard, pickles, sauerkraut, and/or coleslaw, for serving

1. Fire up your smoker, cooker, or grill following the manufacturer's instructions and heat to 250°F. Add the wood as specified by the manufacturer. Place a metal bowl or aluminum foil pan with 1 quart of warm water in the smoker—this creates a humid environment that will help the smoke adhere to the meat and keep your brisket moist.

2. Place the cured brisket fat side up in the smoker. If using an offset smoker, position the thicker end of the brisket toward the firebox. Cook the brisket until the outside is darkly browned and the

internal temperature registers 165°F on an instant-read thermometer, 6 to 8 hours. Refuel your cooker as needed,

A *Brisket Chronicles* first: corned beef in a smoker

following the manufacturer's instructions.

3. Tightly wrap the corned beef in heavy-duty aluminum foil, pleating the edges to make a hermetic seal. Continue cooking the corned beef until the internal temperature reaches 205°F, another 2 hours, or as needed.

4. Place the wrapped corned beef in an insulated cooler and let it rest for 1 to 2 hours. (This allows the meat to relax and the juices to redistribute.)

5. Transfer the corned beef to a welled cutting board and unwrap it. At this point, you can serve it hot or cold. For hot corned beef, use a long sharp knife to slice the meat across the grain into ¼-inch-thick slices. For cold corned beef, let it cool to room temperature, then wrap it in plastic wrap and refrigerate it until cold and firm. Cut it into paper-thin slices on a meat slicer or by hand. Serve on rye bread with mustard, pickles, sauerkraut, and/or coleslaw.

CORNED BEEF AND CABBAGE

Like Italian *bollito misto* (page 167) and French *pot au feu*, corned beef and cabbage is supreme comfort food—Irish in this case. (It's also quintessential St. Patrick's Day fare par excellence here in America—more on that on page 114.) Basically, you put the ingredients in a pot and boil them until tender. There's a little more to the preparation than that, of course, because you want to sequence cooking vegetables so they come out just tender, not boiled to ignominious mush. Another twist on the traditional recipe: buttering the broth. In the best of all worlds, you'd start with home-cured corned beef (such as the Classic Corned Beef on page 111, prepared through step 5). Barring that, use an uncooked corned beef—often available in your supermarket meat department, especially around St. Patrick's Day and Easter. Or order it by mail from Snake River Farms (snakeriverfarms.com) or Mister Brisket (misterbrisket.com).

YIELD: Serves 6 to 8

METHOD: Boiling or braising

PREP TIME: 20 minutes

COOKING TIME: 3 to 3½ hours, or as needed

HEAT SOURCE: Stove (and oven if braising)

INGREDIENTS

1 corned beef (3 to 4 pounds, uncooked)

2 bay leaves, crumbled

1 teaspoon mustard seeds

1 teaspoon whole black peppercorns

1 teaspoon allspice berries

1 savoy cabbage (about 2 pounds)

3 large carrots, trimmed, peeled, and cut crosswise into 2-inch sections

2 medium onions, peeled and quartered

1 pound Yukon gold or boiling potatoes, scrubbed and cut into 2-inch pieces

3 tablespoons unsalted butter

1 tablespoon chopped fresh flat-leaf parsley or chives (optional)

Spicy mustard, for serving

1. Place the corned beef in a Dutch oven. If braising, preheat the oven to 300°F.

2. Tie the bay leaves, mustard seeds, peppercorns, and allspice berries in a square of cheesecloth (alternatively, wrap them in aluminum foil, then perforate the bundle with a fork). Add the spice bundle to the pot and add water to cover by a depth of 2 inches.

3. Bring the corned beef to a boil over high heat, skimming off any foam that rises to the surface with a ladle or slotted spoon. Reduce the heat to low and gently simmer the corned beef, uncovered, until nearly tender, 2 hours. (Alternatively, cover the Dutch oven, place it in the preheated oven, and braise the corned beef until nearly tender, 2 hours.)

4. Remove any wilted or blemished outside leaves from the cabbage. Cut the cabbage in half through the core. Make V-shaped cuts to remove the core, then cut each cabbage half into quarters to obtain 8 wedges.

5. Add the cabbage, carrots, onions, and potatoes to the pot, and continue boiling (or braising, covered) until tender, 1 to 1½ hours more, or as needed. There should be enough liquid to cover the corned beef and vegetables by a depth of 1 inch; add water as needed. (If braising the corned beef and there's too much liquid, keep the Dutch oven uncovered after adding the vegetables.)

6. To serve, remove and discard the spice bundle. Transfer the corned beef to a welled cutting board and use a sharp knife to slice it across the grain as thickly or thinly as you desire. Transfer the slices to a platter or plates, and use a slotted spoon to arrange the boiled vegetables beside the meat, leaving the cooking liquid in the pot.

7. Strain 1½ cups of the cooking liquid into a large heatproof bowl. Whisk in the butter until melted. Spoon this buttery sauce over the corned beef and vegetables. Dust with parsley, if using, and serve plenty of spicy mustard alongside.

IRISH SPICED BEEF

YIELD: Serves 6 to 8

METHOD: Braising or boiling

PREP TIME: 20 minutes, plus 5 to 7 days for curing the brisket

COOKING TIME: 3 hours, or as needed

HEAT SOURCE: Stove (and oven, if braising)

YOU'LL ALSO NEED: A baking dish; spice mill or clean coffee grinder (for the spice rub); butcher's string; a Dutch oven or roasting pan; a brick wrapped in aluminum foil or another weight (if serving cold)

I came across this singular dish in a book called *The Complete Book of Irish Country Cooking* by Darina Allen. Founder of the renowned Ballymaloe Cookery School in Shanagarry, County Cork, Allen dispels the common notion that Irish food is straightforward, even bland. Consider spiced beef, a brisket rubbed with a fragrant mixture of salt, sugar, peppercorns, juniper berries, and allspice. "Spices were difficult and expensive to procure, which meant that spiced beef was a once-a-year indulgence," writes Allen. That indulgence was traditionally served at Christmastime, and although few Americans have heard of it (I hadn't), it appears in James Joyce's short story "The Dead." Peppercorns, allspice, and juniper berries also figure in pastrami and corned beef, of course, lending vigor and excitement to what otherwise would have been a drab diet of salt beef. My assistant, Nancy Loseke, notes a similar dish her Danish grandmother used to make for Christmas. She used flank steak, not brisket, and called it *rullepølse*.

INGREDIENTS

1 brisket flat (3 to 4 pounds)

6 to 8 tablespoons Irish Spice Rub (recipe follows)

1 bay leaf

1 medium onion, peeled and quartered

1 whole clove

3 carrots, trimmed, peeled, and cut into 2-inch pieces

3 ribs celery, cut into 2-inch pieces

1 bottle (11.2 ounces) Guinness or other dark beer

Your favorite fruit chutney and/ or coarse-grained mustard, for serving

1. Using a sharp knife, trim the brisket, leaving a layer of fat at least ¼ inch thick (see page 14). Be careful not to over-trim. It's better to err on the side of too much fat than too little.

2. Place the brisket in a large nonreactive baking dish. Generously season it on all sides with the spice rub (you'll need about 6 tablespoons for a 3-pound piece of brisket or 8 tablespoons for 4 pounds), rubbing it into the meat with your fingertips.

3. Cover the brisket with plastic wrap and cure in the refrigerator, turning it daily, for 5 to 7 days (the longer the cure, the richer the flavor). After a few days, liquid may accumulate in the bottom of the baking dish: This is normal, as the salt draws liquid out of the meat. Discard this liquid before you roll the beef.

4. If braising, preheat the oven to 300°F.

5. Place the brisket on a wire rack over a sheet pan for 30 minutes to drain off the liquid and dry the meat (the surface will be tacky).

6. Roll the brisket (long side to long side) into a compact cylinder, and using butcher's string, tie the brisket crosswise every 2 inches. Place it in a Dutch oven or roasting pan. Pin the bay leaf to one of the onion quarters with a clove. Add the onion, carrots, and celery to the pot with the Guinness and enough water to cover the meat and vegetables by a depth of 1 inch. (Note: If you like your carrots and celery with a little chew to them, add them after 2 hours of braising.)

7. Gradually bring the spiced beef to a boil over high heat. Lower the heat and gently

WHAT ELSE: Like Jewish pastrami (page 93) and Montreal Smoked Meat (page 123), spiced beef was originally designed to preserve meat in the age before refrigeration. You can serve it hot out of the pot or pressed under a weight and chilled, to be sliced and eaten cold. Tradition calls for boiling the beef, but braising it in the oven requires less supervision.

simmer the beef, uncovered, until cooked and tender, 3 hours, or as needed. (Alternatively, cover the pot, place it in the oven, and braise until tender, 3 hours, or as needed.)

8. Transfer the spiced beef to a welled cutting board, discarding the cooking liquid. (You can serve the vegetables on the side and spoon some of the cooking liquid over the beef by way of a sauce.) Remove and discard the butcher's string. For hot spiced beef, use a long sharp knife to cut it across the grain into ¼-inch-thick slices. Serve with chutney and/or mustard. For cold spiced beef, place it in a large loaf pan or baking dish and top with a brick wrapped in foil or another weight. (This compacts the meat.) Let cool to room temperature, then cover and refrigerate overnight. Remove the weight, transfer the meat to a cutting board, and thinly slice it crosswise. Serve it with chutney and/or mustard alongside.

VARIATION

Smoked Irish Spiced Beef: Okay, you saw this one coming. Season and cure the beef as described in steps 2 and 3. Drape it with strips of bacon and smoke it as directed in the Bacon-Smoked Brisket Flat recipe on page 44. Think of it as pastrami with an Irish brogue, and, yes, you should serve it with Guinness.

IRISH SPICE RUB

YIELD: Makes about 1¼ cups

One doesn't normally think of Irish food as spicy or highly seasoned, but this spice rub fairly explodes with the flavor of allspice and juniper berries. Sometimes I like to add Prague Powder #1 (sodium nitrite) to give the spiced beef the handsome rose color and umami flavor of corned beef. It isn't traditional, but it makes one heck of an Irish spiced beef.

INGREDIENTS

¼ cup whole black peppercorns

¼ cup allspice berries

¼ cup juniper berries

9 tablespoons (½ cup plus
    1 tablespoon) coarse sea salt
    or kosher salt

½ cup sugar

1 teaspoon Prague Powder #1
    (pink curing salt; optional;
    see box, page 106)

Coarsely grind the peppercorns, allspice berries, and juniper berries in a spice mill. Transfer to a mixing bowl and mix in the salt, sugar, and Prague Powder #1 (if using).

Irish Spice Rub will keep, in a sealed jar away from heat and light, for several weeks. It makes an invigorating seasoning not just for brisket, but for pork shoulder, poultry, and ribs.

MONTREAL SMOKED MEAT

Smoked meat is pastrami with a French Canadian accent. One taste of the meat—spicy, salty, subtly smoked, and supremely succulent—and you'll sign up for a Rosetta Stone French course. Although closely related, smoked meat differs from pastrami in several key ways: It's not brined but dry-cured with salt, sugar, and spices, which makes it more fragrant and aromatic. (The allspice in the rub may make you think of Jamaican jerk seasoning; see page 73.) It starts as a whole packer brisket, not the point or flat, which means that every smoked meat sandwich has an irresistible ratio of fat to lean meat. Until recently, you had to travel to Montreal to experience smoked meat, but native son Joel Tietolman serves the real deal at his Mile End Deli in Brooklyn, and more recently, in Manhattan's West Village and Tennessee. (A great source for smoked meat in Chicago is Fumare.) "A lot of people who

YIELD: Serves 12 to 14

METHOD: Barbecuing/smoking, steaming

PREP TIME: 20 minutes, plus 12 days for curing the brisket, plus 4 hours for soaking

COOKING TIME: 6 to 8 hours for smoking, plus 2½ to 3 hours for steaming

HEAT SOURCE: Smoker or charcoal grill, steamer

find corned beef boring will find smoked meat extraordinarily tasty," says Tietolman. That might be the understatement of the year. The following has been adapted from the *Mile End Cookbook* by Noah and Rae Bernamoff, who opened the Mile End Deli in Brooklyn with Tietolman.

INGREDIENTS

1 packer brisket
(12 to 14 pounds)

FOR THE CURING RUB

4 heads garlic (yes, you're reading this right—the original recipe called for 12!), broken into cloves and peeled

¾ cup kosher salt

1½ tablespoons Prague Powder #1 (pink curing salt; see box, page 106)

½ cup sugar

1 cup whole black peppercorns

6 tablespoons coriander seeds

¼ cup mustard seeds

2 tablespoons whole allspice berries, cracked (a cast-iron skillet works well for this)

3 tablespoons dehydrated onion flakes

3 tablespoons sweet paprika

12 dried bay leaves, crumbled

FOR THE FINISHING RUB

¾ cup black peppercorns

6 tablespoons coriander seeds

¼ cup sweet paprika

FOR SERVING

Sliced rye bread (or grilled French bread)

French's mustard (to be authentic) or deli-style mustard or Dijon

YOU'LL ALSO NEED:
A rimmed sheet pan; a food processor; a baking dish; a jumbo (2.5-gallon) heavy-duty resealable plastic bag (optional); a large stockpot or roasting pan; a spice mill; a wire rack; hardwood chunks or chips (if using the latter, soak in water to cover for 30 minutes, then drain); a metal bowl or aluminum foil pan; a digital instant-read thermometer (preferably remote); pink butcher paper (unlined; optional); a welled cutting board.

WHAT ELSE: Smoked meat isn't all that difficult to make, but you will need almost two weeks from start to finish. During that time, you'll dry-cure the brisket, then soak it, then smoke it, then steam it. So plan ahead accordingly. (Once it is smoked, you can hold the beef in the refrigerator for up to 3 days before steaming and serving it, Joe Tietolman says.)

1. Using a sharp knife, trim the brisket, leaving a layer of fat at least ¼ inch thick (see page 14). Be careful not to over-trim. It's better to err on the side of too much fat than too little. Place the brisket on a rimmed sheet pan.

2. Make the curing rub: Place the garlic in a food processor and pulse to finely chop. Add the salt, Prague Powder #1, sugar, peppercorns, coriander seeds, mustard seeds, allspice berries, onion flakes, and paprika, and process to mix. Work in the bay leaves, running the processor in short bursts.

3. Spread the curing rub on the brisket on both sides, patting it into the meat with your fingertips. Cover with plastic wrap. (Alternatively, place the rubbed meat in a jumbo, 2.5-gallon resealable plastic bag along with any remaining rub.) Cure the brisket in the refrigerator for 12 days, turning the brisket over each day so it cures evenly.

4. Rinse the brisket to remove the curing rub. Place the brisket in a large stockpot or roasting pan and add cold water to cover by a depth of at least 3 inches. Soak the brisket at room temperature for 4 hours to temper the salt.

5. Meanwhile, make the finishing rub: Grind the peppercorns and coriander seeds in a spice mill. Add the paprika and stir to combine.

6. Drain the soaked brisket and rinse it under cold running water. Arrange it on a wire rack set over a rimmed sheet pan. Pat it dry with paper towels and let it air-dry for 10 minutes.

7. Sprinkle the finishing rub over the brisket, rubbing it into the meat with your fingertips. Be especially generous with the rub on the fat side.

8. Fire up your smoker, cooker, or grill following the manufacturer's instructions and heat to 250°F. Add the wood as specified by the manufacturer. Place a metal bowl or aluminum foil pan with 1 quart of warm water in the smoker—this creates a humid environment that will help the smoke adhere to the meat and keep your brisket moist.

9. Place the brisket fat side up in the smoker. If using an offset smoker, place the thicker end of the brisket toward the firebox. Cook until the internal temperature reaches 170°F on an instant-read thermometer (in the thickest part of the brisket), about 6 to 8 hours. Note: This is a shorter cooking time and lower temperature than are usual for smoked brisket, but the smoked beef will be steamed for several hours.

10. You can steam the brisket right away, which makes this a long continuous cooking process. If so, proceed to step 11. Otherwise, transfer the brisket to a wire rack set on a rimmed sheet pan and let cool to room temperature, then refrigerate it, uncovered, overnight. At this point, the brisket can be wrapped in pink butcher paper and stored in the refrigerator for several days before steaming.

11. When you are ready to steam the beef, set up a steamer following the instructions on page 96.

12. Unwrap the brisket, if necessary, and separate the point from the flat (see page 34); wrap the flat in aluminum foil and refrigerate it. Place the point section fat side up on the steaming rack and steam for 1½ hours.

13. Unwrap the flat and place it atop the steamed point. Continue steaming until both sections of the brisket are very tender, 1 to 1½ hours more.

14. To serve, transfer the smoked meat to a welled cutting board. Use a long sharp knife to separate the point and the flat, then cut each across the grain into thin slices. When building sandwiches or serving, include slices from both the lean flat section and the fatty point section. (According to Joel, the perfect ratio is 60 percent lean to 40 percent fat.) Serve on rye bread or grilled French bread with the mustard of your choice.

NOTE: Tradition calls for steaming, as it does for pastrami, but you can also make excellent Montreal-style smoked meat by smoking the brisket the whole time and omitting the steaming step. In this case, you'll need 10 to 14 hours of smoking to reach an internal temperature of 205°F (follow the method used in The Big Kahuna Barbecued Packer Brisket, page 41).

MONTREAL SMOKED MEAT

Two Jewish butchers left the Old Country bound for North America. One settled in New York City, where he introduced a Romanian specialty: pastrami. The other moved to Montreal, where the same specialty became smoked meat.

That's how Joel Tietolman, owner of the Mile End Deli in Brooklyn (and elsewhere), explains the difference between the most famous deli meat in America and the most famous Canadian deli meat that most Americans have never heard of.

Mile End Deli, Brooklyn, NY

Tietolman wants to set us straight. So in 2010, he and his then partner, Noah Bernamoff, opened Mile End (it's named for a Jewish neighborhood in Montreal). Talk about chutzpah! Here were two guys—best friends growing up in Montreal—who proposed to put a French Canadian cold cut up against New York's beloved pastrami. Sure, they'd serve corned beef (house-cured and freshly steamed) and poutine (that essential French Canadian dish of French fries topped with gravy and cheese curds—it tastes better than it sounds). But the real reason Tietolman wants you to trek out to Brooklyn—or to the new locations in Manhattan's West Village and Nashville—is to try the smoked meat.

Classic smoked meat sandwich on rye. Yes, the mustard is French's.

Believe me, it's worth it. Picture a moist slab of brisket, darkly crusted with spice on the outside, shocking pink inside, salty and garlicky the way all good pastrami is salty and garlicky, but with a subtly different texture and flavor. It's sweeter than pastrami and simultaneously leaner and fatter. A kissing cousin, but distinct in its own way.

As it turns out, there are other differences between smoked meat and pastrami.

- Smoked meat is dry-cured with a spice rub; pastrami is wet-cured in a brine.

- Smoked meat is made with a whole packer brisket, while pastrami often starts with only the flat or the point (see New School Pastrami on page 100). This gives you both lean and fatty smoked meat; a proper sandwich will contain both.

- Pastrami traditionally comes with a slather of spicy deli mustard, like Gulden's, whereas in Montreal, the only mustard worthy of smoked beef is an American import: French's. A few years ago, Canadian prime minister Justin Trudeau stopped by Mile End for a smoked meat sandwich. He loved the experience but had one complaint: They served deli mustard—with nary a bottle of French's on the premises.

Smoked meat arrived in Montreal early in the last century with Jewish immigrants from Eastern Europe. Once such immigrant was Reuben Schwartz, whose namesake restaurant—founded in 1928—remains *the* go-to place for smoked meat in Montreal. (Tietolman calls it the Katz's Deli of Quebec.)

So the next time you're in Montreal, here's where to try smoked meat:

- Schwartz's Deli
- The Main Deli Steak House
- Reuben's Deli & Steakhouse
- Snowdon Deli
- Smoke Meat Pete

And now you can make it at home, following the recipe on page 123.

Snowdon Deli

Schwartz's Deli

The Main Deli

Chapter 4

BRISKET BRAISED

I have a confession to make. I didn't experience barbecued brisket until I was in my twenties. We didn't have barbecue in Baltimore in the 1960s. But we did have brisket. Every Rosh Hashanah and many a Sabbath, my grandmothers and aunts would braise brisket with dried fruits and root vegetables to make a dish that anchors the Jewish culinary pantheon. And no family gathering would be complete without brisket sandwiches on challah or rye bread, the meat sliced thin as tissue and no less delectable for being a drab shade of gray. Brisket thrives with moist, slow, low-heat cooking—a technique used around the planet. Braising is what transforms brisket, bacon, and wine into French *boeuf à la mode*; turns brisket, beer, and onions into Germany's beloved *Bierfleische*. Chinese "red-cooked" brisket is nothing more than meat braised with soy sauce, rice wine, and star anise. In this chapter, you'll master the world's best braised brisket dishes.

AUNT ANNETTE'S HOLIDAY BRISKET
WITH SWEET WINE AND DRIED FRUITS

Long before my indoctrination into barbecue, I ate brisket. So did every other Jewish kid in the neighborhood. Brisket was the ultimate holiday dish, and nobody made it better than my aunt, Annette Farber. Working in a kitchen that would be deemed hopelessly primitive today, Aunt Annette grated mountains of potatoes on a hand grater to produce latkes that defied physics. (They were simultaneously featherlight and rib-stickingly leaden.) She hand-cranked a meat grinder to turn out gefilte fish I still dream about. But the star of her repertory was brisket—braised for hours with onions and carrots and sweet red kosher wine (was there any other kind?). Lavished with apricots, prunes, and other dried fruits, it was the sort of sweet-salty, meaty-fruity mash-up typical of so much Ashkenazi cuisine. Aunt Annette served it at Rosh Hashanah (the dried fruits presaged a sweet New Year). She served it at Hanukkah and Passover, too. I imagine she serves it still to hungry multitudes in heaven. These days, my family is more likely to eat our brisket slow-smoked like they do in Texas, but at least once a year we dust off Aunt Annette's recipe for a braised brisket that transcends wood smoke.

YIELD: Serves 6 to 8

METHOD: Braising

PREP TIME: 15 minutes

COOKING TIME: Depending on the brisket and other factors, 2½ to 3 hours, or as needed

HEAT SOURCE: Stove, oven

YOU'LL ALSO NEED: A Dutch oven with a tight-fitting lid or a roasting pan with aluminum foil (it should be just large enough to hold the brisket); a gravy boat with a fat separator (the sort that allows you to pour the broth off from the bottom, leaving the fat on top; optional); a welled cutting board

WHAT ELSE: This recipe calls for a technique that may surprise all you barbecue buffs out there. You carve the brisket midway through the cooking process when it's still firm enough to slice neatly. The slices finish cooking in the braising liquid. This ensures even slices and exceptionally tender brisket.

INGREDIENTS

1 brisket flat (3 to 4 pounds)

Sea salt and freshly ground black pepper

2 tablespoons canola oil

1 large onion, peeled and finely chopped

4 carrots, trimmed and peeled (1 diced and 3 cut crosswise into 3-inch chunks)

2 ribs celery, finely chopped

2 cloves garlic, peeled and finely chopped

¼ cup chopped fresh flat-leaf parsley

1½ cups sweet kosher Concord grape wine (such as Manischewitz), or 1½ cups dry red wine plus ¼ cup granulated or brown sugar

2 dried bay leaves

2 to 3 cups beef or chicken broth or stock (preferably homemade or low-sodium) or water

1½ cups dried apricots

1½ cups pitted prunes

1 cup golden raisins

1. Preheat the oven to 300°F.

2. Using a sharp knife, trim the brisket, leaving a layer of fat at least ¼ inch thick (see page 14). Be careful not to over-trim. It's better to err on the side of too much fat than too little. Generously season the brisket on all sides with salt and pepper.

3. Heat the oil in a Dutch oven (or roasting pan—though a Dutch oven is preferred) over medium-high heat. Add the brisket and cook, turning once, until browned on both sides, 4 to 6 minutes per side. Transfer the meat to a platter and pour out and discard all but 3 tablespoons of fat from the pot.

4. Add the onion, chopped carrot, celery, garlic, and 3 tablespoons of the parsley to the pot and cook over medium-high heat until softened and lightly browned, 5 minutes.

5. Return the brisket to the pot and spoon half the vegetables in the pot on top. Add the wine, bay leaves, and enough stock to barely cover the brisket. Cover the pot (if using a roasting pan, cover it tightly with aluminum foil), place it in the oven, and braise until semi-tender, 1½ hours.

6. Remove the pot from the oven and transfer the brisket to a welled cutting board; set the pot aside. Using a sharp knife or electric knife, thinly slice the brisket across the grain. Stir half of the carrot chunks and the apricots, prunes, and raisins into the juices in the pot. Using a spatula, neatly lay the sliced brisket on top. Pour in any juices from the cutting board and arrange the remaining carrot chunks and dried fruits on top. Season with salt and pepper. Add additional stock as needed just to cover the meat and fruit.

7. Put the lid on the pot and return it to the oven. Continue braising the brisket until the meat is tender enough to cut with a fork, another 1 to 1½ hours, or as needed. If there's too much cooking liquid (the brisket should be moist, not soupy), uncover the pot for the last half hour to allow some of the juices to evaporate.

8. Transfer the brisket slices to a platter. Using a slotted spoon, transfer the fruits and vegetables to the platter and arrange them around the meat. Pour the pan juices into a gravy boat with a fat separator. (If you don't have one of these, pour the gravy into a bowl or measuring cup and skim the fat off the top with a soup spoon.) Spoon some of the gravy over the meat and fruit, serving the rest on the side. Sprinkle the remaining 1 tablespoon of parsley over the meat and get ready for Jewish holiday awesomeness.

NOTE: Sometimes, Aunt Annette would add a peeled, seeded, sliced lemon to her brisket to offset the sweetness of the dried fruit. It's a nice touch.

For maximum tenderness, cut the brisket into ¼-inch-thick slices midway through the cooking process.

JEWISH DELI BRISKET
BRAISED WITH VEGETABLES

YIELD: Serves 6 to 8

METHOD: Boiling, braising

PREP TIME: 20 minutes

COOKING TIME: Depending on the brisket and other factors, 3 hours, or as needed

HEAT SOURCE: Stove, oven

YOU'LL ALSO NEED: A Dutch oven with a tight-fitting lid; butcher's string; a colander or sieve; a welled cutting board

WHAT ELSE: Preparing deli-style brisket is a multistep process. The first is to blanch the brisket, that is, boil it to remove the surface impurities. Next, you braise the brisket with aromatic root vegetables in the oven. This gives you a delectable by-product: an intensely beefy broth you can turn into soup by adding cooked barley, noodles, or the diced or pureed vegetables from braising. The brisket itself gets sliced and served hot, usually with horseradish sauce. Or—my

(continued)

P astrami has become a darling of the barbecue world, not just the delicatessen. Corned beef enjoys equal popularity with Jewish Americans, Irish Americans, and deli lovers of other ethnic persuasions. But there's a third meat in the deli trifecta, and the fact that it looks unappetizingly gray in no way diminishes its deliciousness. In fact, you could argue that it represents the purest manifestation of this tough, flavorful muscle from the steer's undercarriage. I speak, of course, of deli brisket, which is nothing more than brisket cooked in water with aromatic vegetables, then thinly sliced for sandwiches. When I was growing up, brisket was the meat I went for on deli platters, and these thin gray slices of beefy bliss still hold a place of reverence in my heart. Think of it as barbecue without the wood smoke. And don't think of turning this page without trying it.

INGREDIENTS

1 brisket flat (3 to 4 pounds)

2 to 3 quarts cold water

2 dried bay leaves

1 medium onion, peeled and quartered

2 whole cloves

3 medium carrots, trimmed, peeled, and cut crosswise into 3-inch lengths

3 ribs celery (or 1 small, peeled celery root), cut into 3-inch lengths

2 leeks, trimmed and washed (see Note, page 138)

1 large or 2 small parsnips, trimmed, peeled, and cut into 3-inch lengths (optional)

1 parsley root (optional; see What Else)

6 sprigs fresh flat-leaf parsley, plus 2 tablespoons chopped to add at the end

6 sprigs fresh dill, plus 2 tablespoons chopped to add at the end

6 sprigs fresh thyme, plus 2 tablespoons chopped to add at the end

Sea salt and freshly ground black pepper

Horseradish Dill Sauce (recipe follows) or your favorite bottled horseradish, mustard, and/or other condiments, for serving

1. Preheat the oven to 300°F.

2. Using a sharp knife, trim the brisket, leaving a layer of fat at least ¼ inch thick (see page 14). Be careful not to over-trim. It's better to err on the side of too much fat than too little.

3. Blanch the brisket: Place it in a Dutch oven with cold water to cover by a depth of 2 inches. Bring the meat to a boil over medium-high heat. Using a ladle or large spoon, skim off any foam that rises to the surface. Reduce the heat to medium-low and simmer the brisket for 10 minutes, skimming conscientiously to remove any foam. Then pour off the excess blanching liquid so that the brisket is submerged halfway.

4. Pin the bay leaves to two of the onion quarters with the cloves. Add the onion quarters to the pot along with the carrots, celery, leeks, and parsnips, and parsley root, if using. (Note: If you like your vegetables with a little bite to them, add the carrots, celery, leeks, parsnips, and parsley root after 2 hours of cooking.) Tie the parsley, dill, and thyme into a bundle with butcher's string and add it to the pot. Bring the mixture back to a simmer. Sprinkle in 2 teaspoons salt and 1 teaspoon pepper.

5. Cover the Dutch oven and place it in the oven. Braise the brisket until very tender (test it by inserting a chopstick—it should pierce the meat easily). Normally this takes about 3 hours, but start testing after 2½. Check the brisket halfway through—the meat and vegetables should be half-submerged in the liquid. If the brisket is too dry, add water. When done, remove the pot from the oven and let the brisket rest in its juices for 10 minutes. Add salt and pepper to taste.

6. Transfer the brisket to a welled cutting board. Strain the cooking liquid through a sieve (save it for another use—for example, it could become the base for a soup—see What Else; it will keep, covered, in the refrigerator for at least 3 days, or it can be frozen in a sealed container). Set the vegetables aside or place them in an airtight container and refrigerate.

7. To enjoy the brisket hot, slice it across the grain into ¼-inch-thick slices, transfer it to a platter, and garnish with the boiled vegetables. To serve it cold, let it cool to room temperature, then wrap it in plastic wrap and refrigerate it until well chilled (preferably overnight). Slice the cold

preferred way—chilled and sliced paper-thin on a meat slicer. Try the latter on slices of challah with Horseradish Dill Sauce (page 138). One bite and you'll wonder why everyone makes such a fuss about corned beef. Note: Your grandmother probably boiled the brisket in a stockpot on the stove. Oven-braising gives you the same result with a lot less supervision. The optional parsley root—available at Jewish food markets— combines the flavor of parsley and celery root. Tip o' the hat to Jewish cooking authority Arthur Schwartz, who inspired this recipe.

brisket paper-thin on a meat slicer or by hand.

8. Whether hot or cold, serve the brisket with the Horseradish Dill Sauce or your favorite bottled horseradish, mustard, or other condiments. Heresy warning: I like to slather my brisket sandwiches with mayonnaise.

NOTE: To clean a leek, trim off and discard the dark green leaves (the top half) and furry roots. Make two lengthwise cuts in the leek, up to but not through root end, rotating the leek 90 degrees after the first cut. Plunge the leek up and down in a bowl of cold water to wash out any dirt. Change the water as needed (leeks tend to hide a lot of grit, so you may need to do this a few times).

HORSERADISH DILL SAUCE

YIELD: Makes 1¼ cups

Gefilte fish without horseradish is punishment enough, goes an old Yiddish saying. You could say the same about horseradish and brisket. There's nothing like this piquant, lemon- and dill-scented horseradish sauce for balancing the richness of the beef.

INGREDIENTS

½ cup mayonnaise (preferably Hellmann's or Best Foods)

½ cup sour cream

A 2-inch piece horseradish root, peeled and finely grated (or to taste) or ¼ cup prepared horseradish

2 tablespoons minced fresh dill

½ teaspoon freshly grated lemon zest

Sea salt and freshly ground black pepper

Place the ingredients in a mixing bowl and whisk to combine.

Horseradish Dill Sauce will keep, in a sealed container in the refrigerator, for at least 3 days.

VENETIAN BRAISED VEAL BRISKET

et Texans have their chopped brisket sandwiches and Carolinians their pulled pork. I raise my fork for Venetian *petto di vitello*. This soulful shredded braised veal—redolent with wine, onions, and juniper—turns up at *bacari* (wine bars) across the city in fall and winter—part of the belt-loosening *cichetti* (tapas-like bar snacks) that comprise my favorite Venetian lunch. And no one serves it better than Francesco Pinto and his son Matteo at All'Arco, a tiny one-room bar where you feast standing up a stone's throw from the Rialto Market. Veal brisket is smaller and more tender than its counterpart on a mature steer, and because it's so lean, Italians insist on a wet cooking method, such as braising or stewing. Dish it up in a shallow bowl with crusty bread for sopping up the juices. Better yet, pile it onto ciabatta rolls with pickled onions—just like they do at All'Arco.

YIELD: Serves 6

METHOD: Braising

PREP TIME: 20 minutes

COOKING TIME: 2½ to 3 hours

HEAT SOURCE: Stove, oven

YOU'LL ALSO NEED: A Dutch oven with a tight-fitting lid; a strainer; meat claws (optional); a welled cutting board

WHAT ELSE: Italians eat a lot more veal than we do, so *petto di vitello* (veal brisket) is relatively easy to find in Italy. In the US, you'll likely have to order it ahead from your butcher. One good mail order source for grass-fed veal brisket is straussdirect.com. If you can't find veal, this will still be delicious with beef brisket—use an equal amount.

INGREDIENTS

1 veal brisket (2 to 2½ pounds)

Sea salt and freshly ground black pepper

2 tablespoons extra virgin olive oil

1 medium onion, peeled and finely chopped

2 ribs celery, finely chopped

2 carrots, trimmed, peeled, and finely chopped

3 juniper berries, lightly crushed with the side of a knife

2 whole cloves

1 dried bay leaf

1½ cups white wine (red wine if using a beef brisket), plus extra as needed

1½ cups veal or beef broth or stock (preferably homemade or low-sodium) or water

FOR SERVING

6 ciabatta rolls, cut almost in half through the side with a serrated knife and opened like a book (optional)

Pickled Onions (recipe follows; optional)

1. Using a sharp knife, trim the brisket, leaving a layer of fat at least ¼ inch thick (see page 14). Be careful not to over-trim. It's better to err on the side of too much fat than too little.

2. Generously season the brisket on all sides with salt and pepper.

3. Preheat the oven to 300°F.

4. Heat the oil in a Dutch oven over medium-high heat. Add the brisket and cook, turning once, until browned on both sides, 3 to 5 minutes per side. Transfer the brisket to a platter.

5. Pour off all but 2 tablespoons of the fat from the pot. Add the onion, celery, and carrots and cook over medium-high heat until lightly browned, 5 minutes.

6. Return the brisket to the pot, spooning half the vegetables on top. Add the juniper berries, cloves, and bay leaf. Stir in the white wine and bring to a boil, then add the stock.

7. Cover the pot, place it in the oven, and braise the brisket until very tender, 2½ to 3 hours. Add additional stock as needed to keep it from drying out.

8. Remove the pot from the oven and let the brisket cool slightly in its juices for 10 minutes. Transfer it to a welled cutting board and use a sharp knife to slice it thinly across the grain. Alternatively, pull it into meaty shreds with meat claws or two forks.

9. Meanwhile, pour the braising liquid through a strainer into a bowl, pressing the veggies with the back of a spoon to release the juices.

10. Pile the brisket onto the ciabatta rolls, if using. Spoon the juices and Pickled Onions on top. Or serve the brisket sliced or shredded with the juices spooned over it and the Pickled Onions on top or on the side.

PICKLED ONIONS

YIELD: Makes 2 cups

Horseradish. Mustard. Pickled onions. Did you ever notice how much better braised brisket tastes when paired with a sharp-tasting condiment? Case in point: these simple pickled onions. Just remember to make them ahead of time so they pickle for at least 6 hours (or as long as overnight).

INGREDIENTS

1 cup distilled white vinegar

2 teaspoons sea salt

1 teaspoon sugar

Freshly ground white pepper

1 large sweet or red onion,
 peeled and thinly sliced
 widthwise

1. Place the vinegar, salt, sugar, and pepper in a nonreactive mixing bowl and whisk until the salt and sugar crystals are dissolved.

2. Add the onion. Cover with plastic wrap and refrigerate.

Let the onion pickle in the refrigerator for at least 6 hours, or as long as overnight.

Pickled Onions will keep, in a sealed container in the refrigerator, for at least a week.

WINE COUNTRY BRISKET
BRAISED WITH BACON AND MUSHROOMS

YIELD: Serves 6 to 8

METHOD: Braising

PREP TIME: 30 minutes

COOKING TIME:
Depending on the brisket and other factors, 3 hours, or as needed

HEAT SOURCE: Stove, oven

YOU'LL ALSO NEED:
A Dutch oven with a tight-fitting lid; a large strainer; a rimmed sheet pan; a welled cutting board

Long before my immersion in barbecue, before my food writing, wine writing, and restaurant reviewing days, I spent a year in Paris learning how to cook. These were the glory days of classical French cuisine, when no amount of butter or wine seemed too excessive to add to a dish, when Julia Child would drop by La Varenne cooking school for a visit. I cook very differently now—starting with my heat source of choice, a grill or smoker. But my mouth still waters at the thought of those slow-braised meats sweet with aromatic root vegetables and rich red wine sauce. What follows is a mash-up of two French wine-braised beef classics: *boeuf bourguignon* and *boeuf à la mode*.

INGREDIENTS

FOR THE BRISKET

1 tablespoon extra virgin olive oil or unsalted butter, plus more as needed

4 thick strips artisanal bacon, such as Nueske's, cut crosswise into ¼-inch slivers

1 brisket flat (3 to 4 pounds)

Coarse sea salt and freshly ground black pepper

8 medium shallots or 4 torpedo onions (each 3 to 4 inches long), peeled and halved lengthwise

1 pound cremini or white button mushrooms, trimmed, wiped clean with a damp paper towel (any large mushrooms halved or quartered so all are the same size)

FOR THE AROMATIC VEGETABLES

1 small onion, peeled and finely chopped

2 carrots, trimmed, peeled, and finely chopped

2 ribs celery, finely chopped

2 cloves garlic, peeled and finely chopped

2 dried bay leaves

2 sprigs fresh thyme (or ½ teaspoon dried)

½ cup Cognac, plus 1 tablespoon for finishing the dish

2 cups red wine (preferably pinot noir)

2 cups beef or chicken broth or stock (preferably homemade or low-sodium), plus extra if needed

2 teaspoons cornstarch

2 tablespoons finely chopped chives or flat-leaf parsley

WHAT ELSE: In France, you'd use a wine from Burgundy for braising the brisket. I'm just as apt to reach for a pinot noir from Australia or the West Coast. You needn't buy a Robert Parker pinup, but do cook with a wine you wouldn't mind drinking. If you have the time, marinate the brisket in the wine overnight, then drain it and blot it well with paper towels—your brisket will be all the more flavorful.

1. Preheat the oven to 300°F.

2. Line a platter with paper towels. Heat the oil in a Dutch oven over medium-high heat. Add the bacon slivers and cook, stirring occasionally, until browned, 3 minutes. Transfer to a large strainer over a bowl.

3. Using a sharp knife, trim the brisket, leaving a layer of fat at least ¼ inch thick (see page 14). Be careful not to over-trim. It's better to err on the side

of too much fat than too little. Generously season the brisket on all sides with salt and pepper.

4. Add the brisket to the pot and brown it on both sides and the edges, 3 to 5 minutes per side. Transfer the brisket to a rimmed sheet pan.

5. Add the shallots to the brisket fat in the pot and cook, stirring, over medium-high heat until browned, 3 to 4

minutes. Transfer the shallots with a slotted spoon to the strainer with the bacon. Add the mushrooms to the pot and cook until browned, 3 to 4 minutes. Transfer the mushrooms to the strainer as well. Pour off and discard all but 3 tablespoons of the fat from the pot. You should have this much, but if extra fat is needed, add a tablespoon or two of olive oil.

6. Return the Dutch oven to medium-high heat and add the onion, carrots, celery, garlic, bay leaves, and thyme. Cook, stirring often, until the vegetables are browned, 4 minutes.

7. Add the ½ cup Cognac and flambé: Heat it just slightly (to body temperature), then carefully touch a match to it. (Stand back, of course. To be extra safe, roll up your sleeves and have the pot lid within easy reach to smother the fire if it gets out of hand.) When the flames die down *completely*, add the wine and bring to a boil, stirring with a wooden spoon to dissolve the brown bits on the bottom of the pot. Stir in the stock, bring to a boil, then remove from the heat. Return the brisket to the pot.

8. Cover the pot and place it in the oven. Braise the brisket for 2½ hours, checking every half hour or so to make sure

the meat doesn't stick to the pan. Add stock as needed so the meat is half-submerged.

9. Uncover the pot, and using a large spoon, spoon off and discard any fat floating on the surface. Stir in the reserved bacon, shallots, and mushrooms and their juices, cover the pot, and return to the oven to continue braising until the meat and vegetables are fork-tender, another 30 minutes, or as needed. If there's too much cooking liquid (the brisket should be moist, not soupy), uncover the pot for the last half hour to allow some of the juices to evaporate. When done, remove the pot from the oven and let the brisket rest in its juices for 10 minutes.

10. Again, skim off any fat that has risen to the surface. While you're at it, fish out and discard the bay leaves and thyme sprigs. Transfer the brisket to a welled cutting board and use a sharp knife to slice it thinly crosswise across the grain.

11. Return the pot with the sauce and vegetables to the stovetop and bring to a boil, uncovered, over medium-high heat. Simmer until about 4 cups of liquid remain, 5 minutes. Meanwhile, place the remaining tablespoon of Cognac in a small bowl, add the cornstarch, and stir with a fork to form a paste.

Whisk this mixture into the sauce and boil for 1 minute. The sauce will thicken slightly. Correct the seasoning, adding salt and pepper to taste; the sauce should be highly seasoned.

12. Return the sliced brisket to the sauce and serve directly from the Dutch oven, or arrange the meat, sauce, and vegetables on a large, deep platter. Sprinkle with chopped chives and dig in.

GERMAN BEER-BRAISED BRISKET (BIERFLEISCHE)

YIELD: Serves 6 to 8

METHOD: Braising

PREP TIME: 20 minutes

COOKING TIME: Depending on the brisket and other factors, 3 hours, or as needed

HEAT SOURCE: Stove, oven

YOU'LL ALSO NEED: A Dutch oven with a tight-fitting lid; a welled cutting board

WHAT ELSE: You'll want a beer that goes easy on hops (which are responsible for a beer's bitterness) but long on flavor. A German dunkel (dark beer) or Belgian red comes to mind.

Germans and Austrians call it *Bierfleische* ("beer-meat"). Belgians and French call it *carbonnade*. I call it one of the best excuses ever to combine brisket and beer in a single dish. In a nutshell, you braise the brisket in beer with a mountain of caramelized onions. Traditionally, you cooked the meat in a Dutch oven in the fireplace, with embers piled on the lid. The French word for coal is *charbon*—hence the name *carbonnade*.

INGREDIENTS

1 brisket flat (3 to 4 pounds)

Coarse sea salt and freshly ground black pepper

2 tablespoons vegetable oil

2 tablespoons unsalted butter

2 pounds onions (3 to 4 large onions), peeled and thinly sliced crosswise

1 tablespoon dark brown sugar, or to taste

1 tablespoon tomato paste

1 tablespoon Düsseldorf-style mustard (or other favorite mustard), plus extra for serving

1 can (14 ounces) plum tomatoes, drained and finely chopped

¼ cup chopped fresh flat-leaf parsley, plus 1 tablespoon for serving

1½ cups dark or red beer or stout (keep some extra beers on ice for serving)

1½ cups beef or chicken broth or stock (preferably homemade or low-sodium) or water, plus extra as needed

2 dried bay leaves

1. Preheat the oven to 300°F.

2. Using a sharp knife, trim the brisket, leaving a layer of fat at least ¼ inch thick (see page 14). Be careful not to over-trim. It's better to err on the side of too much fat than too little. Generously season the meat on both sides with salt and pepper.

3. Heat the oil in a Dutch oven over medium-high heat. Add the brisket and cook, turning with tongs, until browned on both sides and the edges, 3 to 5 minutes per side. Transfer the brisket to a platter. Pour off all but 2 tablespoons of the fat from the pot.

4. Add the butter to the pot and set it over medium heat. When the butter has melted, add the onions and cook, stirring often, until they're a deep golden brown, 8 to 12 minutes. You may need to lower the heat if the onions start to burn.

5. Stir in the brown sugar, tomato paste, and mustard and cook for 1 minute. Stir in the chopped tomatoes, ¼ cup parsley, beer, broth, and bay leaves and bring to a boil. Return the browned brisket to the pan, spooning half the onion mixture on top so it sandwiches the meat.

6. Cover the pot, place it in the oven, and braise the beef until it is fork-tender. Normally this takes 3 hours, but start testing after 2½. Check every half hour or so to make sure it doesn't dry out or burn. If it starts to dry out, add additional stock or water; if there is too much liquid (the brisket should be half-submerged), uncover the pot during the last half hour to allow some of the juices to evaporate. When done, remove the pot from the oven and let the brisket rest in its juices for 10 minutes.

7. Transfer the brisket to a welled cutting board and use a sharp knife to cut it crosswise into ¼-inch-thick slices. Discard the bay leaves. Stir the sauce a few times, adding salt and pepper to taste. Return the sliced brisket to the sauce. Dust with the remaining parsley and serve with mustard and more of the beer you used for cooking.

CHINESE RED-COOKED BRISKET

When it comes to Chinese meat dishes, most Americans think of stir-fries, but braising is popular for tougher cuts, like brisket. Which brings us to a technique called "red cooking": braising meats in a fragrant mixture made sweet with honey, salty with soy sauce, and aromatic with star anise, ginger, cinnamon, and tangerine peel. (The soy sauce gives the meat a reddish tint—hence the name.) Think of this as the Chinese analogue of the Jewish brisket with dried fruits and sweet wine on page 133.

YIELD: Serves 6 to 8

METHOD: Braising

PREP TIME: 20 minutes

COOKING TIME: Depending on the brisket and other factors, 3 hours, or as needed

HEAT SOURCE: Stove, oven

YOU'LL ALSO NEED: A Dutch oven with a tight-fitting lid; a welled cutting board

WHAT ELSE: You'll need a few Asian ingredients for this brisket, most of which can be found at a good supermarket or natural foods store. If you're feeling bucks up, try a premium soy sauce, like Takesan Kishibori Shoyu, a first-pressed Japanese soy sauce aged in wood barrels for more than a year (available from Amazon). Otherwise, use Kikkoman or Eden. If you can't find Shaoxing (Chinese rice wine), substitute Japanese sake. Star anise comes in star-shaped pods with a smoky, licorice-like flavor. Alternatively, substitute Chinese five-spice powder (of which star anise is the main ingredient).

INGREDIENTS

1 brisket flat (3 to 4 pounds)

2 tablespoons vegetable oil

1 cup soy sauce

1 cup Chinese rice wine (Shaoxing) or sake

⅓ cup toasted (dark) sesame oil

¼ cup honey or sugar

4 cloves garlic, peeled and flattened with the side of a cleaver

A 2-inch piece fresh ginger, cut lengthwise into ¼-inch slices, flattened lightly with the side of a cleaver

4 scallions, trimmed, green parts finely chopped, white parts flattened with the side of a cleaver

3 strips fresh tangerine or orange zest (½ by 1½ inches; removed with a vegetable peeler)

2 whole star anise pods or 1 teaspoon Chinese five-spice powder

A 1-inch piece cinnamon stick

1. Preheat the oven to 300°F.

2. Using a sharp knife, trim the brisket, leaving a layer of fat at least ¼ inch thick (see page 14). Be careful not to over-trim. It's better to err on the side of too much fat than too little.

3. Heat the vegetable oil in a Dutch oven over medium-high heat. Add the brisket and cook, turning with tongs, until browned on all sides, 3 to 5 minutes per side. Remove the brisket to a plate, pour off any excess fat, then return the meat to the pot.

4. Add 1 cup water, the soy sauce, rice wine, sesame oil, honey, garlic, ginger, scallion whites, and all but 2 tablespoons of the scallion greens (keep the remainder chilled for serving), tangerine zest, star anise, and cinnamon. Bring the mixture to a boil over medium-high heat.

5. Cover the pot, place the brisket in the oven, and braise until very tender (test it by inserting a chopstick—it should pierce the meat easily). Normally this takes about 3 hours, but start testing after 2½. Stir from time to time to make sure the brisket doesn't stick to the bottom or dry out. (The brisket should be half-submerged—if it starts to dry out, add more water.) Uncover the pot for the last half hour or so to concentrate the braising liquid.

6. Remove the pot from the oven, cover it, and let the brisket rest in its juices for 10 minutes. Transfer the brisket to a welled cutting board and use a sharp knife to cut it against the grain into ¼-inch-thick slices.

7. Meanwhile, use a large spoon to skim off and discard any visible fat that pools on the top. If the sauce still seems too liquidy, place the pot on the stove and boil until the sauce is reduced and slightly thickened, 5 to 10 minutes.

8. Serve the brisket in the pot (or on a deep platter with cooking liquid spooned over it) with the reserved scallion greens sprinkled on top. (You can fish out the chunky seasonings, like the ginger, cinnamon stick, and star anise, if you like, but I leave 'em in— they're tasty to nibble.)

Chapter 5

BRISKET BOILED, STEWED, AND FRIED

When you think of high-adrenaline cooking methods—smoking, grilling, stir-frying—boiling probably never crosses your mind. After all, what could be less exciting than throwing meat and vegetables into a pot and simmering them into submission? Yet boiling produces three of the world's most beloved brisket dishes: Italian *bollito misto* (boiled dinner), Vietnamese pho (beef noodle soup), and Spanish Caribbean *ropa vieja* ("old clothes," literally)— shredded brisket in spicy Creole sauce. Without it, we wouldn't have new school brisket ramen or Cuban *vaca frita* (literally "fried cow"). In this chapter, you'll learn how to harness this seemingly primitive cooking method to create brisket dishes of surprising sophistication. So, haul out your stockpot: Brisket bliss will soon be bubbling up on your stove.

PHO FROM SCRATCH
(VIETNAMESE BRISKET RICE NOODLE SOUP)

"**N**o talking when you eat pho," says chef John Nguyen. "The worst sin is to let the soup get cold—even at the expense of conversation." Born in Ho Chi Minh City and raised in "Little Vietnam" (Orange County, California), Nguyen is nothing if not serious about Vietnamese beef noodle soup. I met him at my favorite pho restaurant in New York City—Hà Nội House on St. Marks Place in the East Village—where he presides over a waist-high stockpot. Brisket, oxtail, and marrow bones have been simmering for 16 hours (!) to make a broth that Nguyen fortifies with fistfuls of fire-charred ginger and onions.

Pho is served throughout Vietnam. According to Nguyen, the spiciest soup (*bun bo hue*) comes from the former imperial city of Hue in central Vietnam, where the broth is electrified with lemongrass, chiles, and shrimp paste. The Saigon version comes with sliced chiles, Thai basil, cilantro, and invigorating splashes of Vietnamese chile paste and hoisin sauce. But Nguyen prefers the classic simplicity of Hanoi-style pho. The high ratio of noodles and vegetables to meat makes pho a great dish for health-conscious eaters. "We keep the garnishes to a minimum," Nguyen says. "The star of the show is the broth."

YIELD: Serves 6 (can be multiplied as desired)

METHOD: Boiling

PREP TIME: 40 minutes

COOKING TIME: 3 hours, or as needed

HEAT SOURCE: Stove, charcoal or gas grill, or a broiler

YOU'LL ALSO NEED: 2 large stockpots; a fine-mesh strainer or chinois; cheesecloth; butcher's string; a rimmed sheet pan

INGREDIENTS

FOR THE BROTH

3 to 3½ pounds brisket (preferably both flat and point)

1 pound oxtails, cut into 2-inch sections (optional—if you don't use oxtails, increase the brisket to 4 pounds)

Vegetable oil, for oiling the grill grate

4 medium onions, unpeeled, cut in half lengthwise

2 pieces unpeeled ginger (each about 3 inches long), cut in half lengthwise

FOR THE SEASONING

5 whole star anise pods

3 cinnamon sticks, each about 3 inches long

2 tablespoons coriander seeds

1 tablespoon fennel seeds

6 whole cloves

½ cup Asian fish sauce (preferably Vietnamese, such as Red Boat brand), or to taste

½ cup packed dark or light brown sugar, or to taste

TO FINISH THE SOUP

1 pound dried rice sticks (rice noodles; see What Else)

1 red onion, peeled and very thinly sliced crosswise into rounds

4 scallions, trimmed, white and green parts thinly sliced crosswise

1 cup fresh cilantro leaves

Fried Shallot or Garlic Chips (optional; recipe follows)

1. Using a sharp knife, trim the brisket, leaving a layer of fat at least ¼ inch thick (see page 14). Be careful not to over-trim. It's better to err on the side of too much fat than too little. Cut the brisket into 4 pieces, slicing it in half lengthwise (with the grain), then in half again widthwise.

2. Make the broth: Place the brisket pieces in a large stockpot with the oxtails, if using. Add cold water to cover by a depth of 6 inches. Bring the mixture to a rolling boil over medium-high heat and boil for 3 minutes, skimming the foam off the top with a ladle or large spoon. (You are blanching the meat to remove the impurities, which gives you a cleaner, clearer broth.) Drain the meat in a large colander and rinse it well with cold water. Wipe out the stockpot with a paper towel.

3. Return the blanched meats to the stockpot. Add 1 gallon of cold water or enough to cover the meat by a depth of 2 inches. Gradually bring the mixture to a gentle simmer over medium heat. Small bubbles should just break the surface throughout the cook; at no time after blanching the meats do you want a rolling boil. Skim the broth often with a ladle or large spoon to remove any fat or impurities that rise to the surface. Add water as needed to keep the meat covered.

4. Meanwhile, char the onions and ginger: Set up a grill for direct grilling (see page 81) and heat to medium-high. Brush and scrape the grill grate clean and oil it well. Arrange the onions and ginger, cut sides down, on the grate and cook until the surface is darkly browned, even charred, 3 to 5 minutes. (Alternatively, char the veggies under a hot broiler or in a dry cast-iron skillet over medium-high heat.) When they're ready, add the onions and ginger to the broth. Cook for 1 hour, skimming occasionally.

5. Prepare the seasoning: Heat a dry skillet over medium-high heat. Add the star anise, cinnamon sticks, coriander seeds, fennel seeds, and cloves and roast until fragrant and toasted, 1 minute, stirring so the spices roast evenly. Tie the spices in a square of cheesecloth, or wrap them in aluminum foil that you perforate with a fork to release the flavor. Stir the spice bundle, fish sauce, and brown sugar into the broth.

Hà Nội House on St. Marks Place in New York City's East Village

6. Continue to simmer the broth until it is richly flavored and the brisket is very tender (but not so soft that it falls apart), another 2 to 2½ hours, or 3 to 3½ hours in all.

7. Using tongs, transfer the brisket and oxtails to a rimmed sheet pan and let them cool to room temperature, then cover with plastic wrap and refrigerate until well chilled.

8. Meanwhile, using a ladle and a strainer, strain the broth into another large stockpot. Correct the seasoning, adding more fish sauce and brown sugar to taste. The broth should strike an inviting balance between salty and sweet. (The broth can be prepared a day or so ahead to this stage.) Let it cool to room temperature, then cover and refrigerate.

9. Remove the chilled meat from the refrigerator and unwrap it. Use a meat slicer or sharp knife to cut the brisket across the grain into the thinnest possible slices. If using oxtails, pull the meat off the bones and shred it with your fingers into bite-size pieces. Set the meat aside.

10. Finish the soup: Remove any solidified fat from the top of the broth and discard. Reheat the broth in the stockpot over high heat; bring to a boil. While the broth reheats, fill a large bowl with cold water, add the rice noodles, and soak until soft and pliable, 15 to 30 minutes. Bring 3 quarts of water to a boil in another large pot. Just before serving, drain the soaked rice noodles in a colander and add to the boiling water. Boil the rice noodles until tender, 30 to 60 seconds. Do not overcook the noodles or they will become mushy. Strain the noodles in the colander.

11. To serve, use tongs to divide the warm noodles among 6 large soup bowls. Lay the brisket slices, oxtail bits, if using, and sliced red onion on top. Ladle in the hot broth (1½ to 2 cups per bowl). Sprinkle each serving of pho with sliced scallions, cilantro leaves, and fried shallot or garlic chips, if using. Serve the pho scalding hot—it must be scalding hot.

FRIED SHALLOT OR GARLIC CHIPS

YIELD: Makes 1 cup

Fried shallots and/or garlic are traditional Southeast Asian garnishes and flavorings. The oil acquires a haunting flavor, too. Save it for drizzling over pho and other dishes.

INGREDIENTS

1½ cups vegetable oil

1 cup thinly sliced shallots or 12 cloves garlic, peeled and thinly sliced crosswise

1. Heat the oil in a heavy skillet over medium-high heat. Line a plate with paper towels. Dip a shallot slice into the oil: When bubbles dance, the oil is ready. (Or use a deep-fry thermometer: The oil should be 350°F.)

2. Add the shallots and fry, stirring so they color evenly, until golden brown, 2 minutes. Quickly transfer the fried shallots with a wire skimmer or slotted spoon to the prepared plate to drain. Use the shallots within minutes of frying.

Let the oil cool to room temperature, then store it in a sealed jar—use a spoonful or two for seasoning soups and salads. It will keep in the refrigerator for several days.

PHO IN A HURRY

YIELD: Serves 4 (can be multiplied as desired)

METHOD: Boiling

PREP TIME: 30 minutes

COOKING TIME: 20 minutes

HEAT SOURCE: Stove

YOU'LL ALSO NEED: A stockpot

WHAT ELSE: To make Pho in a Hurry, you'll need cooked brisket. There's no reason you can't use leftover barbecued brisket (see pages 41 to 70)—indeed, the resulting smoky flavor will take this traditional Vietnamese beef noodle soup into realms of gustatory wonder. Alternatively, you could use meat from the Jewish Deli Brisket recipe (page 136) or from the Basic Brisket Broth recipe. As for broth, homemade is best, but a low-sodium store-bought brand will land a home run, too.

Okay, I know: The notion of pho in a hurry seems like a contradiction in terms. Doesn't the broth take a half day to simmer, not to mention a special trip to your butcher to source the right meats? Yes, this classic Vietnamese beef noodle soup demands this and more, which is why pho is a dish more people enjoy at restaurants than at home. You purists out there will find the traditional made-from-scratch recipe on page 155. But if you happen to have some leftover brisket on hand or in your freezer (if you're reading this book, I bet you do), you can make a comforting pho in a half hour. You get the same yin-yang of sweet spices and salty fish sauce, of meaty beef and chewy rice noodles—in a fraction of the time.

INGREDIENTS

FOR THE PHO

10 ounces rice sticks (see What Else, page 156)

8 cups Basic Brisket Broth (page 254) or beef broth or stock (preferably homemade or low-sodium)

3 whole cloves

6 thin slices unpeeled fresh ginger

3 whole star anise pods

3 cardamom pods (optional)

1 cinnamon stick, about 3 inches long, lightly crushed with a rolling pin

4 scallions, trimmed, white and green parts thinly sliced crosswise (keep separate)

2 to 3 tablespoons dark or light brown sugar, or to taste

2 to 3 tablespoons Asian fish sauce, or to taste

12 to 16 ounces cooked brisket (see What Else)

FOR SERVING

1 cup fresh mung bean sprouts

12 sprigs fresh Thai or regular basil

12 sprigs fresh cilantro

2 jalapeño or serrano chiles, stemmed and thinly sliced

2 limes, cut into wedges

FOR THE DIPPING SAUCE

6 tablespoons hoisin sauce

6 tablespoons Vietnamese chile sauce, *sambal oelek*, or sriracha

1. Fill a large bowl with cold water, add the rice sticks, and soak until soft and pliable, 15 to 30 minutes.

2. Meanwhile, place the broth in a large stockpot. Stick the cloves in three of the ginger slices. Add the ginger, star anise, cardamom (if using), cinnamon, scallion whites, and 2 tablespoons each of the sugar and fish sauce. Simmer the broth over medium heat until richly flavored, about 15 minutes, adding more sugar or fish sauce as needed. The broth should be simultaneously sweet, salty, and aromatic. When the broth is ready, remove the ginger, star anise, cardamom, and cinnamon with a slotted spoon and discard.

3. Meanwhile, use a sharp knife to slice the brisket crosswise as thinly as possible. At restaurants, they do this on a meat slicer. If you have one, use it. (Thicker slices are okay, too, especially if you're using leftover slices of barbecued brisket.) Arrange the mung bean sprouts, basil, cilantro, chiles, and limes on a platter.

4. Just before serving, bring the broth to a boil. Drain the soaked rice sticks in a colander, add them to the broth, and boil until tender, 30 to 60 seconds. Do not overcook the noodles or they will become mushy. Using tongs, transfer the rice noodles to large soup bowls. Arrange the brisket slices on top. Ladle the hot broth over the noodles and beef and sprinkle with the reserved scallion greens. Serve the vegetable and herb platter on the side.

5. Have each eater add bean sprouts, basil, cilantro, chiles, and lime juice to the soup as desired. Make a dipping sauce by mixing equal parts of the hoisin sauce and chile sauce in tiny bowls for each eater; use this as a dipping sauce for the brisket slices. Eat the solid ingredients with chopsticks and the broth with a spoon. It's so satisfying that maybe next time you'll be inspired to prepare the purist version.

THE JOY OF PHO

Everyone has a favorite comfort food, a dish you crave when you're feeling underappreciated, under the weather, or simply overwhelmed.

For me, the ultimate restorative is pho (pronounced like "fur" without the "r" and with voice rising as for a question). There's no cold so rheumy, no heartbreak so cruel, no hangover so ferocious, and no hunger so fierce that it can't be relieved by a steaming bowl of this Vietnamese beef noodle soup.

Pho is Vietnam's national dish— eaten for breakfast, lunch, dinner, and midnight snack (and just about any time in between) by people on all rungs of the socioeconomic ladder.

Which explains how I found myself in a pedicab, riding up the Avenue Pasteur in Ho Chi Minh City (formerly Saigon) under a blazing sun. We stopped at a nondescript storefront, where I made my way through a phalanx of beggars to one of the most famous noodle soup restaurants in Vietnam: Phở Hòa Pasteur.

Well, "restaurant" overstates it. Picture a tiny dining room crammed with Formica tables. Lime rinds and basil stems litter the floor. You don't come here for the service. As for hygiene—well, when an eater finishes, he simply wipes his chopsticks clean with a basil leaf and returns them to a communal canister.

Phở Hòa Pasteur, Ho Chi Minh City

What you do come here for is the pho. Giant bowls of steaming broth laden with tangled skeins of rice noodles. The sweet scents of cinnamon and star anise mingle with the meaty aroma of long-simmered brisket and oxtail. The source of all these aromas is a mammoth cauldron in which tough but flavorful meats are boiled for hours into fork-tender (make that chopstick-tender) submission.

Pho may refer to a single soup, but there are myriad variations. Some people take their pho with thinly shaved beef tenderloin, so rare it's almost mooing. Others—like me—prefer the richness of brisket boiled for the better part of a day. Accompanying the soup will be a platter of aromatic fresh Asian basil and cilantro, crisp bean sprouts, fiery chiles, and piquant lime wedges.

You'll also be provided with a jar of dark sweet hoisin sauce and a squeeze bottle of Vietnamese chile sauce. Mix them together in the tiny bowls provided for this purpose to make a dipping sauce for the beef.

You don't need to go to a proper restaurant to enjoy pho. Vietnam abounds with noodle stalls—casual eateries, where the cooking, eating, and washing up are done right on the sidewalk. The popularity of pho has given rise to a whole cottage industry—*mi go*, soup boys—who clack sticks together to attract customers. They'll even deliver the soup to your apartment. Every evening, the streets of the city reverberate with the click-clack of their sticks.

Sidewalk gourmet: Some of the best pho in Vietnam is served streetside.

BRISKET RAMEN

YIELD: Serves 4

METHOD: Boiling

PREP TIME: 30 minutes

COOKING TIME:
30 minutes

HEAT SOURCE: Stove

YOU'LL ALSO NEED:
A stockpot; a colander

WHAT ELSE: To be
authentic, you'll need
some special ingredients.
Kombu is Japanese
dried kelp. *Hon dashi* is
smoked, dried tuna broth
(you're going to use the
powdered form—one
good brand is Ajinomoto).
Mirin is sweet rice wine.
Bamboo shoots are
available canned; pickled
mustard greens come in
jars. All are available at
Japanese markets and
stores like Whole Foods.

Call it globalization's upside. Call it melting pot extreme. It's what happens when American barbecue meets traditional ethnic cuisine. And it's happening more and more across the country and around the world. Consider the brisket ramen (Japanese noodle soup) served at Kemuri Tatsu-ya in Austin, Texas. (The restaurant takes its name from the Japanese word for "smoke.") Like all good ramen, it offers a complex interplay of flavors: the rich beefy broth, briny kelp, sweet mirin, creamy egg, crisp bean sprouts, pickled mustard greens, and, of course, chewy noodles. And lording over them all: the smoky awesomeness of Texas brisket. I'd be lying if I said the recipe is easy, but it does break down into a series of manageable steps. Also, you can omit or add various components based on time and availability. As long as you have noodles, brisket, and broth, you've got ramen.

INGREDIENTS

8 cups Basic Brisket Broth (page 254) or beef broth or stock (preferably homemade or low-sodium)

1 piece (2 by 3 inches) *kombu* (dried kelp)

1 tablespoon *hon dashi* powder

4 scallions, trimmed, white and green parts thinly sliced crosswise (keep separate)

3 tablespoons soy sauce, or to taste

3 tablespoons mirin, or to taste

1 tablespoon sugar, or to taste

1 tablespoon Brisket Butter (page 259), butter, or toasted (dark) sesame oil

TO FINISH THE SOUP

2 large eggs (preferably farm-fresh and organic)

1 can (8 ounces) bamboo shoots, drained

4 ounces fresh mung bean sprouts (optional)

12 ounces fresh ramen noodles (available at Asian markets)

12 to 16 ounces of your favorite barbecued brisket (see pages 41 to 70), cut across the grain into ¼-inch-thick slices

8 ounces pickled mustard greens (see What Else)

1. Heat the brisket broth in a large stockpot over medium heat. Add the *kombu* and gently simmer to flavor the broth, 15 to 20 minutes. Remove the *kombu* and discard.

2. Stir in the *hon dashi* and scallion whites and simmer until the *hon dashi* dissolves, 2 minutes. Stir in the soy sauce, mirin, sugar, and Brisket Butter. The broth should be a little sweet and salty. Adjust the soy sauce, mirin, or sugar as needed. Keep the broth hot.

3. Prepare the garnishes: If using eggs, place them in a medium-size saucepan with cold water to cover. Gradually bring to a boil over medium-high heat. Boil the eggs for 7 minutes, then drain in a strainer and rinse with cold water. Shell the eggs under cold running water and set aside.

4. Thinly slice the bamboo shoots widthwise and rinse and drain in a strainer or colander. Rinse and drain the bean sprouts, if using.

5. Bring 3 quarts of water to a rolling boil in a large pot. Add the ramen and boil until just tender, 1 to 3 minutes. Drain the ramen in a strainer or colander.

6. To serve, divide the ramen among 4 large soup bowls. In each of the bowls, arrange the brisket slices in one quadrant on top. Cut the eggs in half lengthwise and place a half egg, yolk side up, in each of the second quadrants. Add the bamboo shoots and pickled mustard greens to the third quadrants. Ladle hot broth into each bowl. If using the mung bean sprouts, place them in the fourth quadrant of each bowl and sprinkle the scallion greens over all. Serve the ramen with chopsticks and Asian-style soup spoons.

BOLLITO MISTO
TWO BRISKETS AND A BIRD
BOILED IN THE STYLE OF THE PIEMONTE

M eat boiled with root vegetables scarcely sounds like the stuff of epicurean reverie. Unless you come from the Piemonte in northern Italy, where you'll recognize it as *bollito misto* ("mixed boil") and you'll salivate at its mere mention. The meats in this version are two types of brisket (beef and veal), their flavor augmented with a farm chicken and cotechino sausage. (The traditional version also contains tongue.) Italians fetishize the dish to the point of serving *bollito misto* at fancy restaurants from gleaming silver trolleys designed expressly for that purpose. The meats are sliced with ceremony and moistened with broth and *salsa verde* (a piquant green sauce of parsley, capers, and anchovies). *Bollito misto* belongs to a venerable family of boiled dinners that include French *pot au feu*, German *Eintopf*, and, of course, New England boiled dinner. It definitely deserves a place in your brisket repertory.

YIELD: Serves 8 with leftovers (and you'll definitely want leftovers)

METHOD: Boiling

PREP TIME: 30 minutes

COOKING TIME: 3 hours, or as needed

HEAT SOURCE: Stove

YOU'LL ALSO NEED: A stockpot; cheesecloth; butcher string; a welled cutting board

Serving *bollito misto* at a restaurant involves great ceremony.

WHAT ELSE: *Bollito misto* is about the easiest dish you'll ever make: You stick everything in a pot and boil it. But proper sequencing is required so all the meats are ready at the same time. One way to do this is to stagger adding the meats to the broth. The other is to start all at once, removing each when it's ready and reheating the ensemble in the broth at the last minute. I prefer the first method here, but both techniques work great. Piemontese tradition accords scant respect to the vegetables, which are added at the beginning solely to flavor the broth. I like to add more vegetables toward the end, so as to serve them alongside the meat rather than cooking them to mush; I've made this optional. Note: Cotechino is a soft garlicky Italian pork sausage. If unavailable, substitute another favorite fresh Italian sausage.

INGREDIENTS

FOR THE BROTH

1 dried bay leaf

1 medium white onion, peeled and quartered

1 whole clove

2 large carrots, peeled, trimmed, and cut into 2-inch chunks

2 ribs celery, scrubbed and cut into 2-inch sections

1 head garlic, skins intact, cut in half widthwise

4 large Roma tomatoes, halved and seeded (squeeze the halves to wring out the seeds)

2 large sprigs fresh rosemary, plus 3 tablespoons finely chopped rosemary needles for serving

2 tablespoons sea salt, or to taste

2 gallons cold water

2 tablespoons whole black peppercorns

1 tablespoon coriander seeds

FOR THE MEATS AND VEGETABLES

1 beef brisket flat (3 pounds), trimmed (see page 14)

1 veal brisket flat (2 pounds, see Note), trimmed (see page 14)

1 small skin-on chicken (3 to 3½ pounds)

8 carrots, trimmed and peeled

8 ribs celery, trimmed and washed

2 medium turnips, trimmed, scrubbed, and quartered

1 pound baby onions, trimmed and peeled (optional)

1 pound cotechino or other fresh Italian pork sausage

Sea salt and freshly ground black pepper

Salsa Verde (recipe follows), for serving

1. Make the broth: Pin the bay leaf to one of the onion quarters with a clove. Place the onion quarters, carrots, celery, garlic, tomatoes, rosemary sprigs, and salt in a large stockpot and add the water. Tie the peppercorns and coriander seeds in a piece of cheesecloth (alternatively, wrap them in a piece of aluminum foil, poking holes in the resulting bundle with a fork to release the flavor). Add the spice bundle to the pot.

2. Add the beef brisket and bring to a boil over medium-high heat. Boil for 3 minutes, skimming off and discarding any foam that rises to the surface with a ladle.

3. Lower the heat and gently simmer the brisket, uncovered, for 1 hour. Skim the broth often to remove any foam or fat that rises to the surface. (Conscientious skimming is essential to a clean, clear broth.)

4. Add the veal brisket and simmer for 1 hour more, skimming the broth often.

5. Add the chicken and simmer for 30 minutes. Add the carrots, celery, turnips, baby onions (if using), and the cotechino or other sausage, and continue to simmer, skimming often, for 30 to 60 minutes more, about 3 hours in all.

6. At this point, both briskets and the chicken should be very tender. Lift the meats one by one out of the pot with tongs, drain well, and transfer to a welled cutting board. Cut the briskets across the grain into ¼-inch-thick slices. Arrange them on a large warm platter. Carve the chicken into 8 pieces and arrange on the platter. Slice the sausage into 8 equal pieces and arrange on the platter next to the chicken. Transfer the vegetables with a slotted spoon to the platter, placing them beside the sausage. Re-season the broth, adding salt and pepper to taste.

7. Serve the *bollito misto* with hot broth ladled over the meat and vegetables to moisten them, and additional broth in soup bowls on the side. Pass the Salsa Verde at the table.

NOTE: If you cannot find a veal brisket flat, substitute a beef brisket flat and add it in step 2, when you add the other beef brisket. In step 4, simply continue to simmer and skim the broth as directed.

SALSA VERDE
(PARSLEY CAPER SAUCE)

YIELD: Makes 2 cups

Think of this "green sauce" as Italian chimichurri. Brisket and other boiled meats electrify in its presence.

INGREDIENTS

1 bunch fresh flat-leaf parsley, stemmed

1 bunch fresh mint or basil, stemmed

4 oil-packed anchovy fillets, drained (optional)

2 tablespoons brined capers, drained

2 scallions, trimmed, white and green parts coarsely chopped

1 clove garlic, peeled and roughly chopped

1 teaspoon freshly grated lemon zest

3 tablespoons fresh lemon juice

2 tablespoons red wine vinegar

1 cup extra virgin olive oil

1 teaspoon hot red pepper flakes, plus extra as needed

Sea salt and freshly ground black pepper

Finely chop the parsley, mint, anchovies (if using), capers, scallions, garlic, and lemon zest in a food processor, running the machine in short bursts. Work in the lemon juice, vinegar, olive oil, hot red pepper flakes, and salt and pepper to taste—again, running the machine in short bursts. If the salsa is too thick, add a few tablespoons of water. Correct the seasoning, adding more salt, pepper, hot red pepper flakes, or lemon juice to taste. The salsa should be highly seasoned. The salsa is best made no more than an hour or two before serving. (Store it at room temperature.)

ROPA VIEJA ("OLD CLOTHES")
"PULLED" BRISKET IN CREOLE SAUCE

North Carolinians have pulled pork. The Spanish Caribbean revels in *ropa vieja*. The "old clothes" in question are meaty shreds of brisket brightened with bell peppers and a garlic- and cumin-scented Creole sauce. The recipe turns up throughout the Spanish-speaking Caribbean and Central America. It's as colorful as a Caribbean market and as comforting as dinner at your grandmother's. Some versions are served chilled as salad. Others are sautéed, like the one here. Serve it over rice and get ready for Spanish Caribbean soul food.

YIELD: Serves 4

METHOD: Boiling, sautéing

PREP TIME: 30 minutes

COOKING TIME: 2½ to 3 hours for boiling the brisket, plus 15 minutes for the sauce

HEAT SOURCE: Stove

YOU'LL ALSO NEED: A stockpot; a baking dish; a strainer; a large skillet

WHAT ELSE: *Ropa vieja* requires a two-step cooking process: First you boil the brisket until tender, then you shred and sauté it in Creole sauce. So it requires a bit of time to make in one day (what else is new with brisket?) or advance planning so you can make it over two days. The effort will reward you not only with *ropa vieja*, but with a soulful broth for future soups and stews.

INGREDIENTS

FOR THE BEEF

2 pounds brisket flat, trimmed (see page 14)

1 dried bay leaf

1 medium onion, peeled and quartered

1 whole clove

1 luscious ripe tomato, stemmed and quartered

1 carrot, trimmed, peeled, and cut crosswise into 1-inch pieces

2 cloves garlic, peeled

Cilantro stems (reserved from the chopped fresh cilantro, see Creole Sauce)

FOR THE CREOLE SAUCE

3 tablespoons extra virgin olive oil

1 small onion, peeled and thinly sliced crosswise

1 cubanelle or green bell pepper, stemmed, seeded, and cut into pencil-width strips

1 red bell pepper, stemmed, seeded, and cut into pencil-width strips

2 cloves garlic, peeled and minced

1 teaspoon ground cumin

1 teaspoon ground oregano

⅓ cup dry white wine

1 cup tomato sauce

¼ cup chopped fresh cilantro or flat-leaf parsley, plus 2 tablespoons for serving (save the stems for the broth)

Sea salt and freshly ground black pepper

1. Make the broth: Place the brisket in a large stockpot. Pin the bay leaf to an onion quarter with the clove and add the onion quarters to the pot with the tomato, carrot, garlic, and cilantro stems. Add 3 quarts of cold water and bring to a boil over medium-high heat. Skim off the scum that rises to the surface with a ladle or large spoon. Reduce the heat and gently simmer the brisket, skimming often, until very tender, 2½ hours, or as needed.

2. Transfer the brisket to a baking dish and let it cool slightly. (It's easier to shred when it's hot.) Pour the broth through a strainer into a large bowl, pressing the vegetables to extract the juices. You'll need about 1 cup of broth to finish the *ropa vieja* (save or freeze the remainder in a sealed container for future soups or stews; it will keep in the refrigerator for several days, and up to 6 months in the freezer).

3. Tear the brisket into meaty strips about 3 inches long and the thickness of a pencil.

4. Meanwhile, make the Creole sauce: Heat the oil in a large skillet over medium-high heat. Add the onion and peppers and sauté until softened slightly, 2 minutes. Add the garlic, cumin, and oregano and cook until fragrant and the peppers are lightly browned, 2 minutes more. Add the wine and boil to reduce slightly, 1 minute. Stir in the tomato sauce, 1 cup broth, ¼ cup chopped cilantro, and ½ teaspoon each of salt and pepper. Simmer for 2 minutes.

5. Stir the shredded brisket into the sauce. Simmer until the sauce is reduced and the mixture is richly flavored, 10 minutes. Correct the seasoning, adding salt and pepper as needed. Sprinkle the *ropa vieja* with the remaining chopped cilantro and serve at once.

VACA FRITA
"FRIED COW"

YIELD: Serves 6 to 8

METHOD: Frying/
sautéing

PREP TIME: 15 minutes
(plus 1 hour for drying the
beef in the refrigerator)

COOKING TIME:
2½ hours for boiling the
brisket (see page 254),
plus 6 to 9 minutes for
frying

HEAT SOURCE: Stove

YOU'LL ALSO NEED:
Meat claws (optional);
a large skillet; a strainer

WHAT ELSE: There are
two ways to crisp the
brisket—by pan-frying
or by deep-frying. The
former is easier to execute
in most kitchens, but if
you're comfortable with
deep-frying, the resulting
vaca frita will be even
crispier.

Vaca frita ("fried cow") is a Cuban delicacy, not to mention a close cousin of the Ropa Vieja on page 171. Both start with shredded, boiled brisket. But instead of simmering the brisket in Creole sauce as you do for the latter, in the former you fry the meat shreds in hot oil with onions and garlic. The finer you shred the brisket, the crispier the filaments of beef will be.

INGREDIENTS

2 pounds boiled brisket flat
(see page 254)

1 cup vegetable oil, or as needed

1 medium onion, peeled and
thinly sliced crosswise

3 cloves garlic, peeled and thinly
sliced lengthwise

Sea salt and freshly ground
black pepper

1. Tear the brisket into meaty shreds using meat claws, two forks, or your fingers. At a maximum, the shreds should be pencil-thick and about 3 inches long. If you have the patience, shred the meat as thin as spaghetti. Let the shredded brisket dry on a platter or wire rack set over a sheet pan in the refrigerator for 1 hour (drying makes it crispier and less likely to splatter when fried).

2. Set a large strainer over a bowl. Add the oil to a depth of ½ inch in a large skillet. Heat the oil over medium-high heat until a shred of brisket dipped in the oil has bubbles dancing around it.

3. Add a couple handfuls of brisket shreds to the oil and fry until crisp, 2 minutes. Transfer the meat with a skimmer to the strainer to drain. Repeat with the remaining brisket, working in batches to avoid crowding the pan. Fry the onions and garlic until browned and crisp, 1 to 2 minutes, and transfer to the strainer.

4. Transfer the fried brisket, onions, and garlic to a platter. Generously season with salt and pepper and serve.

Chapter 6

BRISKET FOR BREAKFAST

Forget bacon and eggs. Forget biscuits with sausage gravy. When it comes to a breakfast you can really sink your teeth into, I pass my plate for brisket. Who needs steak and eggs when you can scramble those eggs with shredded brisket? Hash? It's about to get a lot more awesome enriched with pastrami or barbecued brisket. In this chapter, you'll learn how to make some of my favorite brisket breakfasts, from the Real Deal Holyfield (brisket breakfast tacos with smoky fiery "gangsta" salsa) to a brisket breakfast sandwich—the egg properly runny—you need to grip with both hands in order to raise it to your mouth. You'll even find brisket scones that beat conventional breakfast pastries hollow. So wake up and smell the brisket.

REAL DEAL HOLYFIELD BRISKET BREAKFAST TACOS

When early morning hunger strikes in Austin, you head for a parking lot filled with sheds, trailers, barbecue pits, and sky-blue picnic tables clustered around a cinderblock roadhouse known as Valentina's Tex Mex BBQ. Proprietor Miguel Vidal grew up in San Antonio, where his dad, like most Texans, staged family barbecues every weekend and his mom made the salsas and tortillas by hand. He worked at various restaurants in Austin prior to opening Valentina's (named for his daughter) in 2013. "I wanted to elevate the Tex-Mex food I grew up on, while marrying it with Texas barbecue," says Vidal, who runs the restaurant with his wife, Modesty, and brother, Elias. To this end, he built three massive barbecue pits (named Cobain, Cornell, and Maynard after his favorite musicians). He burns mesquite—not the post oak customary in these parts—resulting in meats with a decisive smoke flavor. His briskets (seasoned with a triple blast of spices, pepper, and salt) go on at 1 a.m. and cook for 14 to 16 hours. On a typical Saturday, he'll serve 400 pounds of brisket, 200 pounds of pork ribs, and 1,500 house-made tortillas. One morning, Miguel's father asked for some huevos rancheros. Miguel decided to up the ante, adding brisket and a smoked vegetable salsa. The result was the Real Deal Holyfield, and it delivers a wallop.

YIELD: Serves 4

METHOD: Pan-frying

PREP TIME: 20 minutes

COOKING TIME: 20 minutes

HEAT SOURCE: Stove

YOU'LL ALSO NEED: A rimmed sheet pan

Brisket for breakfast at Valentina's awaits you.

WHAT ELSE: Like much Tex-Mex street food, the Real Deal Holyfield features commonplace ingredients—tortillas, eggs, potatoes, refried beans, and salsa—staples of Mexican American cooking. But it takes a little choreography to put them together for breakfast. I've tried to streamline the recipe to the point where you can make it in a single frying pan. (You keep the various components warm on a rimmed sheet pan in the oven.) You'll need some leftover barbecued brisket and a large cooked potato. A purist would make the tortillas, refried beans, and salsa from scratch, but your favorite commercial versions deliver a pretty awesome breakfast, too. The recipe can be multiplied as you desire—given the setup, it's easier (or at least more efficient) to make breakfast tacos for many people rather than just a few.

INGREDIENTS

2 tablespoons butter, olive oil, or Brisket Butter (page 259), or as needed

4 slices barbecued brisket (each slice ¼ inch thick; about ½ pound total; see pages 41 to 70)

1 baked or boiled russet (baking) potato, cut into ¼-inch dice (use whatever cooked potato you might have on hand)

Sea salt and freshly ground black pepper

4 flour or white corn tortillas (each 6 inches in diameter)

4 large eggs (preferably farm-fresh and organic)

1 cup warm refried beans, canned or homemade

1 cup Gangsta Salsa (recipe follows), or your favorite salsa

¼ cup thinly sliced scallion greens

1. Preheat the oven to 250°F.

2. Melt 1 tablespoon butter in a skillet over medium-high heat. Warm the brisket slices, about 30 seconds per side. Transfer to a rimmed sheet pan and keep warm in the oven.

3. Melt the remaining 1 tablespoon butter in the skillet. Add the potatoes and pan-fry, stirring with a spatula, until hot, browned, and crisp, 3 minutes. Season with salt and pepper. Transfer the potatoes to the sheet pan with the brisket and keep warm.

4. Warm the tortillas in the skillet, 30 seconds per side. (Alternatively, warm the tortillas on your grill.) Transfer to the sheet pan with the brisket and potatoes and keep warm.

5. You'll need at least 2 tablespoons of fat in the skillet to fry the eggs. If enough butter remains in the skillet, heat it over a medium-high flame; if not, add butter, oil, or brisket butter to equal 2 tablespoons. When the fat starts sizzling, crack in the eggs. Fry until cooked to taste, 2 to 3 minutes on one side if you like them sunny-side up, or 2 minutes per side for over easy.

6. Assemble the tacos: Lay a tortilla on a plate. Spread it with a quarter of the refried beans. Top with a quarter of the fried potatoes and a slice of brisket. Slide an egg on top. Spoon salsa on top and sprinkle with a quarter of the scallion greens. Assemble the remaining tacos the same way. Serve the tacos open-face, with any remaining salsa on the side.

GANGSTA SALSA

YIELD: Makes 2 cups

This pyrotechnic salsa shows how Miguel Vidal blends Tex-Mex with Hill Country barbecue. He cooks the veggies in the smoker—long enough to infuse them with mesquite smoke, but short enough to keep their vegetal crunch. You can certainly smoke the vegetables ahead of time at a previous smoke or grill session.

INGREDIENTS

2 large tomatoes, stemmed and cut in half widthwise

2 large tomatillos, husked, rinsed, and cut in half widthwise (or more tomatoes)

½ small onion, peeled and halved

3 serrano chiles, stemmed and cut in half lengthwise (for milder salsa, remove the seeds)

1 habanero chile, stemmed and cut in half lengthwise (for milder salsa, remove the seeds)

¼ cup freshly squeezed lime juice, or to taste

½ cup chopped fresh cilantro

Coarse sea salt

1. If using a smoker for this recipe, set it up following the manufacturer's instructions and heat to 275°F. Alternatively, set up your grill for indirect grilling (see page 22) and heat to medium-low.

2. Arrange the tomatoes, tomatillos, onion, and chiles, cut sides up, in foil pans. Place in the smoker or away from the heat on the grill. If using a grill, add 1 cup unsoaked wood chips or 2 wood chunks to the coals. Cover and smoke the veggies until they are just beginning to soften, 20 minutes. Keep some crispness—the vegetables should remain raw in the center. Let cool.

3. Cut the veggies into 1-inch cubes and place in a food processor. Puree as coarsely or smoothly as you desire. Work in the lime juice, cilantro, and salt to taste. The salsa should be highly seasoned.

4. Transfer the salsa to a serving dish or bowl. Serve at once, or cover and refrigerate—it will keep for several days.

THE ULTIMATE BREAKFAST HASH
(YES, THERE WILL BE BRISKET)

YIELD: Serves 2 (can be multiplied as desired)

METHOD: Sautéing

PREP TIME: 20 minutes

COOKING TIME: 15 minutes

HEAT SOURCE: Stove or grill side burner

YOU'LL ALSO NEED: A 10-inch cast-iron skillet or other heavy-bottomed skillet; another skillet (medium-size; if you're frying the eggs)

WHAT ELSE: This recipe calls for barbecued brisket, but equally delectable hash can be made from homemade corned beef (the classic—see page 111) or pastrami (Old School, page 93, or New School, page 100).

I don't know about you, but I believe in the afterlife. The afterlife of brisket, that is—the resurrection of this rich smoky barbecued beef in salads, stuffings, and stir-fries. Above all, I believe in leftover brisket for breakfast—especially in hash. Named for the French verb *hacher* ("to chop"—the same etymological root that gives us our word *hatchet*), hash requires little more than a sharp knife and a cast-iron skillet. This one derives its firepower from poblano peppers and sriracha. Hash is infinitely customizable: Swap the poblanos for bell peppers, for example, or the potatoes for yams or yucca. If you're used to the usual corned beef hash, the intense smoky flavor of this brisket hash will come as a revelation.

INGREDIENTS

2 tablespoons butter, Brisket Butter (page 259), or extra virgin olive oil

2 or 3 shallots or 1 small onion, peeled and finely chopped (to equal ¾ cup)

1 poblano, stemmed, seeded, and diced

2 jalapeños, stemmed, seeded, and diced (for spicier hash, leave the seeds in)

2 cups coarsely or finely diced barbecued brisket (see pages 41 to 70)

2 cups coarsely or finely diced cooked potatoes or other root vegetables

2 tablespoons butter or extra virgin olive oil, for frying eggs (optional)

2 to 4 large eggs (preferably farm-fresh and organic; optional)

1 tablespoon Worcestershire sauce

1 tablespoon sriracha or your favorite hot sauce

Sea salt and freshly ground black pepper

2 tablespoons finely chopped fresh chives, parsley, cilantro, and/or other fresh herb, for garnish

1. Heat the butter in a 10-inch cast-iron skillet over medium-high heat. Add the shallots, poblano, and jalapeños and cook, stirring with a wooden spoon, until browned, 3 minutes.

2. Stir in the brisket and potatoes and continue cooking until the potatoes are browned, 3 to 5 minutes more.

3. Meanwhile, if you want to serve the hash with eggs (and I think you should!), melt the butter or heat the olive oil in a medium skillet over medium-high heat. When the fat starts sizzling, crack in the eggs. Fry until cooked to taste, flipping once with a spatula, 2 minutes per side for yolks that are still a little runny (that's how I like them).

4. Stir the Worcestershire sauce and sriracha into the hash and cook for 1 minute. Correct the seasoning, adding salt and pepper to taste. The hash should be highly seasoned. Serve the hash right from the skillet, sliding the fried eggs on top. Sprinkle with chopped chives and dig in.

VARIATION

Corned Beef or Pastrami Hash: Prepare as described above, substituting corned beef or pastrami for the brisket. Use onions instead of shallots and red or yellow bell peppers (or a mix) instead of poblanos. Replace the sriracha with Louisiana-style hot sauce such as Crystal or Tabasco.

THE BRISKET BREAKFAST SANDWICH

Brisket for breakfast? It may sound excessive in some circles, but here in Raichlendia, it's just how we start our day. As always, it's the attention to detail that differentiates an unforgettable breakfast sandwich from a merely good one. Brioche rolls (and, yes, you should butter and griddle them). Organic farm eggs. And sun-warmed garden tomatoes that have never seen the inside of a refrigerator. The arugula may sound elitist—it's not. Its peppery bite beats the usual iceberg lettuce hollow.

YIELD: Makes 2 sandwiches (can be multiplied as desired)

METHOD: Pan-frying

PREP TIME: 20 minutes

COOKING TIME: 5 minutes

HEAT SOURCE: Stove or grill side burner

YOU'LL ALSO NEED: A 10-inch skillet

WHAT ELSE: Inspired by the classic Western breakfast of steak and eggs, this breakfast sandwich was conceived with barbecued brisket in mind. But there's no reason you couldn't make an equally compelling breakfast sandwich with homemade pastrami (page 93), smoked meat (page 123), or corned beef (page 111). I've made the avocado optional—you don't want to go to too much trouble for breakfast—but it definitely keeps the bottom of the bun from getting soggy and adds another texture and layer of flavor.

INGREDIENTS

3 tablespoons butter, at room temperature, or extra virgin olive oil

2 brioche rolls or hamburger buns, sliced

3 tablespoons Chipotle Mayonnaise (recipe follows) or regular mayonnaise (preferably Hellmann's or Best Foods)

1 ripe avocado, peeled, pitted, and sliced (optional)

4 slices barbecued brisket (each slice ¼ inch thick; about ½ pound total; see pages 41 to 70)

3 ounces thinly sliced pepper Jack cheese

2 large eggs (preferably farm-fresh and organic)

Sea salt and freshly ground black pepper

1 luscious ripe red tomato, stemmed and thinly sliced

1½ cups arugula leaves, washed and dried

1. Heat a 10-inch skillet over medium-high heat.

2. Spread half the butter on the cut sides of the brioche rolls. Toast the rolls, cut sides down, in the skillet until lightly toasted, 2 minutes.

3. Transfer the rolls to a cutting board. Slather the cut sides of the rolls with Chipotle Mayonnaise and arrange the avocado slices, if using, on the bottoms.

4. Heat the remaining butter in the skillet over medium-high heat. Add the brisket slices and fry, turning once, until crusty and hot, 2 minutes per side. Arrange the hot brisket on the rolls. Lay the cheese slices on top.

5. Crack the eggs into the skillet and fry in the remaining butter and brisket drippings until cooked to taste, 2 minutes per side for yolks the way I like them: still a little runny. Season the eggs with salt and pepper as they cook. Using a spatula, slide the eggs atop the cheese. (The hot brisket and eggs will melt the cheese.)

6. Top the eggs with the sliced tomato and arugula. Replace the tops of the rolls. Get ready to bite into a breakfast sandwich that makes all others pale in comparison.

CHIPOTLE MAYONNAISE

YIELD: Makes about 1½ cups

Chipotles add a slow smoky burn to creamy mayonnaise. You'll want to use canned chipotles so you can add some of the adobo, the aromatic can juices.

INGREDIENTS

2 to 3 canned chipotles in adobo, with 2 tablespoons of the sauce

1½ cups mayonnaise (preferably Hellmann's or Best Foods)

3 tablespoons chopped fresh cilantro

1 tablespoon fresh lime juice

½ teaspoon ground cumin

Mince the chipotles with a chef's knife and place in a mixing bowl. Whisk in the chipotle sauce, mayonnaise, cilantro, lime juice, and cumin. Chipotle Mayonnaise will keep, in a sealed container in the refrigerator, for at least 3 days.

BRISKET AND EGGS
WITH CRISPY GRILLED SCALLION TORTILLA CHIPS

Machaca con huevos, shredded dried beef with scrambled eggs, is a beloved breakfast in northern Mexico. It's a high-voltage twist on American steak and eggs made with a sort of Mexican beef jerky called *machaca*. It's about to get a lot more interesting thanks to the addition of—you guessed it—barbecued brisket. I like to serve brisket and eggs with crisp, grilled scallion tortilla chips brushed with—you guessed it again—Brisket Butter. The latter isn't traditional, but it sure is tasty.

YIELD: Serves 4 (can be multiplied as desired)

METHOD: Pan-frying

PREP TIME: 10 minutes

COOKING TIME: 10 minutes

HEAT SOURCE: Stove or grill side burner for the eggs; grill or broiler for the tortilla chips

YOU'LL ALSO NEED: A large nonstick skillet

INGREDIENTS

2 tablespoons Brisket Butter (page 259) or extra virgin olive oil

1 bunch scallions, trimmed and thinly sliced crosswise (set aside 3 tablespoons of the greens for the tortilla chips)

1 clove garlic, peeled and minced

2 jalapeños, stemmed, seeded, and finely chopped (for extra heat, leave the seeds in)

1 luscious ripe red tomato, stemmed, seeded, and diced

1 cup shredded or finely chopped barbecued brisket (see pages 41 to 70)

8 large eggs (preferably farm-fresh and organic)

3 tablespoons chopped fresh cilantro

Sea salt and freshly ground black pepper

FOR SERVING (ANY OR ALL OF THE FOLLOWING)

½ cup sour cream or Mexican *crema*

1 ripe avocado, peeled, pitted, and sliced

Crispy Grilled Scallion Tortilla Chips (optional; recipe follows)

1. Heat the Brisket Butter or oil in a large nonstick skillet over medium-high heat. Add the scallions, garlic, and jalapeños and cook over medium-high heat until lightly browned, 4 minutes. Stir in the tomato and cook until most of the juices are evaporated, 2 minutes. Stir in the brisket and cook for 1 minute.

2. Meanwhile, beat the eggs in a bowl with a fork or whisk until frothy. Beat in the cilantro and some salt and pepper. Stir the eggs into the brisket mixture and cook, stirring with a rubber spatula, over medium-high heat until gently scrambled, 1 to 2 minutes. Add salt and pepper to taste.

3. Serve the brisket and eggs with sour cream and avocado on top, and Crispy Grilled Scallion Tortilla Chips for dipping.

CRISPY GRILLED SCALLION TORTILLA CHIPS

YIELD: Makes 24 chips

Sure, you could serve Brisket and Eggs with packaged tortilla chips. But that wouldn't be *The Brisket Chronicles* way. I like to brush fresh tortillas with Brisket Butter, crust them with scallion greens, and sizzle them on the grill. The texture and flavor are off the charts.

INGREDIENTS

4 flour or white corn tortillas (each 6 inches in diameter)

2 tablespoons Brisket Butter (page 259) or melted butter

3 tablespoons thinly sliced scallion greens

Vegetable oil, for oiling the grill grate

1. Set up your grill for direct grilling (see page 81) and heat it to medium-high. Alternatively, preheat your broiler to medium-high.

2. Brush the tortillas on both sides with Brisket Butter or melted butter. Sprinkle both sides with scallion greens, pressing them in with a fork.

3. Brush or scrape the grill grate clean and oil it well. Arrange the scallion-crusted tortillas on the grate and grill until sizzling and browned on both sides, about 1 minute per side. (Watch carefully, as they can burn easily.) Alternatively, broil the tortillas until sizzling and browned, 1 to 2 minutes per side.

4. Transfer the tortillas to a cutting board. Cut each into 6 wedges. The chips will crisp as they cool. The chips can be made up to several hours ahead.

BRISKET SCONES

YIELD: Makes 16 scones

METHOD: Baking

PREP TIME: 20 minutes, plus 1½ hours for chilling the dough

COOKING TIME: 20 minutes

HEAT SOURCE: Oven

YOU'LL ALSO NEED: A stand mixer with a paddle or a food processor; a rimmed sheet pan; parchment paper; a rolling pin

WHAT ELSE: These scones are easy to make if you have leftover brisket on hand, and incredibly tasty, but leave yourself enough time to chill the dough. Corned beef or pastrami scones? Just saying.

State Road is one of our favorite restaurants on Martha's Vineyard—the sort of place that had a wood-burning grill before it was fashionable for restaurants to have wood-burning grills. (And a chef-owner—Jackson Kenworth—who knows how to use it.) Where the corned beef for the hash is house-cured and where the eggs Benedict ride on smoked brisket instead of the usual Canadian bacon. So I was only half surprised to find brisket scones on the brunch menu recently. "I came up with these scones while thinking about how much I missed the brisket in Texas," says pastry chef Lindsey McCloskey. "The mix of local woods from the island gives our brisket a smoke flavor you can only find here on Martha's Vineyard." Amen.

INGREDIENTS

4¾ cups all-purpose flour, plus extra for rolling out the dough

¼ cup sugar

1 tablespoon baking powder

2¼ teaspoons fine sea salt

2 sticks (8 ounces) cold unsalted butter, cut into ½-inch slices

1 cup finely chopped barbecued brisket (see pages 41 to 70)

½ cup finely diced red onion

3 large eggs (preferably farm-fresh and organic), lightly beaten

1⅓ cups buttermilk, or as needed

FOR THE GLAZE

1 egg yolk

3 tablespoons heavy cream or milk

1. Place the flour, sugar, baking powder, salt, and butter in a stand mixer fitted with a paddle. Mix on low speed until the butter pieces are pea-size. Alternatively, place these ingredients in a food processor fitted with a chopping blade. Run the processor in short bursts to cut in the butter until it's in pea-size pieces. Mix in the brisket and onion. (If using a food processor, run it in short bursts to mix.)

2. Add the beaten eggs and buttermilk and mix or process until the dough just holds together. Wrap the dough in plastic wrap and refrigerate it for 1 hour.

3. Lightly dust a work surface with flour. Line a rimmed sheet pan with parchment paper. Remove the dough from the refrigerator and lay it on the prepared work surface. Using a lightly floured rolling pin, tap and then roll the dough into an 8-by-12-inch rectangle that is 1 inch thick. Cut the rectangle in half lengthwise, then cut each half in fourths widthwise. Cut each of the resulting smaller rectangles in half on the diagonal (from corner to opposite corner) to obtain 16 triangles. Alternatively, roll the dough into a large circle 1 inch thick and cut into 16 wedges. Arrange the scones on the prepared sheet pan and chill for 30 minutes.

4. Preheat the oven to 375°F.

5. Make the glaze: Combine the egg yolk with the cream in a small bowl and beat with a fork.

6. Remove the scones from the refrigerator and brush the tops with the glaze. Bake until lightly browned and cooked through, 20 to 30 minutes, rotating the sheet pan halfway through so the scones bake evenly.

Chapter 7

BRISKET TO BEGIN

Consider the perfect starter. Big-flavored enough to rouse your appetite. Yet small enough to eat in a single bite. There'll be salt and spice in abundance—the better to spur your thirst for a cocktail. And it wouldn't hurt if one or two of those starters were salads—to cool off the chile hellfire. Well, if such is your notion of the perfect appetizer, you're in the right place, because in this chapter you'll learn how the strategic addition of barbecued brisket can breathe new life into commonplace starters and take offbeat appetizers over the top. Poppers? Forget the bacon and stuff those jalapeños with smoky brisket. Tater Tots? Forgo the frozen food version for homemade potato morsels flecked with tiny nuggets of barbecued brisket, making them fit fare for hungry grown-ups. Hot Pockets? Just wait until you try them made from scratch, stuffed with smoky brisket and pepper Jack cheese. What follows are my favorite brisket starters. Let the party begin.

BACON-GRILLED BRISKET BITES
WITH CILANTRO LIME SAUCE

Sometimes, less is more. Sometimes, more is more. Consider these bacon-grilled brisket bites. You start with luscious smoky brisket, which you cook a second time, wrapped in bacon, sizzled on the grill. Think crisp crust, beefy richness, and the smoky goodness of bacon. Think of a finger food so wantonly delectable that eating just one would be inconceivable. To give credit where due, the idea for bacon-grilled brisket bites comes from Shawn Henry of the Missouri barbecue team Smoking and Drinking BBQ. I'll take responsibility for stoking the fire with jalapeños.

INGREDIENTS

1 pound unsliced barbecued brisket (see pages 41 to 70)

3 jalapeños, stemmed, seeded, and thinly sliced crosswise (leave the seeds in for spicier bites)

1 bunch cilantro, stemmed (optional)

1 pound artisanal thin-cut bacon, such as Nueske's, each strip cut crosswise in half

Vegetable oil, for oiling the grill grate

Cilantro Lime Sauce (recipe follows)

1. Cut the brisket into ¾-inch cubes. Place a jalapeño slice and a cilantro sprig on top of each. Wrap each cube in bacon, securing it to the brisket with toothpicks.

2. Set up your grill for direct grilling (see page 81) and heat it to medium-high. Brush and scrape the grill grate clean and oil it well.

3. Arrange the brisket bites on the grill and grill until sizzling and browned on all sides, 8 to 12 minutes, or as needed.

4. Serve with the Cilantro Lime Sauce for dipping. Remind people to remove the toothpicks.

YIELD: Serves 4 to 6

METHOD: Direct grilling

PREP TIME: 15 minutes

COOKING TIME:
8 to 12 minutes direct grilling

HEAT SOURCE: Grill

YOU'LL ALSO NEED:
Toothpicks

WHAT ELSE: You can also indirect grill the brisket bites (thereby eliminating the risk of flare-ups): Set up your grill for indirect grilling (see page 22) and heat to medium-high. Indirect grill the bites for 30 minutes, or as needed. Do you want to take the merely extravagant over the top? Do you own shares in the company that manufactures Lipitor? There's another way to cook these brisket bites— to give them even more snap and crackle. Yes, deep-frying. Heat your oil to 350°F and fry until the bacon and brisket are crisp.

CILANTRO LIME SAUCE

YIELD: Makes 1½ cups

This piquant cream sauce roars with the southwestern flavors of cilantro, cumin, and lime. Cholula would make an appropriate hot sauce.

INGREDIENTS

¾ cup sour cream

¾ cup mayonnaise (preferably Hellmann's or Best Foods)

⅓ cup chopped fresh cilantro

1 teaspoon ground cumin

1 teaspoon freshly grated lime zest

2 tablespoons freshly squeezed lime juice

1 to 2 teaspoons your favorite hot sauce (optional)

Sea salt and freshly ground black pepper to taste

Combine the ingredients in a serving bowl and whisk to mix. Cover and refrigerate if not using immediately.

The sauce will keep, in a sealed container in the refrigerator, for at least 3 days.

TEXAS TORPEDOES
(BRISKET POPPERS)

The Jalapeño Popper burst onto the American food scene in 1992 (the year Anchor Food Products trademarked the term), but I suspect Texans have been stuffing and deep-frying or smoking jalapeños much longer. Start with grated cheese and you wind up with a respectable popper. Add meaty shreds of smoked brisket—appropriately seasoned with cilantro and scallions—and you get poppers that redefine the genre.

INGREDIENTS

12 large jalapeños

12 ounces barbecued brisket (see pages 41 to 70), shredded or finely chopped

12 ounces coarsely grated pepper Jack cheese

¼ cup roughly chopped fresh cilantro

¼ cup thinly sliced scallion greens

½ cup mayonnaise (preferably Hellmann's or Best Foods)

1. Cut each jalapeño in half lengthwise leaving the stem intact. Scrape out the seeds and veins with a small spoon (a grapefruit spoon or melon baller works well). Arrange the jalapeño halves on a wire rack set over a rimmed sheet pan. (Line the pan with aluminum foil for easier clean-up.)

2. Make the filling: Place the brisket, cheese, cilantro, and scallions in a mixing bowl and stir to combine. Stir in the mayonnaise. Spoon the filling into the jalapeño halves, mounding it toward the center.

3. Meanwhile, set up your grill for indirect grilling (see page 22) and heat to medium-high.

4. Place the wire rack with the poppers directly on the grill grate over the drip pan and away from the heat. Add the wood to the coals or to your gas grill's smoker box.

5. Smoke-roast the poppers until the filling is sizzling and browned and the jalapeños are tender, 20 to 25 minutes.

6. Transfer the poppers to a platter. Let cool slightly before serving.

YIELD: Makes 24 jalapeño halves, enough to serve 6

METHOD: Smoke-roasting (indirect grilling with wood smoke)

PREP TIME: 20 minutes

COOKING TIME: 20 to 25 minutes

HEAT SOURCE: Grill or smoker

YOU'LL ALSO NEED: A rimmed sheet pan with wire rack; 2 hardwood chunks or 1½ cups chips (if using the latter, soak in water to cover for 30 minutes, then drain)

WHAT ELSE: If you're reading this book, chances are you've smoked a brisket or two already. So you probably have some leftover brisket in your refrigerator or freezer. (It's magical stuff—next time, smoke some extra.) Many people like to cook poppers in the smoker, but I like the fresh jalapeño crunch you get from smoke-roasting (indirect grilling) the poppers at a higher heat.

BRISKET TOTS

YIELD: Makes about 100 tots; serves 8 to 12 as a starter

METHOD: Deep-frying

PREP TIME: 30 minutes

COOKING TIME: About 25 minutes

HEAT SOURCE: Stove

YOU'LL ALSO NEED: A box grater; a deep-fry thermometer; a skimmer

WHAT ELSE: The chef of the EastSide Tavern in Austin, Texas, fries his potatoes twice—first to cook them through, then to crisp the tots. I always try to keep frying to a minimum, so I call for first boiling the spuds here. But fry them if you prefer. Likewise, the chef forces the mixture through a churros mold, which gives them a handsome ridged finish. It's even simpler to roll and cut them as you would gnocchi.

This may be a book on brisket, but never let it be said that I don't encourage you to eat your vegetables. The vegetable in question here is potato, which the owners of the EastSide Tavern in Austin transform into their take on Tater Tots. This being Texas, these are no ordinary tots: They come enriched with smoky bits of brisket, which EastSide cooks in a custom pit fashioned from a 1,500-pound propane tank. Serve with Chipotle Mayonnaise (page 186) and you've got a starter or side dish that will have people clamoring for more.

INGREDIENTS

2½ pounds baking potatoes (3 to 4 potatoes), scrubbed and unpeeled

Sea salt

1 teaspoon freshly ground black pepper, plus extra as needed

2 tablespoons potato starch, plus extra for dusting your work surface

1 large egg (preferably farm-fresh and organic), beaten with a fork

2 cups finely diced or chopped barbecued brisket (about ½ pound; see pages 41 to 70)

2 cups coarsely grated cheddar cheese

2 scallions, trimmed, white part minced, green part thinly sliced on a sharp diagonal and set aside for garnish (optional)

About 2 cups vegetable oil, for frying

1 cup Chipotle Mayonnaise (page 186)

1. Place the potatoes in a large pot with 1 teaspoon salt and water to cover by a depth of 3 inches. Briskly simmer the potatoes over medium-high heat until just tender when pierced with a bamboo skewer, 12 to 18 minutes. Drain the potatoes in a colander. When cool enough to handle, slip off and discard the skins.

2. Grate the potatoes on the large holes of a box grater into a large bowl. (Alternatively, use a food processor fitted with a grating disk. Do not use a chopping blade.)

3. Sprinkle the potatoes with 1½ teaspoons salt, 1 teaspoon black pepper, and 2 tablespoons potato starch. Gently fold to mix. Fold in the beaten egg, brisket, cheese, and scallion whites (be careful not to over-fold or the tots will be gummy). Correct the seasoning, adding salt and/or pepper to taste.

4. Form the tots as you would gnocchi. That is, lightly dust your work surface with potato starch. Take a 4-ounce piece of the potato mixture (about the size of a lemon) and roll it into a rope about 12 inches long and ½ inch thick. Cut it crosswise into 1½-inch pieces. Continue rolling and cutting the potato mixture until all is used up. The tots can be formed several hours ahead and stored in the refrigerator on a sheet pan lined and covered with plastic wrap.

5. Just before serving, pour oil into a deep frying pan or heavy-bottomed pot to a depth of 2 inches and heat over medium-high heat. Fry the tots in batches (don't crowd the pan) until golden brown on all sides, turning with a skimmer or slotted spoon, 4 to 6 minutes in all. Transfer the tots to a plate lined with paper towels to drain. Continue frying until all the potato mixture is used up.

6. Sprinkle the tots with the scallion greens, if using, and serve immediately, with a bowl of Chipotle Mayonnaise (page 186) on the side for dipping.

SMOKY BRISKET CHEESE POCKETS

Leave it to Tako Matsumoto to come up with brisket "hot pockets." Born in Japan and raised in Texas, the chef-owner of Kemuri Tatsu-ya in Austin, Texas, gleefully merges *izakaya* (Japanese pub) fare with traditional Hill Country barbecue. The pockets in question are tofu skins, and he fills them with barbecued brisket and smoky cheese. A quick sizzle in a contact grill or panini press makes them crisp on the outside, gooey-cheesy inside, with a rich, smoky beef flavor that doesn't quit.

INGREDIENTS

- 6 ounces smoked Gouda or other smoked cheese, shredded
- 6 ounces cheddar cheese, shredded (Tako likes the Tillamook brand)
- ½ pound barbecued brisket (see pages 41 to 70), shredded or finely chopped (about 2 cups)
- 18 tofu skin pockets (see What Else)
- 1 to 2 tablespoons vegetable oil or butter

YIELD: Makes 18, enough to serve 4 to 6

METHOD: Pan-frying/griddling

PREP TIME: 6 to 9 minutes

COOKING TIME: 6 minutes

HEAT SOURCE: Stove

YOU'LL ALSO NEED: A rimmed sheet pan lined with parchment paper; a griddle, skillet, or plancha with a grill press or a contact grill, sandwich grill, or panini press

WHAT ELSE: You'll need to know about one special ingredient: tofu skins, aka bean curd skins, aka *yuba* or *abura age*—papery skins that form when you simmer soybeans to make soy milk. The skins make natural pockets for stuffing with cheese and brisket. Look for tofu skins at Asian markets. You want the kind that come in small rectangles for stuffing.

1. Combine the Gouda, cheddar, and brisket in a bowl and stir to mix.

2. Line a rimmed sheet pan with parchment paper. Open the tofu skin pockets one by one and spoon a tablespoon or two of the brisket-cheese mixture into each; transfer them to the prepared pan. The skins can be stuffed several hours ahead, covered with plastic wrap, and refrigerated.

3. Just before serving, heat a griddle, skillet, or plancha over medium-high heat. Add the oil or butter and heat it as well. Add the stuffed pockets in batches and cook, turning once, until sizzling and lightly browned on both sides, 1 to 2 minutes per side. Alternatively, use a contact grill or panini press, in which case brush the outsides of the pockets with the oil or melted butter and cook for 2 to 4 minutes. Serve at once, hot off the griddle. I dare you to eat just one.

VIETNAMESE CRISPY BRISKET SALAD

This aromatic salad pinballs that traditional Vietnamese quintet of flavors—salty fish sauce, sour lime juice, sweet sugar, pungent garlic, and fiery chiles—with crispy, meaty shreds of smoky brisket and fresh mint, cilantro, and other fragrant herbs. It's the perfect way to enjoy brisket on a hot day.

YIELD: Serves 4 to 6

METHOD: Deep-frying

PREP TIME: 20 minutes

COOKING TIME:
2 minutes for frying the brisket

HEAT SOURCE: Stove

YOU'LL ALSO NEED:
A deep saucepan; a deep-fry thermometer (optional); a slotted spoon or skimmer

WHAT ELSE: Fish sauce is a malodorous condiment made from fermented anchovies. Look for it in the Asian foods section of your local supermarket.

INGREDIENTS

FOR THE DRESSING

1 clove garlic, peeled and minced

2 tablespoons sugar, plus extra as needed

5 tablespoons freshly squeezed lime juice, plus extra as needed

2 tablespoons Asian fish sauce, plus extra as needed

2 tablespoons cold water

1 teaspoon freshly ground black pepper

FOR THE SALAD

1 cup vegetable oil, or as needed, for frying

½ pound barbecued brisket (see pages 41 to 70), torn into slender shreds

1 seedless cucumber (such as Persian), cut crosswise into ¼-inch slices

2 serrano chiles (preferably red), or to taste, stemmed and thinly sliced crosswise

2 scallions, trimmed, white and green parts thinly sliced on a sharp diagonal

2 cups stemmed mixed fresh herbs, including cilantro, Thai or conventional basil, and fresh peppermint or spearmint (at least two, ideally all three)

3 tablespoons chopped dry-roasted peanuts

1. Place the garlic and 1 teaspoon of the sugar in a small mixing bowl and mash to a paste with the back of a spoon. Add the remaining sugar, lime juice, fish sauce, cold water, and pepper, and whisk until the sugar is dissolved. Correct the seasoning, adding lime juice, fish sauce, and sugar to taste. The dressing should be highly seasoned. The dressing can be made ahead and stored in a sealed container in the refrigerator for up to 1 hour until serving (longer than that and the garlic tends to take over).

2. Just before serving, line a plate with paper towels. Heat the oil in a deep saucepan or wok to 350°F. Working in batches, deep-fry the shredded brisket until sizzling and crisp, 2 minutes. Transfer the brisket with a slotted spoon to the prepared plate to drain.

3. Pour the dressing into a large serving bowl. Stir in the fried brisket shreds. Add the cucumber, chiles, scallions, and herbs. Toss to mix. Sprinkle with the peanuts and serve.

TWO CRISPY ASIAN-FLAVOR BRISKET SALADS

Deep-frying is one of the less familiar ways to cook brisket, but it's definitely one of my favorites (see Vaca Frita, on page 174). I love how the meat acquires a crackling crispness—without losing its soulful smoke flavor. To balance the fat, I like to pair it with cucumbers or other crisp vegetables and tons of aromatic fresh herbs. On these pages I offer two versions—one that riffs on a popular Vietnamese salad, the other with a Singapore-inspired tamarind-based sweet-and-sour dressing. (Tip o' the hat to San Antonio restaurateur Jason Dady for the latter. More on Jason on page 61.) I think of these as salads you eat as finger food, or appetizers you can eat with chopsticks.

SINGAPORE CRISPY BRISKET SALAD

Tamarind makes this salad tart, while hoisin sauce makes it sweet and aromatic, with soy sauce providing the requisite umami flavors and salt. Brisket and pineapple may seem like an odd couple; they're not. Jalapeños crank up the heat; toasted cashews provide the crunch.

INGREDIENTS

FOR THE DRESSING

¼ cup tamarind puree

2 tablespoons soy sauce, plus extra as needed

2 tablespoons hoisin sauce

2 tablespoons sugar, plus extra as needed

FOR THE SALAD

1 cup vegetable oil

½ pound barbecued brisket (see pages 41 to 70), torn into slender shreds

1 seedless cucumber (such as Persian), halved, seeded, and cut crosswise into ¼-inch slices

1 cup diced pineapple (cut into ½-inch cubes)

2 jalapeños, stemmed and thinly sliced crosswise

2 scallions, trimmed, white and green parts thinly sliced on a sharp diagonal

1 cup chopped fresh cilantro leaves

3 tablespoons chopped, toasted cashews (see What Else, page 68), for serving

YIELD: Serves 4 to 6

METHOD: Deep-frying

PREP TIME: 20 minutes

COOKING TIME:
2 minutes for frying the brisket

HEAT SOURCE: Stove

YOU'LL ALSO NEED:
A deep saucepan; a deep-fry thermometer (optional); a slotted spoon or skimmer

WHAT ELSE: Tamarind is a fruit pod that tastes sweet, sour, fruity, and smoky all at once. Look for frozen puree (the easiest form to use) at Asian or Latino markets. To make your own, peel 1 pound of fresh tamarind pods. Place the pulp (seeds and all) in a blender with 2 cups of boiling water. Blend at low speed to obtain a brown puree. Strain it and you're in business.

1. Combine the tamarind puree, soy sauce, hoisin sauce, and sugar in a large bowl and whisk to mix. If too thick, add a spoonful or two of water. Correct the seasoning—the dressing should be sweet, sour, and salty. The dressing can be made 1 hour ahead and stored in a sealed container in the refrigerator.

2. Line a plate with paper towels. Heat the oil in a deep saucepan or wok to 350°F. Working in batches, deep-fry the brisket until sizzling and crisp, 2 minutes. Transfer the brisket with a slotted spoon to the prepared plate to drain.

3. Stir the fried brisket into the dressing. Add the cucumber, pineapple, jalapeños, scallions, and cilantro. Toss to mix. Sprinkle with the cashews and serve.

Chapter 8

BRISKET SANDWICHES

Ever since an inveterate gambler, one John Montagu, had the idea to pile roast beef between bread slices (the better to lunch at the gaming table), the sandwich (Montagu's title was the Earl of Sandwich) has been essential to human happiness. And wherever you find great sandwiches, you're sure to find brisket. The deli would be a glum place without pastrami or corned beef on rye; the world in general would be poorer without the Reuben—that glorious melting pot sandwich of Swiss cheese, German sauerkraut, Russian dressing, and Jewish corned beef (doubled down here with pastrami). To these classics add cross-cultural mash-ups, such as the Texas French Dip (made with Camembert or Brie cheese and barbecued brisket), Southern "cheesesteak" (brisket lavished with homemade pimento cheese), and Vietnamese-style brisket banh mi. The "Smoky Joe"—a saucy chopped brisket sandwich—blows the traditional sloppy Joe off its bun. And speaking of buns, try the Korean-style brisket steamed bun from Hometown Bar-B-Que in Brooklyn.

JAKE'S DOUBLE BRISKET CHEESEBURGERS

The double brisket bratwurst created by sausage master Jake Klein is one of the world wonders of wurst—succulent, spicy, and smoky, with just the right snap to the casing. Nepotism alert: Jake Klein is my stepson, but if you don't believe me, here's how *New York Times* restaurant critic Pete Wells described it: "a phenomenal piece of barbecue, packing more smoke into a sausage than I'd thought possible." That's the good news. The bad news is that the formula is a trade secret, and Jake isn't talking—even to me. He will provide the next best thing—the recipe for his double brisket burgers—made with a similar filling. In addition to being exceedingly tasty, it's one of the rare briskets you can direct grill.

YIELD: Makes 4 burgers

METHOD: Direct grilling

PREP TIME: 10 minutes

COOKING TIME: 6 to 8 minutes

HEAT SOURCE: Grill

YOU'LL ALSO NEED: A grill spatula (but no pressing) and a digital instant-read thermometer

WHAT ELSE: You'll likely need to special-order ground brisket from your local butcher shop. Ask them to grind it from a section containing some of the fattier point. Alternatively, grind your own (you must use a meat grinder, not a food processor). You're looking for a fat content of around 20 percent. And ideally, you'll grill these over wood or a wood-enhanced fire.

INGREDIENTS

FOR THE BURGERS

1½ pounds ground brisket (cut from the fatty point section—you want about 20 percent fat), well chilled

½ pound of your favorite barbecued brisket (see pages 41 to 70), chilled and chopped

Vegetable oil, for oiling the grill grate

Coarse sea salt and freshly ground black pepper

4 thin slices sharp provolone cheese (optional)

FOR SERVING

4 sesame hamburger buns or pretzel rolls, cut in half

2 tablespoons melted butter or Brisket Butter (page 259)

OPTIONAL EMBELLISHMENTS

Lettuce leaves—for example, Boston or butter lettuce

Tomato slices

Dill or sweet pickle chips

Chipotle Mayonnaise (page 186) or your favorite condiments (ketchup, mustard, relish, and so on), for serving

1. Place the ground brisket and chopped cooked brisket in a large bowl and mix with a wooden spoon. Moisten your hands with cold water and form the mixture into four equal patties, each ¾ inch thick. Dimple the center slightly with your thumb (burgers rise more in the center as they cook, so this will help them retain a uniform thickness). Line a plate with plastic wrap, set the burgers on it, and chill in the refrigerator for 1 hour.

2. Set up your grill for direct grilling (see page 81) and heat to high. Brush or scrape the grill grate clean and oil it well.

3. Generously season the burgers on both sides with salt and pepper. Arrange on the grate and grill until the bottoms are sizzling and browned, 3 to 4 minutes. Give each a quarter turn after 1½ minutes so they grill evenly. Flip the burgers and lay the provolone slices (if using) on top. Close the grill lid and continue grilling until the cheese is melted and the burgers are cooked to taste, 3 to 4 minutes more. The USDA recommends an internal temperature of 160°F (medium to medium-well). Cook as your conscience and common sense dictate. Insert the probe of an instant-read thermometer through the *side* of the burger to check it.

4. Meanwhile, brush the cut sides of the buns with butter. Toast the buns, cut sides down, on the grill, about 30 seconds.

5. To assemble the burgers, line the bottom of each toasted bun with a lettuce leaf, if using (this keeps the burger juices from making the bun soggy). Add the burger and any of the remaining embellishments, including Chipotle Mayonnaise or your favorite condiments. Add the top bun and dig in.

DOUBLE-DOWN REUBEN

Invented in 1914, the Reuben has become one of the great American sandwiches. Its melting pot immigrant roots are obvious: Irish American corned beef, German sauerkraut, Swiss cheese, Russian dressing. It took a New York Jewish delicatessen owner—one Arnold Reuben—to put them together. Tradition calls for corned beef, but in recent years I've taken to making my Reubens with pastrami—a twist that adds blasts of garlic, pepper, and wood smoke. The following sandwich uses both meats—the contrast of salty and sweet (cured meats and Russian dressing) and crunchy and gooey (the crisp sauerkraut and melted cheese) remains as wondrous as ever.

YIELD: Makes 2 sandwiches (can be multiplied as desired)

PREP TIME: 10 minutes

COOKING TIME: 5 minutes

HEAT SOURCE: Stove or contact grill

YOU'LL ALSO NEED: A contact grill, sandwich grill, or panini press, or a skillet, griddle, or plancha with a grill press

INGREDIENTS

- 4 slices dark or marbled rye bread
- 2 tablespoons salted butter, at room temperature
- 6 tablespoons Russian Dressing (recipe follows)
- 3 to 4 ounces corned beef (see What Else), sliced paper-thin
- 3 to 4 ounces pastrami beef (see What Else), sliced paper-thin
- ⅔ cup well-drained sauerkraut (see What Else)
- 4 ounces thinly sliced Gruyère cheese

1. Slather two rye bread slices with half the butter and place buttered side down on a plate. Spread the tops of these slices with half the Russian Dressing. Lay the corned beef and pastrami on top of the dressing, followed by the sauerkraut and Gruyère.

2. Spread the remaining two bread slices with the remaining Russian Dressing. Place them dressing side down on the sandwiches and spread the tops with the remaining butter.

3. If using a contact grill, preheat it. Grill the sandwiches until the bread crisps and browns, the cheese melts, and the meats are hot, 3 to 5 minutes. Alternatively, if using a skillet, griddle, or plancha,

WHAT ELSE: With a sandwich this simple, perfection lies in the details. For the ultimate Reuben, you'd use my Classic Corned Beef (page 111) and Old School or New School Pastrami (pages 93 and 100)— thinly sliced. Otherwise, order freshly and thinly sliced meats from your favorite delicatessen. For cheese, I recommend cave-aged Gruyère (it has a lot more bite than generic Swiss cheese). The sauerkraut should be artisanal (use the homemade version on page 240 or source kraut at your local farmers' market). And while you're at it, make your own Russian dressing. And, of course, you'll griddle the rye bread with real butter to give it the requisite richness and crunch.

heat it over medium-high heat. Add the sandwiches and place a grill press on top. Cook until the bread crisps and browns, the cheese melts, and the meats are hot, 3 to 5 minutes per side, carefully turning with a spatula.

4. Cut each sandwich in half on the diagonal and serve at once.

RUSSIAN DRESSING

YIELD: Makes 1⅓ cups

Russian dressing is easy to make from scratch at home, requiring only four ingredients (one of which is pepper). Another bonus: There's no added sugar.

INGREDIENTS

⅔ cup mayonnaise (preferably Hellmann's or Best Foods)

¼ cup chili sauce (such as Heinz)

¼ cup sweet pickle relish

Freshly ground black pepper

Combine the mayonnaise, chili sauce, relish, and black pepper in a bowl and stir to mix.

Russian Dressing will keep, in a sealed jar in the refrigerator, for at least 3 days.

SOUTHERN "CHEESESTEAK"

YIELD: Makes 2 sandwiches (can be multiplied as desired)

METHOD: Pan-frying

PREP TIME: 30 minutes

COOKING TIME: 5 minutes for the poblano pan-fry

HEAT SOURCE: Stove

YOU'LL ALSO NEED: A food processor with grating disk and chopping blade (for pimento cheese)

WHAT ELSE: A fully loaded Philly cheesesteak comes with sautéed onions, mushrooms, and peppers. I've pared the toppings back to keep the focus on the brisket. Sure, you could buy prepared pimento cheese. But it's easy to make from scratch and a lot more flavorful.

I magine if the cheesesteak had originated in Charleston or Dallas, not Philadelphia. You'd top it with spicy pimento cheese in place of Cheez Whiz or provolone. You might light it up with poblanos instead of bell peppers. Above all, you'd make it with barbecued brisket in place of steak so cheap and tough that you have to shave it paper-thin to make it palatable. Well, feast your imagination on this Southern cheesesteak.

INGREDIENTS

FOR THE POBLANO PAN-FRY

2 tablespoons extra virgin olive oil

1 large poblano, stemmed, seeded, and cut into matchstick slivers

1 shallot, thinly sliced crosswise

¼ cup chopped fresh cilantro

FOR ASSEMBLY

2 hoagie rolls

Chipotle Mayonnaise (page 186), regular mayonnaise (preferably Hellmann's or Best Foods), or the condiment of your choice

½ pound hot barbecued brisket (see pages 41 to 70), sliced ¼ inch thick and warm (see Note)

½ cup Made-from-Scratch Pimento Cheese, or to taste (recipe follows)

1. Heat the olive oil in a frying pan over medium-high heat. Add the poblano, shallot, and cilantro and fry until the poblano and shallot are browned at the edges and tender, 3 to 5 minutes. Keep warm.

2. Cut the hoagie rolls almost in half through the sides, opening each like a book. Slather the inside of each with Chipotle Mayonnaise or the condiment of your choice. Add the sliced brisket and poblano pan-fry. Spoon the pimento cheese on top and dig in.

NOTE: There are a couple of ways to reheat brisket: Lightly fry the slices in melted butter or olive oil in a skillet over medium-high heat. Or wrap the brisket in foil and warm it in a 250°F oven.

MADE-FROM-SCRATCH PIMENTO CHEESE

YIELD: Makes 1 cup

Pimento cheese is one of the glories of Southern cuisine— sharp cheddar, tangy Tabasco, creamy mayonnaise, and sweet pimentos pureed to a piquant spread that utterly transforms the common brisket sandwich.

INGREDIENTS

8 ounces aged orange cheddar cheese, chilled

1 jar (2 ounces) pimentos, drained and blotted dry

¼ cup mayonnaise (preferably Hellmann's or Best Foods)

2 tablespoons Dijon mustard

1 tablespoon Tabasco sauce or your favorite hot sauce, or to taste

Sea salt and freshly ground black pepper

1. Coarsely grate the cheese in a food processor. (A grating disk works best for this.)

2. Using the chopping blade, work in the pimentos, mayonnaise, mustard, and hot sauce, running the processor in short bursts. Do not overprocess. The mixture should be coarse, not smooth. Add salt and pepper to taste. The mixture should be highly seasoned.

Made-from-Scratch Pimento Cheese will keep, in a sealed container in the refrigerator, for at least 3 days.

SMOKY JOE
(THE BRISKET SLOPPY JOE SANDWICH)

YIELD: Serves 4

METHOD: Sautéing

PREP TIME: 20 minutes

COOKING TIME:
20 minutes

HEAT SOURCE: Stove;
grill, panini press, or
contact grill for the buns

WHAT ELSE: Traditional
sloppy Joes come on
soft industrial hamburger
buns. You're going to up
the ante by using brioche
rolls that you butter and
grill like garlic bread. For
that matter, you could
also serve the Smoky Joe
on 1-inch-thick slices of
grilled garlic French bread
or Lone Star Toast (page
242).

Remember the sloppy Joe? That sweet, saucy, hamburger-based loose-meat stew ladled onto squishy hamburger buns by the cafeteria ladies at your school? Hardly the stuff of epicurean panegyric. But suppose you replaced the ground beef with chopped smoked brisket? Added barbecue sauce instead of ketchup and cut way back on the sugar? Fortified the mixture with poblano and jalapeño chiles instead of bell peppers? You'd wind up with something you might call the brisket version of pulled pork. Your tailgating buddies will be very glad you thought of it.

INGREDIENTS

FOR THE BRISKET MIXTURE

2 tablespoons butter or
    extra virgin olive oil

3 to 4 large shallots, finely
    chopped (about ¾ cup)

1 poblano chile, stemmed,
    seeded, and finely chopped

2 jalapeños, stemmed,
    seeded, and finely chopped
    (for spicier Smoky Joes,
    leave the seeds in)

¼ cup chopped fresh cilantro

1½ pounds barbecued brisket
    (see pages 41 to 70),
    shredded or chopped

1 cup canned tomato sauce

½ cup of your favorite barbecue
    sauce (I'm partial to the
    Chipotle Molasses Barbecue
    Sauce on page 248)

2 tablespoons Worcestershire
    sauce

2 tablespoons brown sugar
    (optional)

Sea salt and freshly ground
    black pepper

FOR SERVING

4 tablespoons (½ stick) butter

1 clove garlic, minced

2 tablespoons chopped fresh
    cilantro or parsley

4 brioche buns, cut in half
    crosswise

Sweet pickle chips or dill pickle
    chips (optional)

1. Heat the butter or oil in a skillet. Add the shallots, poblano, jalapeños, and cilantro and cook over medium-high heat until sizzling and browned, 4 minutes.

2. Stir in the brisket and cook, stirring occasionally, until browned, 3 to 4 minutes. Stir in the tomato sauce, barbecue sauce, Worcestershire sauce, brown sugar (if you like your Smoky Joes sweet), and salt and pepper to taste. Simmer the mixture until thick and richly flavored, 10 minutes.

3. Meanwhile, make the garlic butter: Melt the butter in a small saucepan. Add the garlic, cilantro, and a pinch of salt and cook until the garlic is fragrant and golden, 2 minutes. Don't let it burn. Brush the cut sides of the buns with the garlic butter.

4. Set up your grill for direct grilling (see page 81) and heat to high, or heat a contact grill or panini press. Grill the buns, cut sides down, until toasted, 30 seconds to 1 minute.

5. To serve, spoon the Smoky Joe mixture onto the toasted buns. Top with pickle chips, if desired, and dig in.

TEXAS FRENCH DIP SANDWICH

Name notwithstanding, the French dip sandwich originated not in Paris or Lyon, but at a sandwich shop in Los Angeles. The year was 1918. The place: Philippe the Original (still in business on Alameda across from Union Station in downtown LA). The inventor, one Philippe Mathieu, was indeed a Frenchman, who, as legend has it, accidentally dropped a roll into a pan of roast beef drippings while preparing a sandwich for a local policeman. The cop ate it anyway and returned the next day to order another one. The "French dip" sandwich quickly became the house specialty and it remains so to this day. You're about to give it a Texas twist by replacing the roast beef with—you guessed it—barbecued brisket. To reinforce the smoke flavor, I suggest a nontraditional

YIELD: Serves 2 (can be multiplied as desired)

METHOD: Boiling

PREP TIME: 15 minutes

COOKING TIME:
5 minutes

HEAT SOURCE: Stove

condiment—Chipotle Mayonnaise. The cheese isn't traditional, but I like the way it rounds out the sandwich. In keeping with Mathieu's origins, I suggest Camembert or Brie.

INGREDIENTS

1 crusty baguette, cut in half crosswise, or 2 mini baguettes or soft French bread rolls

4 to 6 tablespoons Chipotle Mayonnaise (page 186)

½ pound thinly sliced barbecued brisket (see pages 41 to 70), at room temperature or warm (see Note, page 217)

6 ounces Camembert or Brie cheese (optional), at room temperature—it is very important to use cheese that isn't cold

2 cups beef broth or stock (preferably homemade or low-sodium; see What Else)

2 tablespoons brisket drippings (optional)

Sea salt and freshly ground black pepper

1. Cut each piece of bread almost in half through one side and open it like a book. Spread the inside of each on the top and bottom with Chipotle Mayonnaise, and layer in the sliced brisket and cheese.

2. Meanwhile, bring the beef broth and brisket drippings, if using, to a boil in a saucepan over medium-high heat. Add salt and pepper to taste. The broth should be highly seasoned. Transfer the broth to two deep bowls.

3. Serve the sandwiches with bowls of piping-hot broth for dipping. When you get it right, the hot broth will heat the brisket and melt the cheese.

WHAT ELSE: In the best of all possible worlds, you'd dip the sandwich in homemade beef stock reinforced with brisket drippings. There are several options in this book: the Jewish Deli Brisket broth on page 136, for example; the Bollito Misto broth on page 167; or the Basic Brisket Broth on page 254. Alternatively, use a good commercial beef broth—preferably low-sodium. Note: Tradition calls for a soft French roll, but I prefer a crusty baguette.

BRISKET BANH MI

Vietnam's banh mi occupies a sacred place in the world's sandwich pantheon—meaty pâté, crisp lettuce, and sweet-sour carrot and radish slaw, all piled onto a crusty baguette (the latter a legacy of the French, who occupied Vietnam for a century). And that's *before* you add the fireworks of sliced chiles, fresh cilantro, and Sriracha Mayonnaise. In other words, it's a kaleidoscope of aromas, textures, and tastes. The following banh mi was inspired by one of my favorite Los Angeles carry-outs, Gjelina Take Away, in Venice. They use braised brisket, but I've taken the smoky route with Texas-style barbecued brisket.

YIELD: Serves 2 (can be multiplied as desired)

METHOD: Pickling for the slaw

PREP TIME: 20 minutes

COOKING TIME: 30 minutes for marinating the slaw

WHAT ELSE: This banh mi calls for barbecued brisket, but you could also use a braised brisket from chapter 4 (I suggest the Jewish Deli Brisket on page 136). For even more flavor, replace the sliced cucumber with the Korean Cucumber Salad on page 237.

INGREDIENTS

FOR THE VIETNAMESE SLAW

2 carrots, trimmed, peeled, and cut into matchstick slivers

1 medium-size daikon radish (about 8 ounces), peeled and cut into matchstick slivers

½ teaspoon sea salt

3 tablespoons sugar

½ cup rice vinegar

1 tablespoon Asian fish sauce

2 allspice berries, lightly crushed

Freshly ground black pepper

TO FINISH THE SANDWICHES

1 large crusty baguette, cut in half crosswise, or 2 mini baguettes

4 to 6 tablespoons Sriracha Mayonnaise (see page 224)

1 head Boston lettuce, separated into leaves, washed, and spun dry

1 cucumber (preferably Kirby), thinly sliced

6 to 8 ounces your favorite barbecued brisket (see pages 41 to 70), thinly sliced

8 sprigs fresh cilantro, washed and shaken dry

1 scallion, trimmed, white and green parts thinly sliced on a sharp diagonal

1 to 2 jalapeños, stemmed and sliced paper-thin (for milder banh mi, remove the seeds)

1. Make the Vietnamese slaw: Place the carrots and daikon in a mixing bowl and stir in the salt and sugar. Let the vegetables marinate for 5 minutes. Add the rice vinegar, fish sauce, allspice berries, and pepper, and stir until the sugar dissolves. Let the slaw marinate for at least 30 minutes or as long as overnight (cover and refrigerate until serving). Discard the allspice berries before serving.

2. Cut each piece of bread almost in half through one side and open like a book. Slather the insides of each piece with Sriracha Mayonnaise and line with lettuce and sliced cucumber. Pile on the brisket. Add the slaw with some of the juices, and cilantro, scallion, and sliced jalapeños. Close the sandwiches if you can and get ready for one of the best East-West flavor fusions on Planet Barbecue.

SRIRACHA MAYONNAISE

YIELD: Makes 1 cup

Sriracha Mayonnaise gives this banh mi the perfect dose of creaminess, piquancy, and spice. It's pretty compelling slathered on brisket sandwiches of all stripes.

INGREDIENTS

¾ cup mayonnaise (preferably Hellmann's or Best Foods)

3 tablespoons sriracha

½ teaspoon finely grated lime zest

1 tablespoon freshly squeezed lime juice

Combine the ingredients in a bowl and whisk to mix.

Sriracha Mayonnaise will keep, in a sealed container in the refrigerator, for at least 3 days.

BRISKET WHISPERER—BILLY DURNEY

Billy Durney remembers the exact moment he took barbecue as the true religion: "I walked into Louie Mueller Barbecue in Taylor, Texas. One bite of brisket and I knew—this is who I want to be and this will be my life's work."

So the security expert (a former bodyguard for Oscar-nominated actresses and Grammy Award–winning musicians) found a century-old former woodworker's warehouse in Red Hook, Brooklyn—vacant for decades—and turned it into a cavernous dining room fitted with timbers and paneling from an antique barn. He installed an Ole Hickory carousel smoker in the back corner and parked an oversize Lang barrel smoker by the front door. He perfected his brisket recipe and hired local bands for entertainment.

Then Hurricane Sandy struck, flooding his dining room with 6 feet of water. The restoration took more than a year, and Hometown formally opened on September 12, 2013. By the end of the week, they had waiting lines and were selling out of meat.

Like most of the new wave pit masters, Durney takes an ecumenical approach, cooking his ribs St. Louis–style and his pork shoulders in the manner of North Carolina. He powers the house hot sauce with Thai sriracha. He serves barbecued lamb belly Vietnamese banh mi–style— with house pickles on a crusty baguette.

But the heart and soul of Hometown is the brisket. Coal-black slabs of steaming meat so smoky it smells like a fireplace and so moist it squirts when you cut into it. Tender? Let's just say you can cut it with the side of a fork.

The secret? "We start with Niman Ranch natural briskets and use only two seasonings: salt and pepper," explains Durney. "We burn white oak in our pits. We cook hotter than most restaurants—275°F—and we smoke for up to 15 hours."

Of course, great brisket is made not just with seasonings and wood smoke, but with the dozens of personal touches developed over time and experience. Durney cooks his slabs on rectangles of perforated cardboard—a way to protect the lean meat of the flat from drying out or burning on the hot grate. (See box on page 30.)

"Resting the meat is one of the most important things you can do to ensure moist, tender brisket," says Durney. Hometown's rests for 5 hours in a professional meat warmer called an Alto-Shaam. At home, Durney recommends a minimum 2-hour rest in an insulated cooler.

So how do you know when the brisket is ready? "We never use a meat thermometer," explains Durney. "It's all done by touch and feel. Poke each slab (wear heatproof gloves) and watch how it jiggles. Imagine Jell-O comprised of animal protein and beef fat. *That's* how a properly cooked brisket should feel."

BRISKET STEAMED BUNS

YIELD: Makes 12 buns, enough to serve 4 to 6

METHOD: Steaming (for the buns)

PREP TIME: 20 minutes

COOKING TIME: 10 minutes

HEAT SOURCE: Stove

YOU'LL ALSO NEED: A bamboo steamer; parchment paper; a wok or pot

WHAT ELSE: The easiest way to source steamed buns is frozen from an Asian market. While you're at it, buy some *gochujang* (Korean chile paste). *Sambal oelek* is a fiery chili sauce from Indonesia—sriracha will work in a pinch. Note: The traditional way to warm the buns is in a Chinese bamboo steamer over a wok. Line the steamer with a circle of parchment paper to keep the buns from sticking.

I n Texas (and Brooklyn) the traditional bread served with brisket is a soft puffy white industrial loaf, like Wonder Bread. (An oddly ignominious accompaniment, I've always thought, for this noble slab of steer.) The Asian equivalent is the steamed bun, which is equally soft and puffy, but with more chew and cachet. Billy Durney of Hometown Bar-B-Que in Brooklyn (see page 225) normally packs steamed buns with barbecued lamb belly or short ribs. He created the following brisket steamed bun for *The Brisket Chronicles*. Think smoky beef, sweet-salty barbecue sauce, and pickled cucumbers for crunch. In other words, think heaven on earth on a steamed bun.

INGREDIENTS

12 Asian-style steamed buns, thawed if frozen

1½ pounds your favorite barbecued brisket (see pages 41 to 70), thinly sliced and warm (see Note, page 217)

1 batch Korean Cucumber Salad (page 237) or 2 Kirby cucumbers, thinly sliced

4 scallions, trimmed, white and green parts thinly sliced on a sharp diagonal

3 tablespoons toasted sesame seeds (see What Else, page 68), for serving

Korean Barbecue Sauce (recipe follows), for serving

Sriracha or *sambal oelek*, for serving (optional; see What Else)

1. Set up a bamboo steamer lined with parchment paper over a wok or pot (see page 96). Add the buns and steam until hot, 5 to 10 minutes.

2. Open each bun and add a slice of brisket, a spoonful of cucumber salad (or a couple of cucumber slices), scallions, sesame seeds, and a generous dollop of Korean Barbecue Sauce. If you like spice, add a drizzle of sriracha or a smear of *sambal oelek*.

3. Enjoy immediately, while the buns are piping hot.

KOREAN BARBECUE SAUCE

YIELD: Makes 2 cups

first wrote about Korean barbecue more than 20 years ago, in *The Barbecue! Bible*. But it took a Los Angeles food truck operator turned restaurateur—Roy Choi, creator of the Kogi BBQ taco—to make it a national food fetish. Like its Kansas City counterpart, Korean barbecue plays sweet against salty against spicy (in this case, brown sugar, soy sauce, and ginger). The fireworks come from a Korean chile paste called *gochujang*. If you like a pronounced umami flavor and tongue-tingling heat, this Korean barbecue sauce is your new best friend.

INGREDIENTS

- 1 tablespoon toasted (dark) sesame oil
- A ½-inch piece fresh ginger, peeled and minced
- 1 clove garlic, peeled and minced
- ¼ cup rice vinegar, plus extra as needed
- ½ cup tamari soy sauce, plus extra as needed
- ½ cup brown sugar, preferably dark, plus extra as needed
- ⅓ cup *gochujang* (Korean chile paste)
- 1 teaspoon freshly ground black pepper

Heat the sesame oil in a small saucepan. Add the ginger and garlic and cook over medium heat until lightly browned, 2 minutes. Stir in the rice vinegar and bring to a boil. Stir in the tamari, ⅓ cup water, brown sugar, *gochujang*, and black pepper and bring to a boil. Gently simmer the sauce, whisking from time to time, until richly flavored, 5 to 8 minutes. If sauce is too thick, thin it with a little water. Correct the seasoning, adding more tamari, vinegar, or sugar to taste. The sauce should be a little sweet and a little salty with just a touch of acidity.

Korean Barbecue Sauce will keep, in a sealed container in the refrigerator, for at least 1 week.

Chapter 9
BRISKET SIDES

Tradition calls for certain sacrosanct side dishes to accompany brisket. You know the suspects: baked beans, coleslaw, some sort of potato. What you may not realize is how much brisket itself can enhance a conventional side dish. Baked beans? Obvious. Baked beans laced with smoky brisket chunks? Inspired. Ditto baked stuffed potatoes, which you, barbecue fiend, are going to enrich with burnt ends. Other sides are designed to counterpoint brisket's belt-loosening richness. Like the cool, crisp cucumber salad served with Korean grilled brisket, or the most innovative cucumber salad of all—the buttermilk, cuke, and rye berry salad served with the New School pastrami sandwich at Harry & Ida's Meat & Supply Co. in New York. The dishes in this chapter may be served on the side, but when it comes to big flavors, they definitely take center stage.

BRISKET-STUFFED BAKERS
(BAKED POTATOES)

YIELD: Makes 8 halves, enough to serve 8 (or 4 really hungry people as a main course)

METHOD: Indirect grilling

PREP TIME: 15 minutes

COOKING TIME: 1½ hours

HEAT SOURCE: Grill

YOU'LL ALSO NEED: 2 hardwood chunks or 1½ cups chips (if using the latter, soak in water to cover for 30 minutes, then drain); a vegetable brush; a bamboo or metal skewer (for testing doneness)

WHAT ELSE: Don't have a grill or it's too cold and snowy to fire it up? You can certainly bake these in the oven. You just won't get a smoke flavor. I call for Gruyère cheese here (ideally, cave-aged), but white cheddar makes awesome stuffers, too. Ditto for smoked cheese—especially when you're cooking the potatoes indoors. Note: Sometimes I sauté thinly sliced shallots or onions in place of the scallions.

Bacon and baked potatoes are longstanding bedfellows. But spuds stuffed with smoked brisket? Well, it was only a matter of time before someone brought them together. Brisket makes these larger-than-life bakers beefy and smoky, with scallions and Gruyère cheese rising to a flavor crescendo. They may just be the most outrageous stuffed baked potatoes on Planet Barbecue.

INGREDIENTS

FOR THE POTATOES

Vegetable oil, for oiling the grill grate

4 jumbo baking potatoes (14 to 16 ounces each)

2 tablespoons Brisket Butter (page 259), melted butter, or extra virgin olive oil, for brushing the skins

Coarse sea salt and freshly ground black pepper

FOR THE STUFFING

2 tablespoons butter, Brisket Butter (page 259), or extra virgin olive oil, plus 2 tablespoons butter, thinly sliced, for topping

1 bunch of scallions, trimmed and thinly sliced crosswise (set aside 3 tablespoons of the green parts for garnish)

1 cup shredded or chopped barbecued brisket (see pages 41 to 70)

3 cups (12 ounces) coarsely grated cave-aged Gruyère or white cheddar

¾ cup sour cream

Sea salt and freshly ground black pepper

Pimentón (Spanish smoked paprika), for sprinkling

1. Set up your grill for indirect grilling see page 22) and heat to medium-high. Brush or scrape the grill grate clean and oil it well.

2. Scrub the potatoes thoroughly with a vegetable brush. Rinse well and blot dry with paper towels. Prick the skin of each potato all over 4 to 6 times with a fork.

(This vents the potatoes and prevents them from exploding from steam buildup.) Brush the potatoes on all sides with the Brisket Butter and season very generously with salt and pepper.

3. Place the potatoes on the grill over the drip pan away from the heat. Toss the wood chips on the coals or, if using a gas grill, place in the smoker box. Cover the grill. Smoke-roast the potatoes until tender, about 1 hour. To test for doneness, pierce a potato through the top with a skewer. It should pierce easily. Transfer the potatoes to a cutting board and let cool slightly (cool enough to handle but still hot).

4. Meanwhile, make the stuffing: Melt 2 tablespoons of butter or heat 2 tablespoons of olive oil in a large saucepan over medium-high heat. Add the sliced scallions and cook, stirring occasionally, until lightly browned, 4 minutes. Remove the pan from the heat and let it cool to room temperature.

5. Cut each cooked potato in half lengthwise. Using a spoon, scrape out most of the potato flesh, leaving a ¼-inch-thick wall next to the skin. Very roughly chop the scooped potato flesh and place it in the saucepan with the scallions. Gently stir in the brisket, 2 cups of the grated cheese, the sour cream, and salt and pepper to taste. The mixture should be highly seasoned. Stir as little as possible to leave some texture to the potatoes.

6. Scoop the potato mixture back into the potato skins, mounding it in the center of each. Sprinkle the remaining cheese over the potatoes and top with the 2 tablespoons thinly sliced butter. Sprinkle each stuffed potato with pimentón. The potatoes can be prepared up to 24 hours ahead to this stage, covered with plastic wrap, and refrigerated.

7. Just before serving, reheat the potatoes on your grill (still set up for indirect grilling) until the stuffing is browned and bubbling, 20 to 30 minutes, or as needed. Sprinkle with the reserved scallion greens and dig in!

BRISKET BAKED BEANS
(FOUR BEANS, MUCHO BRISKET)

Like barbecued brisket, baked beans have deep roots in American food culture. Native Americans cooked them with maple sap and bear fat, using fire-scorched stones for heat. European colonists adopted the dish, adding salt pork for fat and molasses as a sweetener. Today, baked beans are inextricably woven into the fabric of American barbecue and they're about to get a lot better. With brisket. Lots of brisket. This is a great place to use up all those burnt ends and brisket trimmings. Sweet, salty, smoky, and, above all, meaty, these are everything you hunger for in baked beans—and more.

YIELD: Makes 12 cups; serves 10 to 12

METHOD: Smoking (though you can also indirect grill or bake the beans)

PREP TIME: 20 minutes

COOKING TIME: 1½ to 2 hours

HEAT SOURCE: Smoker (or grill or oven)

YOU'LL ALSO NEED: A Dutch oven or heavy-bottomed pot with a tight-fitting lid or a large heavy-duty aluminum foil roasting pan

INGREDIENTS

4 strips thick-sliced artisanal bacon, such as Nueske's, cut crosswise into ¼-inch slivers

1 large onion, peeled and cut into ¼-inch dice

1 poblano chile, stemmed, seeded, and cut into ¼-inch dice

1 red or yellow bell pepper, stemmed, seeded, and cut into ¼-inch dice

3 jalapeños, stemmed, seeded, and diced

2 cloves garlic, peeled and minced

½ cup chopped fresh cilantro

1 can (15 ounces) baked beans (preferably organic) with can juices

1 can (15 ounces) black beans (preferably organic), drained

1 can (15 ounces) red kidney beans (preferably organic), drained

1 can (15 ounces) navy beans (preferably organic), drained

1½ cups your favorite sweet red barbecue sauce (for options, see pages 53, 77, and 248)

⅔ cup packed brown sugar, plus extra as needed

½ cup dark beer, plus extra as needed

⅓ cup Dijon mustard

2 cups chopped barbecued brisket (see pages 41 to 70)

Coarse salt (sea or kosher) and freshly ground black pepper

WHAT ELSE: Sure, you can simmer or bake the beans in a large pot (see Variations), and you'll get good smoke flavor from the brisket. But for even more smoke flavor, barbecue them in an open Dutch oven (or a large, heavy-duty aluminum foil pan) in your smoker. As you cook your way through the recipes in this book, you'll make a lot of brisket. I hope you'll accumulate the trimmings and odd pieces in the freezer, so you always have brisket on hand for this and the other recipes in this chapter. Note: You drain the canned beans, but not the canned baked beans.

1. Place the bacon in a large Dutch oven or heavy-bottomed pot. Place over medium-high heat and cook, stirring occasionally, until sizzling and golden, 3 minutes.

2. Add the onion, poblano, bell pepper, jalapeños, garlic, and ¼ cup of the chopped cilantro and cook, stirring occasionally, until lightly browned 3 to 4 minutes more.

3. Stir the beans into the bacon mixture. Stir in the barbecue sauce, sugar, beer, mustard, and brisket. You can cook the beans in the Dutch oven, or transfer them to a large heavy-duty aluminum foil roasting pan.

4. Set up your smoker following the manufacturer's instructions and heat to 275°F. Smoke the beans, uncovered, until thick, concentrated, and richly flavored, 1½ to 2 hours. If they start to dry out, stir in a little water or more dark beer and put the lid on the Dutch oven or cover the pan tightly with aluminum foil.

5. Correct the seasoning, adding salt, pepper, or sugar to taste. The beans should be very flavorful. Sprinkle the remaining ¼ cup chopped cilantro on top. Dig in!

Brisket Baked Beans will keep, in a sealed container in the refrigerator, for at least 3 days.

VARIATIONS

Grill method: Set up your grill for indirect grilling (see page 22) and heat to medium. If using a charcoal grill, toss 1½ cups wood chips (soaked in water to cover for 30 minutes, then drained) or 2 hardwood chunks on the coals. If using a gas grill, place wood chunks under the grate over the heat diffusers. In step 4, smoke-roast the beans, uncovered, until they are thick, concentrated, and richly flavored, 40 to 60 minutes.

Oven method: Preheat the oven to 275°F. In step 4, bake the beans, uncovered, until thick, concentrated, and richly flavored, 1½ to 2 hours.

BRISKET YORKSHIRE PUDDING

Yorkshire pudding. Dutch babies. Popovers. Three names for one simple eye-popping pastry—a flour, milk, and egg batter traditionally enriched with roast beef drippings and baked to a towering puff. Did someone say drippings? As good as roast beef drippings are, nothing rivals brisket drippings. Same luscious beefy flavor, but aromatized with wood smoke.

YIELD: Makes 1 Yorkshire pudding (serves 4 to 6)

METHOD: Baking

PREP TIME: 10 minutes

COOKING TIME: 30 to 40 minutes

HEAT SOURCE: Oven

YOU'LL ALSO NEED: A 10-inch cast-iron skillet

WHAT ELSE: This recipe produces a single magisterial Yorkshire pudding, but you can also bake the batter in popover molds to make 6 individual popovers; see the Variation.

INGREDIENTS

6 large eggs (preferably farm-fresh and organic)

2¼ cups cold milk (preferably whole milk)

1 teaspoon sea salt or kosher salt

½ teaspoon freshly ground black pepper

2 cups unbleached all-purpose flour

¼ cup brisket drippings, Brisket Butter (page 259), or melted butter

½ cup finely chopped barbecued brisket (see pages 41 to 70)

1. Combine the eggs, milk, salt, and pepper in a large mixing bowl and whisk or blend to mix. Whisk in the flour and 3 tablespoons of the brisket drippings. Stir in the chopped brisket. Chill the mixture, covered, in the refrigerator for at least 2 hours, or overnight. (For a crispier crust and less dense pudding, allow the batter to sit at room temperature for an hour after chilling and before baking.)

2. Preheat the oven to 450°F.

3. Use the remaining tablespoon of brisket drippings to grease the bottom and side of a 10-inch cast-iron skillet. (Tilt the pan to coat it.) Place the skillet in the oven and heat for 5 minutes.

4. Remove the hot pan and carefully pour the batter into it. Return the pan to the oven and bake for 10 minutes, then lower the heat to 400°F. Continue baking until the pudding is dramatically puffed and handsomely browned on top, about 20 minutes more. Don't open the oven door to peek—at least not for the first 20 minutes, or the cool air will deflate the pudding.

5. Cut the pudding into wedges and serve immediately.

VARIATION

Brisket Popovers: Prepare the pudding batter as directed. In step 3, use the remaining tablespoon of brisket drippings to grease the bottom and sides of a 6-cup popover pan. Place the pan in the oven and heat for 5 minutes. Bake as directed in step 4. Remove the popovers from the pan and serve immediately.

KOREAN CUCUMBER SALAD

This spicy cucumber salad is part of the *banchan*—a table-burying condiment and salad selection—that invariably accompanies Korean barbecue (see page 83). Like the kosher dills traditionally served with pastrami and the sauerkraut piled on corned beef, these crisp sweet-sour cucumber slices bring contrapuntal fire and crunch to the meaty chew of the brisket.

YIELD: Serves 4

PREP TIME: 10 minutes

WHAT ELSE: You want a cucumber with a high flesh-to-seed ratio, like a Kirby, Persian, or European cucumber. Barring that, use conventional cucumbers: Cut them in half lengthwise, scoop out the seeds with a spoon, and thinly slice crosswise. *Gochugaru* is a Korean hot pepper powder. (It's hot, but not brutally so.) Look for it at an Asian market or substitute hot paprika.

INGREDIENTS

2 to 3 Kirby or Persian cucumbers or 1 European cucumber, trimmed and thinly sliced crosswise (2 cups)

2 tablespoons sugar, or as needed

1 tablespoon Korean hot pepper powder (*gochugaru*) or hot paprika

2 tablespoons rice vinegar, or as needed

Sea salt or kosher salt

Place the cucumbers, sugar, and hot pepper powder in a mixing bowl and toss to coat. Let stand for 5 minutes. Stir in the vinegar and add salt to taste. The cucumbers should be a little sweet, a little sour, and pugnacious without quite being incendiary.

Store Korean Cucumber Salad in a sealed container in the refrigerator for 2 days. It tastes best served the day it's made.

A trio of crunchy-crisp salads (clockwise from left): Vietnamese Slaw (page 223), Korean Cucumber Salad (page 237), and Cucumber, Buttermilk, and Rye Berry Salad

CUCUMBER, BUTTERMILK, AND RYE BERRY SALAD

Pastrami and other brisket dishes have a natural affinity for cucumbers and rye. How else do you explain our collective fondness for pickles with pastrami and corned beef, and rye as their preferred sandwich bread? Cukes and rye come together in this cool, crisp, piquant salad, which is served with the extraordinary pastrami sandwiches at Harry & Ida's Meat & Supply Co. in New York—the perfect foil for the fatty richness of the meat.

INGREDIENTS

1 cup rye berries (see What Else)

2 European cucumbers or 4 to 6 Persian cucumbers, trimmed and thinly sliced crosswise (3 to 4 cups)

1 small red onion, peeled, halved, and sliced crosswise paper-thin

½ cup buttermilk

½ teaspoon finely grated lemon zest

2 tablespoons freshly squeezed lemon juice, or to taste

½ teaspoon caraway seeds

Sea salt and freshly ground black pepper

YIELD: Serves 4 to 6

PREP TIME: 15 minutes, plus 1 day for soaking the rye berries

COOKING TIME: 1 to 1½ hours for cooking the rye berries

HEAT SOURCE: Stove

WHAT ELSE: You can buy rye berries (unground rye grain) in bulk at Whole Foods and other natural foods markets. Note: You'll need to soak the rye berries for a day, so plan accordingly.

As in the previous recipe, you want a cucumber with a high ratio of flesh to seeds. European cucumbers (aka hothouse cucumbers)—the sort sold individually shrink-wrapped in plastic—come to mind. So do Persian cukes and small Kirbys. If using conventional cucumbers, peel and seed them as described on page 237.

1. Place the rye berries in a large bowl with cold water to cover by 4 inches. Let soak in the refrigerator for 24 hours.

2. Drain the rye berries. Place in a large pot with water to cover by 3 inches. Boil until just tender, 1 to 1½ hours. Drain the rye berries in a colander and rinse with cold water until cool. Drain again and transfer to a mixing bowl. (The berries can be cooked up to 2 days ahead, then covered and refrigerated.)

3. Stir in the cucumbers, onion, buttermilk, lemon zest, lemon juice, and caraway seeds. Add salt and pepper to taste— the salad should be highly seasoned.

Store Cucumber, Buttermilk, and Rye Berry Salad in a sealed container in the refrigerator. It tastes best served the day it's made.

MADE-FROM-SCRATCH SAUERKRAUT

YIELD: Makes 4 to 6 cups

PREP TIME: 15 minutes

COOKING TIME: 4 hours for salting the cabbage, plus 2 to 4 weeks for curing the sauerkraut

YOU'LL ALSO NEED: A cabbage shredder, mandoline, or food processor with a slicing disk; a large ceramic crock (about 1 gallon); a clean cotton cloth

WHAT ELSE: I prefer sauerkraut with a kick, so I like to add jalapeños and black peppercorns. The purist can certainly omit them. For a more delicate kraut, use savoy cabbage in place of the green cabbage.

Sauerkraut traditionally accompanies two of the world's greatest incarnations of brisket—corned beef and pastrami. Sure, you can buy commercial kraut, but it's easy and immensely satisfying to make your own.

INGREDIENTS

3 pounds (1 to 2 heads) green cabbage

1 to 2 jalapeños, stemmed and thinly sliced (optional)

3 tablespoons coarse sea salt

2 teaspoons caraway seeds

2 teaspoons juniper berries, lightly crushed with the side of a knife

2 teaspoons whole black peppercorns

Spring water

1. Cut each cabbage in quarters from top to bottom using a large chef's knife. Cut out and discard the core. Remove any wilted or blemished leaves. Slice the cabbage crosswise into very thin ribbons by hand, on a cabbage shredder or a mandoline, or in a food processor fitted with a slicing disk.

2. Place the sliced cabbage in a large mixing bowl and sprinkle with the jalapeños (if using), salt, caraway seeds, juniper berries, and peppercorns. Mix well, kneading with your hands. The idea is to bruise the cabbage so it releases its liquid more readily. Lay plastic wrap directly on top of the cabbage, then place a heavy dinner plate or a saucepan filled with canned goods on top of it to act as a weight. Let the pressed mixture macerate at room temperature for 4 hours. The cabbage should feel moist and spongy.

3. Transfer the cabbage mixture to a clean crock and pack it as tightly as possible. Place a clean weight, like a heavy dinner plate, on top. This weight helps force the water out of the cabbage and keep it submerged in the brine. Cover the crock with a clean cotton cloth to keep out airborne debris.

4. Allow the cabbage to ferment in a cool, dark cabinet or basement (60° to 70°F is ideal) overnight, then check it: If the cabbage is not completely submerged in brine, add enough spring water to cover. Replace the weight, cover the crock again, and return it to a cool, dark place to continue fermenting. Check the kraut daily. Sometimes mold appears on the surface of the brine. Skim as much as you can off the surface—it may break up and you might not be able to remove all of it. Don't worry about it—it's just a surface phenomenon. The sauerkraut itself is under the anaerobic protection of the brine.

5. Taste the cabbage every 4 to 5 days. It will start to taste like sauerkraut after about a week. The flavor will continue to deepen over time. The fermentation process typically takes 2 to 4 weeks, though the exact duration will depend on the time of year and precise storage conditions. Once you get the amount of "funk" you like, remove the weight. Your sauerkraut is ready to serve.

Made-From-Scratch Sauerkraut will keep, with its juices, in sealed jars in the refrigerator, for several months.

Pack the shredded cabbage as tightly as possible in an earthenware crock.

LONE STAR TOAST
(GRILLED GARLIC BREAD)

YIELD: Makes 12 slices, enough to serve 6 to 12

METHOD: Direct grilling

PREP TIME: 10 minutes

COOKING TIME: Quick—2 minutes per side

HEAT SOURCE: Charcoal, gas, or wood-burning grill

Lone Star toast is Texan for grilled garlic bread. You'll want a Pullman or country-style loaf—white bread with a denser crumb than the factory white bread that usually accompanies Texas brisket. Buy it at a local bakery. In a pinch, you could use Pepperidge Farm.

INGREDIENTS

FOR THE GARLIC BUTTER

3 cloves garlic, peeled and minced

½ teaspoon sea salt

½ teaspoon freshly ground black pepper

12 tablespoons (1½ sticks) unsalted butter, at room temperature

3 tablespoons minced fresh flat-leaf (Italian) parsley or chives

FOR THE GRILLED BREAD

1 country-style loaf or Pullman white bread, cut crosswise into ¾-inch-thick slices

Vegetable oil, for oiling the grill

1. Place the garlic, salt, and pepper in the bottom of a mixing bowl and mash to a paste with the back of a spoon. Add the butter and parsley or chives and whisk until smooth. Note: Do not use a food processor, or you'll turn the butter green.

2. Using a palette knife or butter knife, spread the bread slices on *both* sides with a thin, even layer of garlic butter.

3. Set up your grill for direct grilling (see page 81) and heat to medium-high. Brush or scrape the grill grate clean and oil it well. Be sure to leave a fire-free safety zone—a section of the grill that is not lit or burning—in case a flare-up occurs or the bread starts to burn.

4. Arrange the bread slices on the grill. Grill until sizzling and golden brown on both sides, 1 to 2 minutes per side, turning with tongs. Serve immediately, hot off the grill.

Chapter 10

A BRISKET MISCELLANY

Somewhere between the brisket kettle corn served at Loro restaurant and the brisket chocolate chip cookies dished up at the LeRoy and Lewis food truck, Austin's barbecue scene went loco. Brisket now turns up not just on meat plates and sandwiches, but in dishes where you'd never expect it. True, the smoky, spicy succulence of Texas's favorite barbecued meat makes everything taste better. But dessert? Yes, even dessert. This chapter looks at some of the more offbeat uses for brisket—actual dishes served by respected pit masters in one of the most brisket-obsessed states in the Union.

In the following pages, you'll also find formulas for barbecue rubs and sauces. Brisket butter? What else would you slather on grilled bread? Brisket broth? You'll find it here, too.

DALMATIAN RUB

YIELD: Makes 1 cup

PREP TIME: 5 minutes

WHAT ELSE: I make my Dalmatian rub with coarse sea salt and cracked black peppercorns, with a handful of hot red pepper flakes for heat.

Dalmatian rub is the name given to that simple mixture of salt and pepper used by pit masters across Texas. (Black and white, the coloring of a Dalmatian—get it?) Elegant in its simplicity, it's in no way simpleminded, because depending on the salt (kosher or sea, coarse or fine) and the pepper grind (cracked, coarsely ground, 16 mesh, or finer), the resulting brisket will have a very different bark and taste. And that's before you add additional flavorings, such as sesame seeds or hot red pepper flakes (the latter making it a newspaper rub—black and white and "read" all over). Here's the basic formula. Tweak it to suit your taste.

INGREDIENTS

½ cup salt (coarse, fine, kosher, sea, smoked, and so on)

½ cup black pepper (cracked, coarse, fine, and so on)

OPTIONAL FLAVORINGS (ADD ANY ONE OR TWO OF THE FOLLOWING)

¼ cup hot red pepper flakes

¼ cup sesame seeds (white, toasted white, or black)

2 to 4 tablespoons chili powder

1 tablespoon ground cumin

Combine the ingredients in a bowl and mix with your fingers.

Dalmatian Rub will keep, in a sealed jar away from heat or light, for several weeks.

RAICHLEN'S RUB
(AKA YOUR BASIC BARBECUE RUB OR 4/4 RUB)

This is it, folks. The only barbecue rub you'll ever need—both basic and universal. I call it a 4/4 rub because it requires only 4 basic ingredients in equal proportions: salt, pepper, paprika, and brown sugar. And Raichlen's Rub because it's my go-to seasoning at home. This simple rub is infinitely customizable: Use smoked salt in place of sea salt, or maple sugar instead of brown sugar. Pump up the smoke flavor with pimentón (Spanish smoked paprika). You get the idea. Sometimes I round out the flavor with a touch of granulated garlic, onion, and celery seed.

YIELD: Makes 1 cup

PREP TIME: 5 minutes

INGREDIENTS

¼ cup salt (coarse, fine, kosher, sea, smoked, and so on)

¼ cup pepper (cracked, coarse, fine, black, white, green, rainbow, and so on)

¼ cup paprika (sweet, hot, or pimentón)

¼ cup sugar (dark brown, light brown, maple, granulated, or Sucanat—granulated sugarcane juice)

OPTIONAL FLAVORINGS (ADD ANY OR ALL OF THE FOLLOWING)

1 tablespoon granulated garlic

1 tablespoon granulated onion

1 teaspoon celery seed

Combine the ingredients in a bowl and mix, breaking up any lumps in the sugar with your fingers.

Raichlen's Rub will keep, in a sealed jar away from heat or light, for several weeks.

CHIPOTLE MOLASSES BARBECUE SAUCE

YIELD: Makes 3 cups

METHOD: Simmering

PREP TIME: 10 minutes

COOKING TIME:
15 minutes

HEAT SOURCE: Stove or grill side burner

WHAT ELSE: I don't normally recommend canned ingredients, but canned chipotles in adobo have a lot more flavor than dried. Two good brands are La Morena and San Marcos.

Smoke and fire are what make brisket barbecue, and they're about to ignite a barbecue sauce to go with it. The smoke here comes from chipotles—Mexican smoked jalapeños. The fire comes from the chiles, plus sriracha and horseradish mustard. There's one unexpected ingredient here—sambuca—an Italian liqueur (similar to French pastis and Greek ouzo) that adds an unexpected anise-y sweetness.

INGREDIENTS

2 cups ketchup

¼ cup sriracha, plus extra as needed

¼ cup rye whiskey

¼ cup brown sugar, plus extra as needed

3 tablespoons horseradish mustard or Dijon mustard

2 tablespoons molasses

1 tablespoon Worcestershire sauce

1 tablespoon sambuca

2 teaspoons soy sauce

1 canned chipotle chile in adobo, minced, plus 1 teaspoon sauce (or to taste)

1 teaspoon granulated garlic

1 teaspoon finely grated lemon zest

3 tablespoons freshly squeezed lemon juice

Sea salt and freshly ground black pepper

1. Combine the ketchup, ¼ cup Sriracha, whiskey, ¼ cup brown sugar, mustard, molasses, Worcestershire sauce, sambuca, soy sauce, minced chipotle and sauce, granulated garlic, lemon zest, and lemon juice in a heavy saucepan and bring to a boil over medium heat. Reduce the heat to medium-low and gently simmer the sauce, uncovered, until thick and richly flavored, 10 to 15 minutes. The sauce should be pourable—if it's too thick, whisk in a little water.

2. Correct the seasoning, adding salt, pepper, sriracha, or sugar as desired—the sauce should be highly seasoned. Let the sauce cool to room temperature before serving.

Chipotle Molasses Barbecue Sauce will keep, in a sealed container in the refrigerator, for at least 1 week.

ASIAN BEER BARBECUE SAUCE

A lot of beer gets served with barbecued brisket. So why not repurpose some of that beer in a barbecue sauce? Beer adds a malty richness and hoppy tang to a sauce that takes its smoky sweetness from Chinese hoisin sauce, available in the Asian food section of most supermarkets. Serve with any of the Asian-style briskets in this book.

INGREDIENTS

2 tablespoons plus 1 teaspoon toasted (dark) sesame oil

2 scallions, trimmed, white and green parts thinly sliced

4 teaspoons peeled, minced fresh ginger

1 clove garlic, peeled and minced

1 cup Asian beer (see What Else)

1 cup hoisin sauce

¼ cup sake or rice wine

3 tablespoons mirin (sweet rice wine)

2 tablespoons *sambal oelek* (see What Else) or sriracha

2 tablespoons plus 1 teaspoon rice vinegar

2 tablespoons brown sugar, plus extra as needed

Lots of freshly ground black pepper

Sea salt (optional)

1. Heat 2 tablespoons of the sesame oil in a heavy saucepan over medium heat. Add the scallions, ginger, and garlic, and cook, stirring occasionally, until lightly browned, 3 minutes.

2. Stir in the beer and bring to a boil. Briskly boil the beer until reduced by half, 5 minutes.

3. Stir in the hoisin sauce, sake, mirin, *sambal oelek*, 2 tablespoons rice vinegar, and brown sugar and gradually bring to a boil.

4. Reduce the heat to medium-low and simmer the sauce until thick and richly flavored, 10 to 15 minutes, whisking from time to time.

5. Remove from the heat and stir in the remaining sesame oil and rice vinegar. The sauce should be pourable—if it's too thick, whisk in a little water.

YIELD: Makes 2 cups

METHOD: Simmering

PREP TIME: 10 minutes

COOKING TIME: 15 minutes

HEAT SOURCE: Stove or grill side burner

WHAT ELSE: You'll want an imported Asian beer for this barbecue sauce. Chinese Tsingtao, Thai Singha, and Japanese Asahi or Sapporo come to mind. Mirin is sweet rice wine. If it's unavailable, use more sake and add a little more sugar. *Sambal oelek* is Indonesian chile paste and is also known as chile-garlic paste. Look for it in the Asian food section of your supermarket—one widely available brand is Huy Fong—or substitute sriracha.

Correct the seasoning, adding a ton of black pepper and salt or sugar as needed—the sauce should be highly seasoned. Let the sauce cool to room temperature before serving.

Asian Beer Barbecue Sauce will keep, in a sealed container in the refrigerator, for at least 1 week.

REDEYE BARBECUE SAUCE

YIELD: Makes 2 cups

METHOD: Simmering

PREP TIME: 10 minutes

COOKING TIME:
15 minutes

HEAT SOURCE: Stove or grill side burner

Perhaps it's the long hours spent tending brisket. Or the wee-hours wake-up calls to fire up the pit. Strong coffee and barbecued brisket have been longstanding companions for nocturnal smoke sessions. Joe Carroll, for example, adds espresso to the barbecue sauce at Fette Sau in Brooklyn and Philadelphia. You're about to do the same in this not-too-sweet Redeye Barbecue Sauce fortified with smoky bacon.

INGREDIENTS

2 tablespoons butter

1 strip artisanal bacon, such as Nueske's, thinly sliced crosswise

1 small onion, peeled and minced

1 jalapeño, stemmed, seeded, and minced (for spicier sauce, leave the seeds in)

1 clove garlic, peeled and minced

3 tablespoons chopped fresh cilantro

¾ cup brewed espresso or strong brewed coffee

¾ cup ketchup

¼ cup Worcestershire sauce

2 tablespoons apple cider vinegar

2 tablespoons Dijon mustard

2 tablespoons molasses

2 tablespoons brown sugar, plus extra as needed

Sea salt and freshly ground black pepper

1. Melt the butter in a heavy saucepan over medium heat. Add the bacon, onion, jalapeño, garlic, and cilantro and cook, stirring occasionally, until lightly browned, 3 to 5 minutes.

2. Stir in the espresso, ketchup, Worcestershire sauce, vinegar, mustard, molasses, and brown sugar and gradually bring to a boil.

3. Reduce the heat to medium-low and simmer the sauce, whisking occasionally, until thick and richly flavored, 10 to 15 minutes. The sauce should be pourable—if it's too thick, whisk in a little water.

4. Correct the seasoning, adding sugar, salt, and/or pepper to taste—the sauce should be highly seasoned, with just a touch of sweetness. Let the sauce cool to room temperature before serving.

Redeye Barbecue Sauce will keep, in a sealed container in the refrigerator, for at least 3 days.

COFFEE BEER MOP SAUCE

A mop sauce is very different from a barbecue sauce. The former gets applied to the brisket during cooking. Consequently, a mop sauce is thinner than a barbecue sauce and much less sweet (excess sugar would burn during the long smoke). This one—loosely inspired by Snow's BBQ in Lexington, Texas (read more about Snow's octogenarian pit mistress Tootsie Tomanetz on page 253)—merges the earthiness of coffee and beer with the piquancy of vinegar and Worcestershire sauce. Butter and beef broth provide additional richness. Unlike barbecue sauce, a mop sauce doesn't taste particularly pleasing by itself. What it does is lay on an essential base layer of flavor and help keep the brisket moist during smoking. Apply it to any of the barbecued brisket recipes on pages 41 to 70 (start mopping after 1 hour of cooking).

YIELD: Makes about 4 cups, enough to mop 2 packer briskets

METHOD: Simmering

PREP TIME: 5 minutes

COOKING TIME: 10 minutes

HEAT SOURCE: Stove or grill side burner

YOU'LL ALSO NEED: A barbecue mop or basting brush

WHAT ELSE: As the name suggests, mop sauces are traditionally applied with a barbecue mop. (For large quantities, you could use a full-size new cotton floor mop.) I'm partial to my Signature Series barbecue mop, which has a removable head for easy cleaning. You could certainly use a basting brush, but it won't look as cool as a mop.

INGREDIENTS

½ cup (1 stick) unsalted butter

1 small onion, peeled and diced

2 cups Basic Brisket Broth (page 254) or beef broth or stock (homemade or low-sodium)

¼ cup Worcestershire sauce

¼ cup strong brewed coffee

¼ cup dark or light beer

¼ cup distilled white vinegar

¼ cup your favorite mustard (I like Dijon)

Your favorite barbecue rub (see pages 246 to 247)

1. Melt the butter in a medium-size saucepan over medium heat. Add the onion and cook until fragrant but not brown, 3 minutes.

2. Stir in the brisket broth, Worcestershire sauce, coffee, beer, vinegar, mustard, and 1 tablespoon barbecue rub or to taste, and simmer, whisking to mix, for 5 minutes.

Use Coffee Beer Mop Sauce within 1 hour of making it (there is no need to refrigerate it).

BUTTER BOURBON INJECTOR SAUCE

YIELD: Makes 1 cup, enough to inject 1 packer brisket

METHOD: Simmering

PREP TIME: 5 minutes

COOKING TIME: 5 minutes

HEAT SOURCE: Stove or grill side burner

YOU'LL ALSO NEED: A saucepan

Injector sauces turn up on the competition circuit, where teams use them to add moistness and flavor to the lean brisket flat. (The flat is the preferred cut for competition on account of its handsome lean, even slices.) This one uses brisket broth to reinforce the beef flavor, with melted butter added for richness and bourbon for kick.

INGREDIENTS

½ cup (1 stick) unsalted butter

½ cup Basic Brisket Broth (page 254) or beef broth or stock (preferably homemade or low-sodium)

1 tablespoon bourbon, Cognac, or Worcestershire sauce

Sea salt and finely ground black pepper

BRISKET WHISPERER—TOOTSIE TOMANETZ

Norma Frances "Tootsie" Tomanetz starts her workday at 2 a.m. For the next ten hours or so, the pit mistress of Snow's BBQ in Lexington, Texas, loads meat into pits, shovels burning oak embers into fireboxes, and generally moves at a pace that would exhaust someone a quarter of her age. (She recently celebrated her eighty-third birthday.) That's after working Monday

through Friday as a groundskeeper at the nearby Giddings High School. When asked the secret of great barbecue, her weathered face cracks a smile. "There is no secret. It just takes patience and hard work."

Experience helps, too, and Tootsie has logged more than fifty years putting wood smoke to meat. It started at the City Meat Market in Lexington, which Tootsie ran with her husband, "White," from 1976 to 1996. "We didn't have boxed meat [butchered, portioned, and packaged at the packing house] back then. We worked with hanging beef, doing the butchering ourselves," she recalls. Whatever was left unsold at the end of the week—be it sirloin or shoulder clod—became barbecue on Saturday morning.

Surprisingly, one meat she didn't cook in her youth was brisket. "It was scrap meat we'd grind into hamburgers," she says. "We didn't fool with it." The brisket moment arrived with the advent of boxed

beef. When Snow's opened in 2003, they sold six to eight briskets on a typical Saturday. Today, they go through ninety briskets in a single morning to serve the 300 to 400 people who flock to Snow's from all over Texas and beyond.

When it comes to cooking brisket, Tootsie and Snow's proprietor, Kerry Bexley, do things a little differently. For starters, they use the Select grade, not costlier Choice or Prime beef. They buy their briskets trimmed down to 7-pound slabs (no additional trimming is required after cooking). They season solely with table salt and 16-mesh (coarsely ground) black pepper. They smoke the brisket over post oak in a pair of oversize stick burners (offset barrel smokers) that Kerry welded himself.

Like many Hill Country barbecue joints, Snow's wraps the brisket two-thirds of the way through the cook (at 160°F internal temperature), but they wrap the meat not in the usual pink butcher paper but in aluminum foil (see page 31). This makes the brisket so tender and moist, it requires an electric knife to slice it.

For Tootsie, what's most important in barbecue is fire management. "Every fire is different and every piece of wood burns differently," she says. "A lot depends on the weather, the humidity, and the dew point. And God decides that."

WHAT ELSE: Use a barbecue injector (it looks like an oversize hypodermic needle; see page 23) to shoot this sauce deep into the brisket. When adding rubs or spices to injector sauces, strain through a fine-mesh strainer so the seasonings don't clog the holes in the needle.

1. Melt the butter in a saucepan over medium heat. Whisk in the broth, bourbon, and salt and pepper to taste. (Whisk until the salt crystals dissolve.)

2. Let the injector sauce cool to room temperature before injecting the meat.

Use Butter Bourbon Injector Sauce within 1 hour of making it (there is no need to refrigerate it).

NOTE: To load an injector, depress the plunger, lower the needle into the pan (tip the pan to create a deeper pool), then slowly raise the plunger. Insert the needle deep in the brisket to inject it. Inject the brisket several times through the same hole, angling the needle in different directions, so as to make as few holes in the meat as possible.

BASIC BRISKET BROTH

YIELD: Makes 8 to 10 cups

METHOD: Simmering

PREP TIME: 15 minutes

COOKING TIME: 2½ to 3 hours

HEAT SOURCE: Stove

YOU'LL ALSO NEED: A stockpot; a fine-mesh strainer

Boiling may not be the first technique most Americans think of to cook brisket. But travel the world's brisket belt and you find boiled brisket among Ashkenazi Jews, Vietnamese soup lovers, and ramen fanatics in Japan. You'll need a good beef broth for many other dishes in this book, such as the German/Austrian *Bierfleische* (beer-braised brisket) on page 146 and the Wine Country Brisket on page 142. So it behooves you to know how to make brisket broth from scratch. Fortunately, it's easy, it stores well in the freezer, and it beats store-bought beef broth hollow. Added benefit: You wind up with a handsome slab of boiled brisket, which you can use in Vaca Frita (page 174) or chill, cut across the grain into paper-thin slices (this works best on a deli-style meat slicer—otherwise use a very sharp knife), and serve with a big-flavored dipping sauce like the ones on pages 256 to 257.

INGREDIENTS

A 2-pound section of brisket flat

1 dried bay leaf

1 medium onion, peeled and quartered

1 whole clove

1 carrot, trimmed, peeled, and cut into 1-inch pieces

1 celery rib, cut into 1-inch pieces

1 clove garlic, peeled and crushed with the side of a knife

2 sprigs fresh flat-leaf parsley or cilantro

1. Place the brisket in a large pot. Pin the bay leaf to one of the onion quarters with the clove and add it to the pot with the remaining onion, carrot, celery, garlic, and parsley. Add 3 quarts of water and bring to a boil over medium-high heat. Using a ladle, skim off any scum that rises to the surface.

2. Reduce the heat and gently simmer, skimming the liquid often, until the brisket is very tender, 2½ to 3 hours. Conscientious skimming and gentle simmering is the secret to a clean, clear broth. Add water as needed to keep the brisket and vegetables covered.

3. Transfer the brisket to a cutting board or baking dish and let it cool completely, then wrap it in plastic wrap and place it in the refrigerator to chill.

4. Strain the broth through a fine-mesh strainer into a large bowl, pressing the vegetables with the back of a wooden spoon to extract the juices. You should wind up with around 2 quarts.

Basic Brisket Broth will keep, in a sealed container in the refrigerator, for at least 3 days, or in the freezer for several months.

WHAT ELSE: This brisket broth is infinitely customizable depending on its final destination. A ramen broth (page 164) will be fortified with *kombu* (dried kelp) and *hon dashi* (smoky dried bonito). Vietnamese pho broth (page 155) boasts ginger and lemongrass. The broth for Ropa Vieja (page 171) comes scented with tomatoes, oregano, and cumin.

THREE DIPPING SAUCES
FOR CHILLED SLICED BRISKET

Making the broth on page 254 gives you a tasty slab of boiled brisket. It's great for thinly slicing and serving with one of the following boldly flavorful dipping sauces.

HORSERADISH SAUCE

YIELD: Makes 1 cup

INGREDIENTS

⅓ cup prepared horseradish or freshly grated horseradish root (use a Microplane or the fine holes on a box grater)

⅓ cup mayonnaise (preferably Hellmann's or Best Foods)

¼ cup sour cream

1 tablespoon Dijon mustard

½ teaspoon finely grated lemon zest

Salt and freshly ground black pepper to taste

Combine the horseradish, mayonnaise, sour cream, mustard, lemon zest, and salt and pepper in a bowl and whisk to mix.

Horseradish Sauce will keep, in a sealed container in the refrigerator, for at least 3 days.

DRAGON SAUCE

YIELD: Makes 1 cup

INGREDIENTS

⅔ cup mayonnaise (preferably Hellmann's or Best Foods)

3 tablespoons *sambal oelek* (see What Else, page 110) or sriracha (or to taste)

2 teaspoons Asian fish sauce or soy sauce (optional)

3 tablespoons minced fresh cilantro

½ teaspoon freshly grated lime zest

1 tablespoon freshly squeezed lime juice

Combine the mayonnaise, *sambal oelek*, fish sauce, cilantro, lime zest, and lime juice in a bowl and whisk to mix.

Dragon Sauce will keep, in a sealed container in the refrigerator, for at least 3 days.

CHINESE CHILE SAUCE

YIELD: Makes 1 cup

INGREDIENTS

¼ cup chile oil or vegetable oil

¼ cup toasted (dark) sesame oil

¼ cup rice vinegar

¼ cup soy sauce

2 tablespoons toasted sesame seeds (see What Else, page 68)

2 scallions, trimmed, white and green parts thinly sliced crosswise

1 serrano or jalapeño chile, thinly sliced crosswise (optional)

Combine the chile oil, sesame oil, rice vinegar, soy sauce, sesame seeds, scallions, and chiles, if using, in a bowl and whisk to mix.

Chinese Chile Sauce tastes best within a few hours of being made.

BRISKET BUTTER

When I was growing up, the gold currency (culinary gold currency, that is) in our family was schmaltz—rendered chicken fat. You cooked it with onion for extra flavor, and my aunts and uncles fought over who got the *gribenes*, or crispy bits. Well, here's the barbecue equivalent—brisket butter, rendered from the fatty brisket trimmings in a foil pan at the same time you cook the brisket. That gives you smoky brisket butter, which is even more precious than schmaltz.

So what do you do with your brisket butter? Slather it on cornbread or sandwich rolls. Use it to make the Yorkshire pudding on page 235. Fry eggs in it. For unforgettable steaks, place a dollop of brisket butter atop a freshly grilled T-bone or rib eye. And don't forget to brush it on grilled corn.

YIELD: Makes ¾ to 1 cup (depending on the amount of brisket trimmings)

METHOD: Barbecuing/smoking

PREP TIME: 5 minutes

COOKING TIME: 3 to 4 hours

HEAT SOURCE: Smoker or charcoal grill

YOU'LL ALSO NEED: Wood logs, chunks, or soaked, drained hardwood chips; a large aluminum foil pan (about 13 by 9 inches); a fine-mesh strainer

INGREDIENTS

Sea salt

2 to 3 pounds trimmed brisket fat (reserved from trimming a whole packer brisket; see Note)

1 small onion, peeled and quartered (optional)

1. Fire up your smoker, cooker, or grill following the manufacturer's instructions and heat to 250°F. Add the wood as specified by the manufacturer.

2. Lightly salt the brisket fat and place the pieces along with the onion (if using) in a large foil pan. Smoke the brisket trimmings until the fat renders, 3 to 4 hours, or as needed.

3. Strain the fat through a fine-mesh sieve into a heatproof bowl. Cool to room temperature, then transfer to a clean jar.

Brisket Butter will keep in a sealed container in the refrigerator for at least 1 week, and can be frozen for several months. Scoop out what you need with a spoon and pop an extra dose of Lipitor.

NOTE: For even more spectacular brisket butter, collect the fat from a Wagyu brisket (see page 49).

KETTLE CORN
WITH CRISPY BRISKET

YIELD: Serves 4 (can be multiplied as desired)

METHOD: Sautéing

PREP TIME: 10 minutes

COOKING TIME: 1 to 2 minutes for reheating the brisket

HEAT SOURCE: Stove or a grill side burner

WHAT ELSE: Franklin laces his kettle corn with bits of dehydrated brisket. For the sake of simplicity, I've rejiggered the recipe, using burnt ends. *Togarashi* is a blend of Japanese peppers, sesame seeds, and nori among other seasonings. Look for it at Asian markets or online, or make it from scratch following the recipe on page 68.

He couldn't. He wouldn't. Brisket kettle corn? If there's one person who has put brisket on the world barbecue map, it's Aaron Franklin of Franklin Barbecue in Austin (see page 262). At this point, he can pretty much put brisket wherever he pleases. His latest venture is Loro, self-described "Asian smokehouse"—run in partnership with Tyson Cole of Austin's renowned Uchi restaurant. Of course, they serve brisket (smoked in J&R Oyler pits)—dressed up Asian-style with Thai herbs and chile gastrique. You'll also find Thai green curry sausage, Malaysian chicken, and even crispy Sichuan tofu. But my favorite dish is a bar snack—candied kettle corn tossed with smoky brisket bits and peppery *togarashi*. It's sweet, salty, spicy, crunchy, and utterly irresistible.

INGREDIENTS

1 tablespoon butter or vegetable oil

1½ cups finely diced barbecued brisket or burnt ends (see pages 41 to 70)

6 cups homemade or store-bought kettle corn, such as Angie's BOOMCHICKAPOP, or even Cracker Jack

1 tablespoon *togarashi* (see What Else)

Sea salt to taste

1. Melt the butter in a large saucepan over medium-high heat. Add the brisket and sauté until hot and crisp, 2 minutes.

2. Take the pan off the heat and stir in the kettle corn, *togarashi*, and salt to combine. Serve at once.

BRISKET WHISPERER—AARON FRANKLIN

If there's one man who's responsible for the world brisket renaissance, it is Aaron Franklin of Franklin Barbecue in Austin. Dressed in his habitual T-shirt, shorts, and black sneakers, he may not look like a James Beard Award–winning chef (the first pit master accorded such an honor). But no one knows more about brisket or cooks it better than this musician turned carpenter turned pit master.

By now the story of how Aaron and Stacy Franklin got their start has acquired mythical status. Aaron grew up in Bryan, Texas, where his father ran a restaurant called Ben's Bar-Be-Que. ("I spent most of the time chopping onions and lemons for the sauce," he recalls.) He also did a stint at Louie Mueller Barbecue in Taylor, Texas.

One day, a friend who owned an abandoned Texaco gas station urged Franklin to open a barbecue joint. So Franklin, 31 at the time, bought a turquoise-blue Aristocrat trailer to use as a kitchen and built a pit from an old propane tank. (He still builds all his pits himself at his welding shop in Austin.) His wife, Stacy, kept her day job to pay the bills.

Word of Franklin's barbecue spread like Texas brush fires, and so did the waiting lines. A year later, the couple signed a lease on its current digs, a turquoise cinderblock building on 11th Street. Today, Franklin serves 500 people a day (more on weekends), and they still close in the early afternoon when the meat runs out. His empire has grown to include a bestselling cookbook, a public television show, and a new restaurant—a self-styled "Asian Smokehouse" called Loro. Next year, Franklin will start selling custom-designed barbecue pits; the waiting list for those extends several years in the future.

I asked Aaron why brisket inspires such reverence and has such a mystique. "Because it takes so darn much work to get it right," he says. "Ribs cook in a few hours. Pork shoulder is virtually impossible to screw up. But brisket—you're looking at a 15-hour cook. You have to wake up early or stay up all night. It requires constant attention and supervision and there are no shortcuts. People know what you had to go through to get it right."

In a field where pit masters guard their recipes like tech companies their algorithms, Franklin is an open book. (The brisket recipe in his *Franklin Barbecue: A Meat Smoking Manifesto* runs eleven pages.) His trim reduces a 15-pound brisket to 5 pounds of servable meat. He wraps his brisket in pink butcher paper when it reaches an internal temperature of 160°F. He cooks his briskets to between 203° and 208°F but goes by feel to check doneness. "Lift it up from the center. If it's supple enough to bend, the brisket is cooked.

"Brisket works on so many different timelines. One timeline to render the fat. Another to cook the flat. A third to cook the point. Your job is to make sure they converge," Franklin says.

Bottom line? "The more labor you put into the process, the greater the potential for quality," Franklin says. Amen!

BRISKET CHOCOLATE CHIP COOKIES

W ell, here's a dish I never expected to put in a book on brisket: dessert. Specifically, brisket chocolate chip cookies. Until, that is, I met Evan LeRoy, co-proprietor of a barbecue food truck called LeRoy and Lewis in Austin. The bearded, soft-spoken chef specializes in "new wave" barbecue, which means you'll find the likes of macaroni and cheese–stuffed quail and beet barbecue sauce served with textbook Hill Country brisket. Of course, I did a double take at the sight of brisket chocolate chip cookies. You're supposed to. But they're really no stranger than the ubiquitous bacon brownies—and in both cases, the smoky saltiness of the meat has an uncanny way of both accentuating and moderating the sweetness of the cookie. It's almost impossible these days to find a dessert not finished with salt in some way. So why not add it in the form of brisket? At first glance, the brown clump atop each cookie looks like a piece of dark chocolate. It's actually brisket glazed with butter and brown sugar. Pass me another.

YIELD: Makes 20 cookies

METHOD: Baking

PREP TIME: 15 minutes, plus several hours to chill the dough

COOKING TIME: About 15 minutes

HEAT SOURCE: Oven, stove

YOU'LL ALSO NEED: A large bowl; an electric mixer (stand or hand); a sifter; a rimmed sheet pan; parchment paper or a silicone baking mat

WHAT ELSE: If you're reading this book, you've probably barbecued a few briskets. In fact, you probably have some left over in your refrigerator or freezer right now. (If you don't, you should.) If you're lucky enough to have some extra burnt ends on hand, use them in place of the ¾ cup chopped brisket in the topping. Cut them into ½-inch chunks, brown them in butter and sugar as described in step 7, and top the cookies with them.

INGREDIENTS

1 cup (2 sticks) unsalted butter, at room temperature

¾ cup packed dark brown sugar

¾ cup sugar

1 tablespoon bourbon

2 large eggs (preferably farm-fresh and organic)

2¼ cups unbleached white all-purpose flour

1 teaspoon baking powder

¼ teaspoon sea salt or table salt

2½ cups semisweet chocolate chips

2½ cups finely chopped barbecued brisket (see pages 41 to 70)

FOR THE TOPPING

2 tablespoons unsalted butter

2 tablespoons dark brown sugar

1. Combine the butter and sugars in a large mixing bowl and cream together with a handheld electric mixer at medium speed until smooth, light, and fluffy, about 3 minutes, periodically scraping down the side of the bowl with a spatula. (Alternatively, use a stand mixer.) Beat in the bourbon, followed by the eggs, one by one.

2. Sift the flour, baking powder, and salt over the butter mixture and fold in with a spatula to mix. Fold in the chocolate chips and 1¾ cups of the brisket.

3. Cover the dough with plastic wrap and refrigerate until firm but still pliable, at least 4 hours or overnight.

4. When ready to bake the cookies, preheat the oven to 375°F.

5. Line a rimmed sheet pan with parchment paper or a silicone baking mat (this prevents sticking and facilitates cleanup). Divide the dough into 20 equal-size balls, about 2 ounces each, and arrange them on the prepared sheet pan, 3 inches apart. Gently flatten the balls with the palm of your hand.

6. Bake the cookies, rotating the pan halfway through, until the dough has spread and the tops are browned, about 14 minutes.

7. Meanwhile, make the topping: Melt the butter in a small saucepan over medium-high heat. Stir in the sugar and heat until bubbling. Stir in the remaining ¾ cup chopped brisket and cook until the sugar mixture thickens and coats the meat, 2 minutes. Set aside to cool slightly.

8. Remove the cookies from the oven and immediately place a spoonful of sugar-coated meat in the center of each. Let cool to room temperature. Use a thin-bladed metal spatula to loosen the cookies from the parchment paper and serve.

In the unlikely event you have any cookies left over, store them in a sealed container in the refrigerator for up to 3 days. Let them come to room temperature before serving.

CONVERSION TABLES

Please note that all conversions are approximate but close enough to be useful when converting from one system to another.

OVEN TEMPERATURES

FAHRENHEIT	GAS MARK	CELSIUS
250	½	120
275	1	140
300	2	150
325	3	160
350	4	180
375	5	190
400	6	200
425	7	220
450	8	230
475	9	240
500	10	260

NOTE: Reduce the temperature by 20°C (68°F) for fan-assisted ovens.

APPROXIMATE EQUIVALENTS

1 stick butter = 8 tbs = 4 oz = ½ cup = 115 g

1 cup all-purpose presifted flour = 4.7 oz

1 cup granulated sugar = 8 oz = 220 g

1 cup (firmly packed) brown sugar = 6 oz = 220 g to 230 g

1 cup confectioners' sugar = 4½ oz = 115 g

1 cup honey or syrup = 12 oz = 350 g

1 cup grated cheese = 4 oz = 125 g

1 cup dried beans = 6 oz = 175 g

1 large egg = about 2 oz or about 3 tbs

1 egg yolk = about 1 tbs

1 egg white = about 2 tbs

LIQUID CONVERSIONS

U.S.	IMPERIAL	METRIC
2 tbs	1 fl oz	30 ml
3 tbs	1½ fl oz	45 ml
¼ cup	2 fl oz	60 ml
⅓ cup	2½ fl oz	75 ml
⅓ cup + 1 tbs	3 fl oz	90 ml
⅓ cup + 2 tbs	3½ fl oz	100 ml
½ cup	4 fl oz	125 ml
⅔ cup	5 fl oz	150 ml
¾ cup	6 fl oz	175 ml
¾ cup + 2 tbs	7 fl oz	200 ml
1 cup	8 fl oz	250 ml
1 cup + 2 tbs	9 fl oz	275 ml
1¼ cups	10 fl oz	300 ml
1⅓ cups	11 fl oz	325 ml
1½ cups	12 fl oz	350 ml
1⅔ cups	13 fl oz	375 ml
1¾ cups	14 fl oz	400 ml
1¾ cups + 2 tbs	15 fl oz	450 ml
2 cups (1 pint)	16 fl oz	500 ml
2½ cups	20 fl oz (1 pint)	600 ml
3¾ cups	1½ pints	900 ml
4 cups	1¾ pints	1 liter

WEIGHT CONVERSIONS

US/UK	METRIC	US/UK	METRIC
½ oz	15 g	7 oz	200 g
1 oz	30 g	8 oz	250 g
1½ oz	45 g	9 oz	275 g
2 oz	60 g	10 oz	300 g
2½ oz	75 g	11 oz	325 g
3 oz	90 g	12 oz	350 g
3½ oz	100 g	13 oz	375 g
4 oz	125 g	14 oz	400 g
5 oz	150 g	15 oz	450 g
6 oz	175 g	1 lb	500 g

INDEX

Note: Page references in *italics* indicate photographs.

A

Airflow controller, 23
Aluminum foil pans, 23
Anchovy mustard, 104
Asian beer barbecue sauce, 249–50
Asian-flavor barbecue sauce, simple, 70
Asian-flavor brisket in the style of Kyu, *66,* 67–70
Attman's Deli, 114
Aunt Annette's holiday brisket with sweet wine and dried fruits, *132,* 133–35
Austrian-style brisket, about, 8

B

Bacon:
  -grilled brisket bites with cilantro lime sauce, *196,* 197–98
  and mushrooms, wine country brisket braised with, 142–46, *144*
  -smoked brisket flat, 44–46, *45*
  smoked Irish spiced beef, 122
Banh mi, brisket, *222,* 223–24
Barbecue mop, 23
Barbecue sauces:
  Asian beer, 249–50
  chipotle molasses, 248
  cider beer, 53
  cool smoke, 77
  Korean, 227
  redeye, 250–51
  simple Asian-flavor, 70
Barbecue University, 82
Barbecuing/smoking brisket:
  the carve, 34–35
  choosing a cooker, 26–27
  choosing fuel, 27–29
  choosing wood smoke, 29
  doneness test, 32–33
  first cook, 29–31
  overview of, 15
  the rest, 33–34
  seasoning meat, 26
  the second cook, 32
  trimming meat, 25
  the wrap, 31
  see also Brisket (barbecued and grilled)
Bark, about, 7, 29, 30
Basic brisket broth, 254–55
Beans:
  brisket baked (four beans, mucho brisket), *232,* 233–34
  Real Deal Holyfield brisket breakfast tacos, *178,* 179–81
Beer:
  Asian, barbecue sauce, 249–50
  cider barbecue sauce, 53
  coffee mop sauce, 251–52
  German, –braised brisket *(bierfleische),* 146–48, *147*
  Irish spiced beef, 120–22
  smoked Irish spiced beef, 122

Vietnamese crispy
brisket salad, *204,*
205–6
Brisket butter:
recipe for, *258,* 259
serving ideas, 257
Broth, basic brisket, 254–55
Buns, brisket steamed,
226–27
Burger:
Jake's double brisket
cheeseburgers, *210,*
211–12
Burnt ends:
about, 7, 78
Tuffy Stone's, 74–77, *75*
Butcher paper, 24
Butter, shallot sage, *80,* 81
Butter, brisket:
recipe for, *258,* 259
serving ideas, 257
Butter bourbon injector
sauce, 252–54

C

Cabbage:
corned beef and, 117–20,
119
double-down Reuben,
213–14, *215*
made-from-scratch
sauerkraut, 240–41
Camp Brisket, 54–55
Caper parsley sauce
(salsa verde), 170
Cardboard smoking
platform, 30

Carrots:
bollito misto (two
briskets and a bird
boiled in the style of
the Piemonte), 167–70
brisket banh mi, *222,*
223–24
corned beef and
cabbage, 117–20, *119*
Irish spiced beef, 120–22
smoked Irish spiced
beef, 122
Vietnamese slaw,
223–24, *238*
Central American–style
brisket, about, 9
Charcoal, 29
Charcoal briquettes, 29
Cheese:
brisket-stuffed bakers
(baked potatoes),
230–31
the brisket breakfast
sandwich, 185–86
brisket tots, 200–202,
201
double-down Reuben,
213–14, *215*
Jake's double brisket
cheeseburgers, *210,*
211–12
pimento, made-from-
scratch, 217
pockets, smoky brisket,
203
Southern "cheesesteak,"
216–17
Texas French dip
sandwich, 219–21, *220*

Texas torpedoes
(brisket poppers),
199
Cheeseburgers, Jake's
double brisket, *210,*
211–212
Chef's knife, 24
Chicken:
bollito misto (two briskets
and a bird boiled in the
style of the Piemonte),
167–70
Chile(s):
bacon-grilled brisket
bites with cilantro
lime sauce, *196,*
197–98
brisket and eggs with
crispy grilled scallion
tortilla chips, 187–89,
188
brisket baked beans
(four beans, mucho
brisket), *232,* 233–34
chipotle mayonnaise,
186
chipotle molasses
barbecue sauce, 248
gangsta salsa, 181
Kung Pao pastrami,
108, 109–11
sauce, Chinese, 257
Singapore crispy brisket
salad, 207
smoky Joe (the brisket
sloppy Joe sandwich),
218–19
Southern "cheesesteak,"
216–17